Table of Contents

W9-BCI-623

Introduction

Basic Math Skills is based on current NCTM standards and is designed to support any math curriculum that you may be using in your classroom. The standard strands (Number and Operations, Algebra, Geometry, Measurement, and Data Analysis and Probability) and skills within the strand are listed on the overview page for each section of the book. The skill is also shown at the bottom of each reproducible page.

Opportunities to practice the process standards (Problem Solving, Reasoning and Proof, Communication, Connections, and Representations) are also provided as students complete the various types of activities in this resource book.

Basic Math Skills is to be used as a resource providing practice of skills already introduced to students. Any page may be used with an individual child, as homework, with a small group, or by the whole class.

Skill Practice

Each skill is covered in a set of six reproducible pages that include the following:

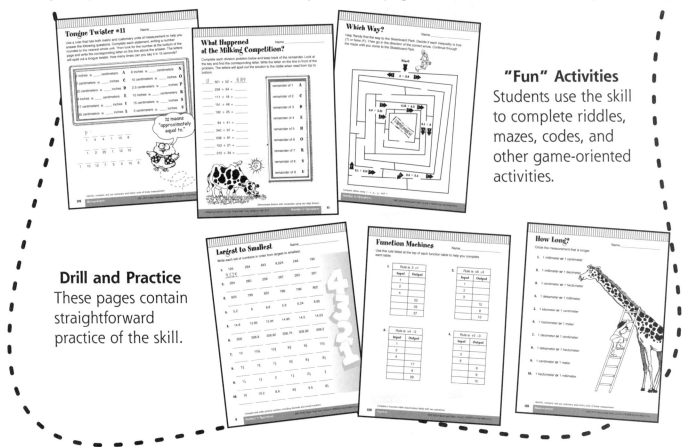

"Fun" Activities
Students use the skill to complete riddles, mazes, codes, and other game-oriented activities.

Drill and Practice
These pages contain straightforward practice of the skill.

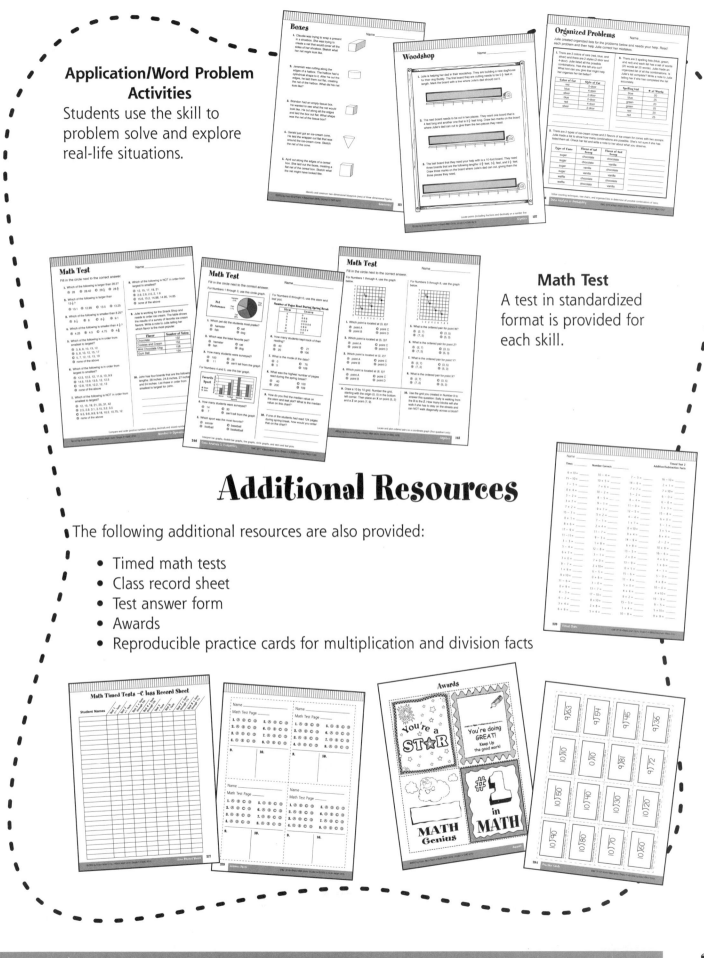

Application/Word Problem Activities

Students use the skill to problem solve and explore real-life situations.

Math Test

A test in standardized format is provided for each skill.

Additional Resources

The following additional resources are also provided:

- Timed math tests
- Class record sheet
- Test answer form
- Awards
- Reproducible practice cards for multiplication and division facts

Number and Operations

Tongue Twister #1

Write the numbers below in order from smallest value to the largest value. Above each value, write the corresponding letter. The letters will spell out a tongue twister. Try to say it quickly three times.

5.31	**C**
5.49	**C**
5.1	**C**
5.53	**E**
5.09	**I**
5.44	**I**
5.21	**K**
5.5	**K**
4.75	**R**
5.42	**R**
5.7	**S**
4.5	**T**
5.61	**T**
5.3	**Y**

T
[4.5] [ ] [ ] [ ] [ ] [ ]

[ ] [ ] [ ] [ ] [ ] [ ] [ ] [ ]

Compare and order positive numbers including decimals and mixed numbers

Number & Operations

Riddle

To solve the riddle, write the values below in order from largest to smallest. Then above each value, write the corresponding letter. The letters will spell out the solution to the riddle.

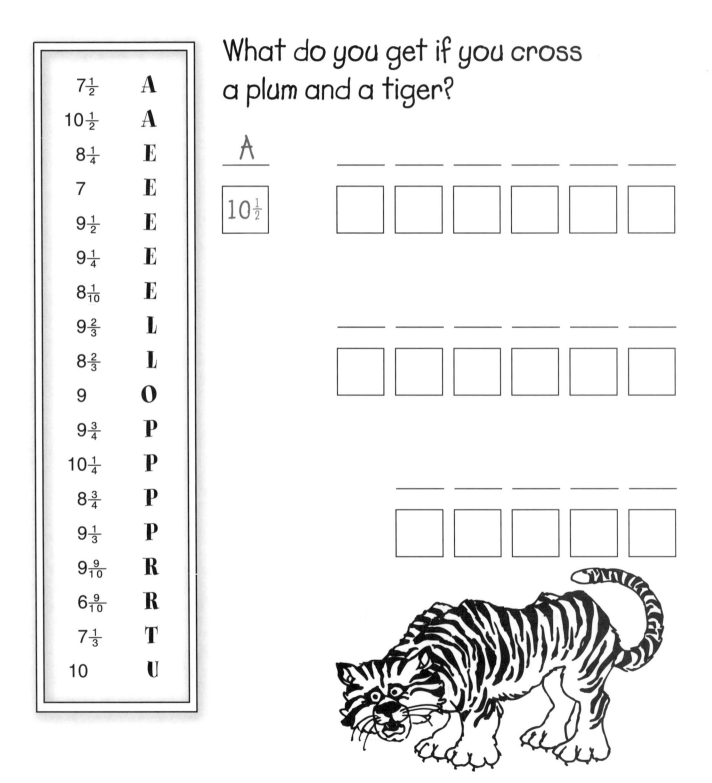

$7\frac{1}{2}$	A
$10\frac{1}{2}$	A
$8\frac{1}{4}$	E
7	E
$9\frac{1}{2}$	E
$9\frac{1}{4}$	E
$8\frac{1}{10}$	E
$9\frac{2}{3}$	L
$8\frac{2}{3}$	L
9	O
$9\frac{3}{4}$	P
$10\frac{1}{4}$	P
$8\frac{3}{4}$	P
$9\frac{1}{3}$	P
$9\frac{9}{10}$	R
$6\frac{9}{10}$	R
$7\frac{1}{3}$	T
10	U

What do you get if you cross a plum and a tiger?

$\dfrac{A}{\boxed{10\frac{1}{2}}}$ __ __ __ __ __ __

Compare and order positive numbers including decimals and mixed numbers

Least to Greatest

Name _____

Write each set of numbers in order from least to greatest.

1. 25   75   34   83   74   17

   _17_   _____   _____   _____   _____   _____

2. 175   37   491   382   170   208

   _____   _____   _____   _____   _____   _____

3. 15.7   26.4   15.9   16.2   17   15.3

   _____   _____   _____   _____   _____   _____

4. $8\frac{1}{2}$ $7\frac{1}{3}$ $7\frac{1}{5}$ 8 $8\frac{2}{3}$ $7\frac{1}{2}$

   _____   _____   _____   _____   _____   _____

5. 6 $6\frac{1}{3}$ $6\frac{3}{4}$ $6\frac{1}{2}$ $6\frac{2}{3}$ $6\frac{1}{4}$

   _____   _____   _____   _____   _____   _____

6. 159   15.9   0.0159   1,590   1.59   0.159

   _____   _____   _____   _____   _____   _____

7. 26   26.34   25.9   25.99   26.25   26.3

   _____   _____   _____   _____   _____   _____

8. $7\frac{9}{10}$ $6\frac{4}{9}$ $6\frac{2}{3}$ $7\frac{3}{5}$ $7\frac{1}{10}$ $8\frac{3}{10}$

   _____   _____   _____   _____   _____   _____

9. 2.56   256   2,560   0.256   0.0256   25.6

   _____   _____   _____   _____   _____   _____

10. 14.8   14.2   14.3   14   14.21   14.19

   _____   _____   _____   _____   _____   _____

Compare and order positive numbers including decimals and mixed numbers

Number & Operations

7

Largest to Smallest

Write each set of numbers in order from largest to smallest.

1. 125   264   843   9,524   249   190

    9,524   ____   ____   ____   ____   ____

2. 264   260   259   267   263   261

    ____   ____   ____   ____   ____   ____

3. 825   795   820   798   799   802

    ____   ____   ____   ____   ____   ____

4. 5.2   6   6.8   5.9   6.24   6.85

    ____   ____   ____   ____   ____   ____

5. 14.9   13.85   13.94   14.95   14.5   14.53

    ____   ____   ____   ____   ____   ____

6. 309   308.9   308.92   308.75   308.95   309.2

    ____   ____   ____   ____   ____   ____

7. 10 $10\frac{1}{10}$ $10\frac{4}{5}$ $9\frac{2}{3}$ $9\frac{1}{4}$ $10\frac{1}{2}$

    ____   ____   ____   ____   ____   ____

8. $7\frac{1}{3}$ $7\frac{3}{4}$ $7\frac{1}{2}$ $6\frac{3}{4}$ $8\frac{1}{3}$ $8\frac{1}{2}$

    ____   ____   ____   ____   ____   ____

9. $1\frac{1}{3}$ $1\frac{3}{4}$ 2 $1\frac{1}{2}$ $2\frac{1}{3}$ $\frac{3}{4}$

    ____   ____   ____   ____   ____   ____

10. 10   10.2   8.9 $8\frac{3}{4}$ 9.5 $9\frac{1}{3}$

    ____   ____   ____   ____   ____   ____

Compare and order positive numbers including decimals and mixed numbers

Number & Operations

EMC 3018 • Basic Math Skills, Grade 5 • ©2003 by Evan-Moor Corp.

Carpenter's World

Name _____

Solve each problem.

1. Shirley and her dad are building a new doghouse. They have several boards that they want to stack in order from shortest to longest. The lengths of the boards are 14 inches, 27 inches, 19 inches, 34 inches, 30 inches, and 21 inches. Write the lengths in order from shortest to longest.

_____

2. Julia is fencing in her backyard. She needs 240 feet of fencing. The roll that she is looking at has 85 yards of fencing. Is the roll long enough to provide Julia with all the fencing she will need?

_____

3. Chuck is cutting a board that is 6 feet long into two pieces. One piece will be two and one-half feet and the other piece will be two feet, five inches. Which one is longer?

_____

4. Jay has three pieces of wire rolled up and labeled with their lengths. The lengths are 75 feet, 84 feet, and 29 feet. His dad wants the longest one first, followed by the medium length one, and then the shortest one. In what order should Jay hand these to his dad?

_____

5. Ian and Brandon are collecting boards to make a fort in their backyard. The lengths of the boards they collected are 29 inches, 25 inches, 28.6 inches, 25.75 inches, 28.5 inches, $28\frac{3}{4}$ inches, and 29.5 inches. Help Ian and Brandon list these boards in order from the longest to the shortest length.

_____

Compare and order positive numbers including decimals and mixed numbers

Bakery World

Solve each problem.

1. Sam is making a five-layer cake and needs to stack the cakes in order with the largest cake on the bottom and the smallest cake on the top. In what order should the cakes be stacked if their diameters are the following lengths: 18 inches, 2 feet, 8 inches, 22 inches, and 1 foot?

   _____

2. George is helping his mom make a wedding cake for George's sister. The bride and groom figures that they want to place on top of the cake are 14 cm and 6 inches tall, respectively. Which figure is the taller one? Justify your response. (Use a ruler to help you decide which is taller.)

   _____

3. Helena is making a cake with pedestals between each layer. She wants to use the tallest pedestals between the bottom two layers, the medium-length ones next, and then the shortest pedestals between the top two layers of cake. The lengths of the pedestals are 14.2 inches, 1.5 feet, and 8.95 inches. In what order will the pedestals be used, starting at the bottom?

   _____

4. Frank wants to buy 5 square pastries that are each 4 inches by 4 inches. He would like to set these pastries on a plate that is $\frac{1}{2}$ foot by $1\frac{1}{2}$ feet. Will the pastries fit on the platter without stacking them or having them hang over the edge?

   _____

Compare and order positive numbers including decimals and mixed numbers

EMC 3018 • Basic Math Skills, Grade 5 • ©2003 by Evan-Moor Corp.

Math Test

Fill in the circle next to the correct answer.

1. Which of the following is larger than 28.5?

   Ⓐ 28   Ⓑ 28.42   Ⓒ $28\frac{1}{3}$ Ⓓ $28\frac{3}{4}$

2. Which of the following is larger than $13\frac{1}{3}$?

   Ⓐ 13.1   Ⓑ 12.99   Ⓒ 13.5   Ⓓ 13.25

3. Which of the following is smaller than 8.25?

   Ⓐ $8\frac{1}{4}$ Ⓑ 8   Ⓒ $8\frac{1}{2}$ Ⓓ 9.1

4. Which of the following is smaller than $4\frac{1}{2}$?

   Ⓐ 4.25   Ⓑ 4.5   Ⓒ 4.75   Ⓓ $4\frac{9}{10}$

5. Which of the following is in order from smallest to largest?

   Ⓐ 3, 6, 8, 10, 13, 12
   Ⓑ 5, 8, 10, 12, 15, 17
   Ⓒ 5, 7, 12, 15, 13, 19
   Ⓓ none of the above

6. Which of the following is in order from largest to smallest?

   Ⓐ 12.5, 12.2, 12, 11.9, 10, 9.9
   Ⓑ 14.6, 13.9, 13.5, 12, 12.5
   Ⓒ 12.8, 12.6, 12.2, 12, 13
   Ⓓ none of the above

7. Which of the following is NOT in order from smallest to largest?

   Ⓐ 12, 15, 19, 21, 25, 31, 42
   Ⓑ 2.5, 2.9, 3.1, 3.15, 3.2, 3.5
   Ⓒ 9.5, 9.6, 9.9, 9.18, 10.2, 10.75, 12
   Ⓓ none of the above

8. Which of the following is NOT in order from largest to smallest?

   Ⓐ 12, 15, 17, 19, 21
   Ⓑ 2.9, 2.8, 2.5, 2, 1.9
   Ⓒ 15.6, 15.2, 14.98, 14.95, 14.85
   Ⓓ none of the above

---

9. Julie is working for the Snack Shop and needs to order ice cream. The table shows the results of a survey of favorite ice-cream flavors. Write a note to Julie telling her which flavor is the most popular.

Flavor	Number of Votes
Chocolate	132
Cookies and Cream	152
Mint Chocolate Chip	158
Gum Ball	139

10. John has four boards that are the following lengths: 28 inches, 24.6 inches, 27 inches, and 24 inches. List these in order from smallest to largest for John.

   _____

   _____

   _____

Compare and order positive numbers including decimals and mixed numbers

Tongue Twister #2

Name _____

Find the place value of the digit **5** in each number. Then write the corresponding letter above the number. The letters will spell out a tongue twister. Try to say it fast three times.

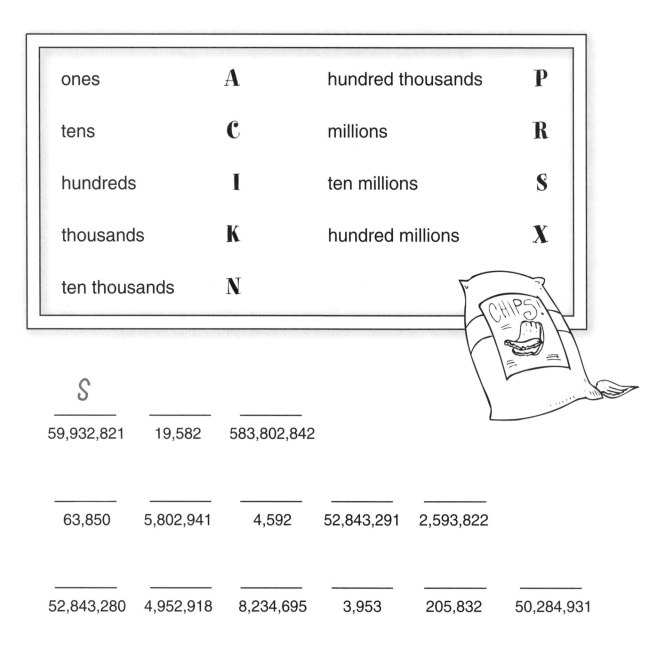

ones	**A**	hundred thousands	**P**
tens	**C**	millions	**R**
hundreds	**I**	ten millions	**S**
thousands	**K**	hundred millions	**X**
ten thousands	**N**		

S
———
59,932,821

———
19,582

———
583,802,842

———
63,850

———
5,802,941

———
4,592

———
52,843,291

———
2,593,822

———
52,843,280

———
4,952,918

———
8,234,695

———
3,953

———
205,832

———
50,284,931

Determine place value and round numbers up to millions

EMC 3018 • Basic Math Skills, Grade 5 • ©2003 by Evan-Moor Corp.

What Bow Can Never Be Tied?

To answer the riddle, draw a straight line between each number on the left and the corresponding number on the right that is rounded to the requested place value. Each line will go through a small number. Write the letter from in front of the number on the left on the numbered line at the bottom of the page. The letters will spell out the solution to the riddle.

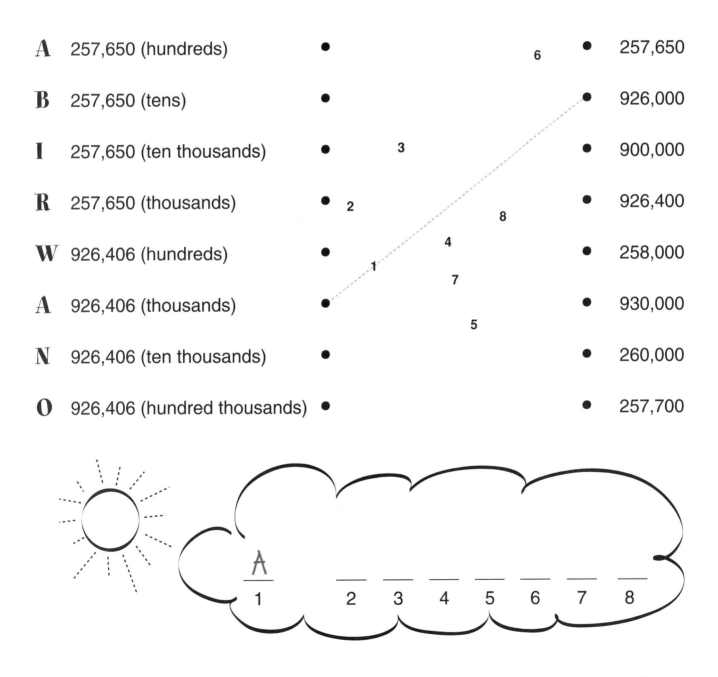

A 257,650 (hundreds)	•	• 257,650
B 257,650 (tens)	•	• 926,000
I 257,650 (ten thousands)	•	• 900,000
R 257,650 (thousands)	•	• 926,400
W 926,406 (hundreds)	•	• 258,000
A 926,406 (thousands)	•	• 930,000
N 926,406 (ten thousands)	•	• 260,000
O 926,406 (hundred thousands)	•	• 257,700

A
‾
1   2   3   4   5   6   7   8

Determine place value and round numbers up to millions

Number & Operations

The Round Table

Round each number to the requested place value.

1. 280 to the nearest hundred _____ *300*

2. 49,305 to the nearest thousand _____

3. 27,539 to the nearest ten _____

4. 184,390 to the nearest ten thousand _____

5. 286,952 to the nearest hundred thousand _____

6. 1,682,842 to the nearest hundred thousand _____

7. 5,930,206 to the nearest million _____

8. 7,502,401 to the nearest hundred thousand _____

9. 3,202,294 to the nearest million _____

10. 15,392,487 to the nearest million _____

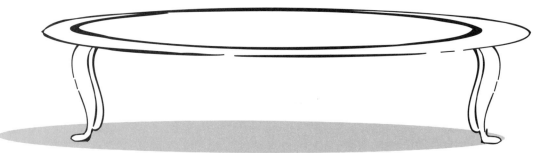

Determine place value and round numbers up to millions

Watch Your Places

Name _____

What place value does the **3** hold in each of the following numbers?

1. 135 _____tens_____

2. 394 _____

3. 1,293 _____

4. 93,649 _____

5. 320,196 _____

6. 194,634 _____

7. 5,462,349 _____

8. 3,579,216 _____

9. 2,634,912 _____

10. 9,616,493 _____

What numeral is in the requested place value in the number 13,495,628?

11. tens _____2_____

12. millions _____

13. hundred thousands _____

14. ones _____

15. ten thousands _____

What numeral is in the requested place value in the number 91,348,762?

16. hundred thousands _____

17. thousands _____

18. millions _____

19. ten thousands _____

20. hundreds _____

Determine place value and round numbers up to millions

Find My Number

Name_____

Find the number that satisfies each set of clues.

1. What is my three-digit number?

   • It has a 6 in the ones place.
   • When it is rounded to the nearest hundred, it becomes 200.
   • The digits in my number are 9, 6, and 1.

   _____

2. What is my four-digit number?

   • If it is rounded to the nearest ten or hundred, they are the same.
   • The digits in my number are 8, 4, 3, and 0.
   • The ones place has a 3 in it.
   • When rounded to the nearest thousand, my number is 8,000.

   _____

3. What is my three-digit number?

   • The digits are 7, 6, and 3.
   • When rounded to the nearest hundred, my number becomes 800.

   _____

4. What is my four-digit number?

   • The digits are 9, 8, 2, and 1.
   • When rounded to the nearest thousand, my number is 9,000.
   • There is a 1 in the tens place.
   • When rounding to the nearest ten, the digit in the tens place doesn't change.

   _____

5. What is my five-digit number?

   • There are two 1s in my number.
   • The other digits are 7, 5, and 4.
   • The largest digit is in the thousands place.
   • When rounded to the nearest ten-thousands place, my number is 20,000.
   • The 4 is in the ones place.
   • When rounded to the nearest hundreds place, the digit in the hundreds place doesn't change.

   _____

Determine place value and round numbers up to millions

EMC 3018 • Basic Math Skills, Grade 5 • ©2003 by Evan-Moor Corp.

Find My Number II

Name _____

Find the number that satisfies each set of clues.

1. What is my three-digit number?

- The sum of the three digits is 3.
- When rounded to the nearest hundreds, the number is 200.
- The ones digit is a 1.

_____

2. What is my three-digit number?

- When rounded to the nearest hundred, the number is 1,000.
- The sum of the three digits is 27.

_____

3. What is my three-digit number?

- The digits are 5, 4, and 2.
- When rounded to the nearest ten, the number is 250.
- The tens digit is less than the ones digit.

_____

4. What is my four-digit number?

- The digits are 6, 3, 2, and 0.
- When the number is rounded to either the nearest tens place or the nearest hundreds place, the answers are the same.
- There is a 2 in the hundreds place.
- The largest digit is in the thousands place.

_____

5. What is my four-digit number?

- The digits are 9, 8, 4, and 3.
- When rounded to the nearest thousand, the number becomes 5,000.
- The 8 is in the tens place.

_____

Determine place value and round numbers up to millions

Math Test

Fill in the circle next to the correct answer.

1. In the number 25,943, which digit is in the tens place?

Ⓐ 2   Ⓑ 5   Ⓒ 9   Ⓓ 4

2. In the number 74,931, which digit is in the hundreds place?

Ⓐ 4   Ⓑ 9   Ⓒ 3   Ⓓ 1

3. In the number 94,382, the digit 4 is in which place?

Ⓐ ones place
Ⓑ tens place
Ⓒ hundreds place
Ⓓ thousands place

4. In the number 264,035, the digit 2 is in which place?

Ⓐ hundreds place
Ⓑ thousands place
Ⓒ ten thousands place
Ⓓ hundred thousands place

5. Round 296,520 to the nearest hundred.

Ⓐ 300,000
Ⓑ 300,500
Ⓒ 296,500
Ⓓ 296,600

6. Round 95,842 to the nearest ten thousand.

Ⓐ 90,000
Ⓑ 100,000
Ⓒ 190,000
Ⓓ 96,000

7. Round 48,251 to the nearest thousand.

Ⓐ 48,000   Ⓒ 48,300
Ⓑ 50,000   Ⓓ 48,200

8. Round 105,842 to the nearest hundred.

Ⓐ 100,000   Ⓒ 105,840
Ⓑ 105,000   Ⓓ 105,800

9. Write a three-digit number that when rounded to the nearest ten and the nearest hundred, the answers are the same.

_____

10. What number satisfies all of the following clues?

- It is a three-digit number.
- The digits are 9, 8, and 2.
- When rounded to the nearest hundred, the number is 300.
- The 9 is in the ones place.

_____

Determine place value and round numbers up to millions

What Is a Sheep's Hairdresser Called?

Name _____

Solve the following problems to find the answer to the riddle. Then look at the key to see what letter corresponds to the answer. Write the letter on the line in front of each problem. The letters will spell out the solution to the riddle.

__A__ 216 × 25 = _5,400_

_____ 29 × 80 = _____

_____ 450 × 12 = _____

_____ 90 × 60 = _____

_____ 116 × 20 = _____

_____ 120 × 45 = _____

_____ 150 × 36 = _____

_____ 678 × 19 = _____

_____ 113 × 27 = _____

_____ 52 × 95 = _____

_____ 412 × 42 = _____

5,400	**A**
2,320	**B**
4,000	**D**
3,051	**H**
10,482	**M**
4,940	**O**
17,304	**P**
12,882	**S**
5,081	**T**

Demonstrate multiplication with whole numbers up to a three-digit number multiplied by a two-digit number

How Do You Prevent Getting Water into Your House?

Name _____

To solve the riddle, complete each problem. Then write the corresponding letter on the line in front of each problem. The letters will spell out the solution to the riddle, reading down the left column first and then down the right column.

_S_ 85 × 35 = _2,975_

____ 84 × 62 = _____

____ 29 × 15 = _____

____ 73 × 27 = _____

____ 219 × 9 = _____

____ 104 × 5 = _____

____ 128 × 5 = _____

____ 429 × 8 = _____

____ 184 × 42 = _____

____ 295 × 41 = _____

____ 168 × 31 = _____

____ 495 × 73 = _____

____ 49 × 80 = _____

____ 51 × 93 = _____

____ 52 × 10 = _____

____ 124 × 42 = _____

____ 98 × 40 = _____

____ 91 × 73 = _____

____ 124 × 8 = _____

____ 858 × 4 = _____

____ 70 × 52 = _____

____ 104 × 35 = _____

520	**A**	3,432	**I**	6,643	**R**
992	**B**	3,640	**L**	2,975	**S**
3,920	**E**	7,728	**N**	5,208	**T**
12,095	**G**	435	**O**	4,743	**W**
36,135	**H**	1,971	**P**	640	**Y**

Demonstrate multiplication with whole numbers up to a three-digit number multiplied by a two-digit number

Number & Operations

EMC 3018 • Basic Math Skills, Grade 5 • ©2003 by Evan-Moor Corp.

Products and Products

Name_____

Find the product of each of the following problems.

1.   25
   × 91

2.   29
   × 17

3.   372
   × 28

4.   827
   × 51

5.   420
   × 38

6. 29 × 63 = _____

7. 10 × 48 = _____

8. 382 × 50 = _____

9. 307 × 28 = _____

10. 429 × 59 = _____

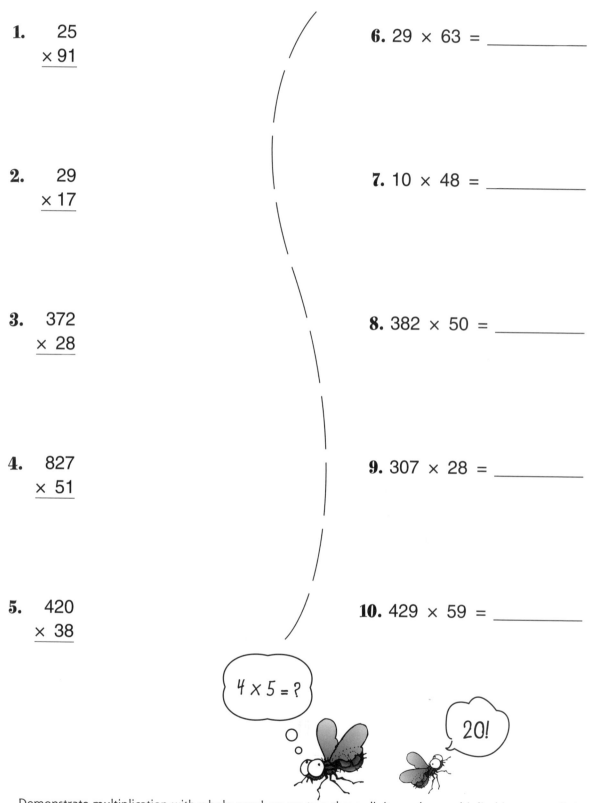

4 × 5 = ?

20!

Demonstrate multiplication with whole numbers up to a three-digit number multiplied by a two-digit number

Products and More Products

Find the product of each of the following problems.

1.
   42
   × 96

2.
   84
   × 25

3.
   761
   × 19

4.
   915
   × 22

5.
   940
   × 64

6. 28 × 94 = _____

7. 42 × 80 = _____

8. 109 × 64 = _____

9. 540 × 60 = _____

10. 349 × 82 = _____

mmm...

10 x 15=?

150!

Demonstrate multiplication with whole numbers up to a three-digit number multiplied by a two-digit number

EMC 3018 • Basic Math Skills, Grade 5 • ©2003 by Evan-Moor Corp.

Pets

Name _____

Solve each problem.

1. Shirley has 26 gerbils and she gives each one 2 sunflower seeds each day. How many sunflower seeds does she need for a week's worth of feedings?

   _____

2. At the City Pet Store, there were 18 fish tanks. In each fish tank there were 35 fish. What was the total number of fish in all the tanks?

   _____

3. On Susie's block there are 5 dogs and 18 cats. Each dog eats 48 ounces of food a day and each cat eats 8 ounces of food a day. Which set of animals goes through more food in a week?

   _____

4. Dolly made a quilt for her father out of square pieces of fabric. Each piece of fabric for the quilt measured 3 inches by 3 inches. The finished quilt was 12 squares wide and 36 squares long. What are the dimensions of the finished quilt?

   _____

5. A peregrine falcon can fly 217 miles per hour. If it flew for 8 hours, how far could it fly? Could it make it all the way from New York to Los Angeles (about 2,800 miles) in 8 hours? Justify your answer.

   _____

Demonstrate multiplication with whole numbers up to a three-digit number multiplied by a two-digit number

Raising Money

Name _____

Solve each problem.

1. Shirley is walking dogs to raise some money. She charges $16 per month to walk one dog 30 minutes per week. She has 21 dogs that she is walking every week. How much money will she earn in one month?

   _____

2. Brendan is mowing lawns over the summer. He mows 14 lawns each week and charges $24 to mow each one. How much will he earn during the 14 weeks of summer?

   _____

3. Andrea is selling boxes of candy for the school fundraiser. The boxes sell for $8 each and she has sold 265 boxes. If the school makes half of the money as profit, how much profit will the school make from Andrea's sales?

   _____

4. Amy and April have been selling magazines for their chess club. The club gets $12 from each magazine sale that is made. Amy sold 15 magazines and April sold 24 magazines. How much will the club earn from these two girls' sales?

   _____

5. Drew is shoveling snow in the winter. He hopes that it will snow a lot this winter so that he can purchase a new television for his bedroom. He wants to buy one that costs $149. He wants to charge $12 for each walk that he shovels, and he has 8 people willing to pay him to shovel their walks. If it snows twice, will he have enough money to buy the TV?

   _____

Demonstrate multiplication with whole numbers up to a three-digit number multiplied by a two-digit number

Number & Operations   EMC 3018 • Basic Math Skills, Grade 5 • ©2003 by Evan-Moor Corp.

Math Test

Fill in the circle next to the correct answer.

1. 27 × 84 = _____

   Ⓐ 2,160   Ⓒ 2,268

   Ⓑ   324   Ⓓ   756

2. 105 × 52 = _____

   Ⓐ   735   Ⓒ   780

   Ⓑ 5,460   Ⓓ 5,250

3. 319 × 30 = _____

   Ⓐ 9,570   Ⓒ 957

   Ⓑ 9,251   Ⓓ 270

4. 927 × 11 = _____

   Ⓐ   927   Ⓒ   9,270

   Ⓑ 1,854   Ⓓ 10,197

5. Which of the following has a solution of 1,512?

   Ⓐ 30 × 50

   Ⓑ 24 × 64

   Ⓒ 33 × 54

   Ⓓ 28 × 54

6. Which of the following has a solution of 6,016?

   Ⓐ 128 × 47

   Ⓑ 231 × 26

   Ⓒ 127 × 47

   Ⓓ 136 × 46

7. Which of the following does NOT have the solution of 3,800?

   Ⓐ 76 × 50

   Ⓑ 38 × 50

   Ⓒ 190 × 20

   Ⓓ 200 × 19

8. Which of the following does NOT have the solution of 840?

   Ⓐ 105 × 8

   Ⓑ 42 × 20

   Ⓒ 18 × 46

   Ⓓ 35 × 24

9. Julie has 24 books on the shelf in her bedroom. Each book has 245 pages in it. If she reads all 24 books, how many pages will she have read?

_____

10. A wild turkey can travel 55 miles per hour. Can it travel 200 miles in four hours? Justify your answer.

_____

_____

Demonstrate multiplication with whole numbers up to a three-digit number multiplied by a two-digit number

Basketball Riddle

Name _____

What does a basketball player do before he blows out the candles on his birthday cake?

To solve this riddle, solve each division problem. Then look at the key and write the corresponding letter on the line in front of the problem. The letters will spell out the solution to the riddle when read from top to bottom.

__H__   7 ÷ 7 = __1__

_____   27 ÷ 3 = _____

_____   4 ÷ 2 = _____

_____   54 ÷ 9 = _____

_____   45 ÷ 9 = _____

_____   36 ÷ 4 = _____

_____   28 ÷ 4 = _____

_____   36 ÷ 6 = _____

_____   42 ÷ 6 = _____

_____   24 ÷ 6 = _____

_____   24 ÷ 8 = _____

_____   35 ÷ 5 = _____

_____   5 ÷ 5 = _____

6	A
9	E
1	H
3	I
5	K
2	M
7	S
4	W

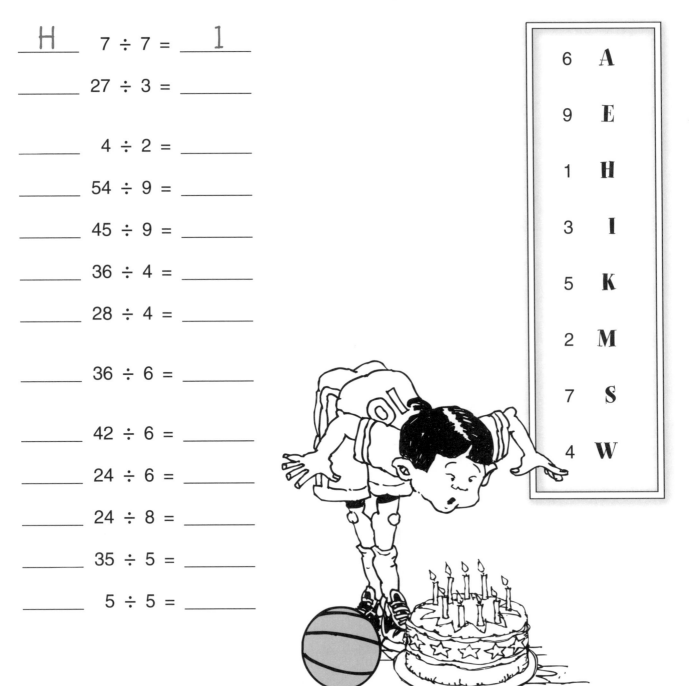

Demonstrate division facts

EMC 3018 • Basic Math Skills, Grade 5 • ©2003 by Evan-Moor Corp.

How Do You Make a Car Smile?

Name _____

To solve this riddle, solve each division problem. Then look at the key at the bottom and write the corresponding letter on the line in front of the problem. The letters will spell out the solution to the riddle when read from top to bottom, starting with the left column.

I   27 ÷ 3 = ____9____

____   0 ÷ 5 = _____

____   20 ÷ 4 = _____

____   16 ÷ 8 = _____

____   24 ÷ 8 = _____

____   36 ÷ 4 = _____

____   42 ÷ 6 = _____

____   36 ÷ 6 = _____

____   0 ÷ 6 = _____

____   32 ÷ 8 = _____

____   49 ÷ 7 = _____

____   90 ÷ 9 = _____

____   64 ÷ 8 = _____

____   6 ÷ 2 = _____

____   8 ÷ 8 = _____

____   12 ÷ 6 = _____

0	A	4	J	8	R
1	D	5	K	9	T
2	E	6	N	10	Y
3	I	7	O		

Demonstrate division facts

Number & Operations   **27**

How Fast Can You Divide?

Name _____

Complete the following division problems as quickly as you can.

1. $27 \div 9 =$ _____ $24 \div 6 =$ _____ $18 \div 3 =$ _____

2. $42 \div 7 =$ _____ $40 \div 5 =$ _____ $50 \div 5 =$ _____

3. $24 \div 8 =$ _____ $48 \div 8 =$ _____ $81 \div 9 =$ _____

4. $35 \div 5 =$ _____ $16 \div 2 =$ _____ $20 \div 4 =$ _____

5. $63 \div 9 =$ _____ $10 \div 10 =$ _____ $21 \div 3 =$ _____

6. $49 \div 7 =$ _____ $5 \div 1 =$ _____ $9 \div 1 =$ _____

7. $18 \div 6 =$ _____ $54 \div 9 =$ _____ $42 \div 6 =$ _____

8. $9 \div 3 =$ _____ $25 \div 5 =$ _____ $12 \div 2 =$ _____

9. $28 \div 7 =$ _____ $12 \div 4 =$ _____ $15 \div 5 =$ _____

10. $45 \div 9 =$ _____ $20 \div 2 =$ _____ $28 \div 4 =$ _____

How long did it take you to complete all the problems? _____

How many did you get correct? _____

Demonstrate division facts

EMC 3018 • Basic Math Skills, Grade 5 • ©2003 by Evan-Moor Corp.

Division Is My Forte

Name _____

Complete these division problems as quickly as you can.

1. $4\overline{)16}$ $2\overline{)12}$ $9\overline{)36}$ $3\overline{)3}$

2. $2\overline{)8}$ $1\overline{)6}$ $3\overline{)21}$ $10\overline{)70}$

3. $6\overline{)36}$ $7\overline{)49}$ $9\overline{)54}$ $8\overline{)16}$

4. $1\overline{)9}$ $6\overline{)42}$ $8\overline{)56}$ $2\overline{)22}$

5. $3\overline{)15}$ $5\overline{)30}$ $1\overline{)12}$ $7\overline{)14}$

6. $5\overline{)45}$ $8\overline{)48}$ $8\overline{)32}$ $9\overline{)45}$

7. $4\overline{)24}$ $7\overline{)35}$ $4\overline{)28}$ $6\overline{)24}$

8. $9\overline{)27}$ $2\overline{)4}$ $9\overline{)63}$ $4\overline{)44}$

How long did it take you to complete all the problems? _____

How many did you get correct? _____

Demonstrate division facts

Sharing

Name _____

Solve each problem.

1. Sally has 72 pencils and she has been given the task of dividing them into bundles of 6 pencils for each student. How many bundles can she make?

   _____

2. Ben and his four siblings were given $40. How much money did each get if they divided the money evenly?

   _____

3. Alex has 24 fish and he needs to divide them evenly among his 3 aquariums. How many fish should he put in each aquarium?

   _____

4. Julia and her 5 friends have a bag of candy that contains 54 pieces. If they split the candy evenly, how many pieces will Julia end up with?

   _____

5. Mike has 32 treats that he wants to share with his reading group of 8 students (including himself). How many treats will each get?

   _____

6. Alice has 4 six-packs of juice boxes. She wants to share them with her bowling team. If there are 8 boys and 4 girls (including herself) on the team, how many juice boxes will each person get?

   _____

Demonstrate division facts

Number & Operations

EMC 3018 • Basic Math Skills, Grade 5 • ©2003 by Evan-Moor Corp.

Division Is Just Sharing

Name_____

Solve each problem.

1. Jack has 35 pieces of candy. Does he have enough to give 7 pieces to each of his 6 friends? Justify your answer.

_____

2. Irene has just been given 49 fish and she needs to put them into 7 glass bowls for centerpieces at a dinner. How many fish does she need to put in each bowl?

_____

3. Josh and his brother each have 28 baseball cards. They want to share them among their 7 cousins. If they divide them equally, how many cards will each cousin receive?

_____

4. Nathan has 15 sticks of gum. He wants to give each of his friends 3 pieces of gum. What is the maximum number of friends that he could give the gum to if he also wants 3 pieces for himself?

_____

5. There are 17 boys and 18 girls in the library. If the same number of people sit at each of the 7 tables, how many people will there be at each table?

_____

6. Lilly picked 14 daffodils and 4 tulips. She wants to give the flowers to 6 of her friends. How many flowers can she give to each of her friends?

_____

Demonstrate division facts

Math Test

Fill in the circle next to the correct answer.

1. 64 ÷ 8 = _____

- Ⓐ 9
- Ⓑ 8
- Ⓒ 7
- Ⓓ 6

2. 32 ÷ 4 = _____

- Ⓐ 9
- Ⓑ 8
- Ⓒ 7
- Ⓓ 6

3. 24 ÷ 2 = _____

- Ⓐ 14
- Ⓑ 13
- Ⓒ 12
- Ⓓ 10

4. 15 ÷ 3 = _____

- Ⓐ 8
- Ⓑ 7
- Ⓒ 6
- Ⓓ 5

5. 6)‾24‾

- Ⓐ 2
- Ⓑ 3
- Ⓒ 4
- Ⓓ 5

6. 9)‾54‾

- Ⓐ 7
- Ⓑ 6
- Ⓒ 5
- Ⓓ 4

7. 12)‾48‾

- Ⓐ 3
- Ⓑ 4
- Ⓒ 5
- Ⓓ 6

8. 7)‾35‾

- Ⓐ 5
- Ⓑ 6
- Ⓒ 7
- Ⓓ 8

9. Jake has four friends over for dinner. They want to divide the 20 pieces of cake evenly among all of them. How many pieces will each one receive?

_____

10. Samantha is saving money to buy a new CD player. She figures that she needs to earn $80 and that she has eight weeks to earn the money. How much does she need to earn each week to have enough to purchase the CD player?

_____

Demonstrate division facts

Where Do You Take a Frog with Bad Eyesight?

Name _____

To solve the riddle, complete each division problem below, noting any remainder. Then use the key to determine the corresponding letter. Write that letter on the line in front of each problem. The letters will spell out the solution when read from top to bottom.

____T____ 80 ÷ 9 = _____

_____ 46 ÷ 8 = _____

_____ 35 ÷ 9 = _____

_____ 15 ÷ 4 = _____

_____ 34 ÷ 8 = _____

_____ 28 ÷ 5 = _____

_____ 48 ÷ 7 = _____

_____ 71 ÷ 8 = _____

_____ 44 ÷ 9 = _____

_____ 24 ÷ 5 = _____

_____ 17 ÷ 8 = _____

_____ 40 ÷ 9 = _____

_____ 36 ÷ 9 = _____

_____ 75 ÷ 7 = _____

remainder of 0	**A**	remainder of 5	**N**
remainder of 1	**C**	remainder of 6	**O**
remainder of 2	**E**	remainder of 7	**P**
remainder of 3	**H**	remainder of 8	**T**
remainder of 4	**I**		

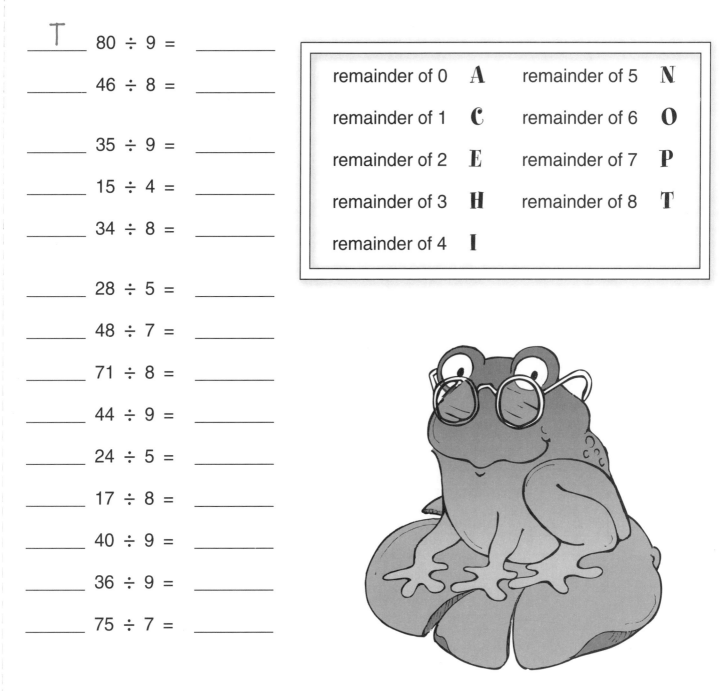

Demonstrate division with remainders using single-digit divisors

Oh, My Stars!

Name_____

Complete each division problem below. As you complete the problem, keep track of each remainder. Look at the key at the bottom, and then color that region according to the key.

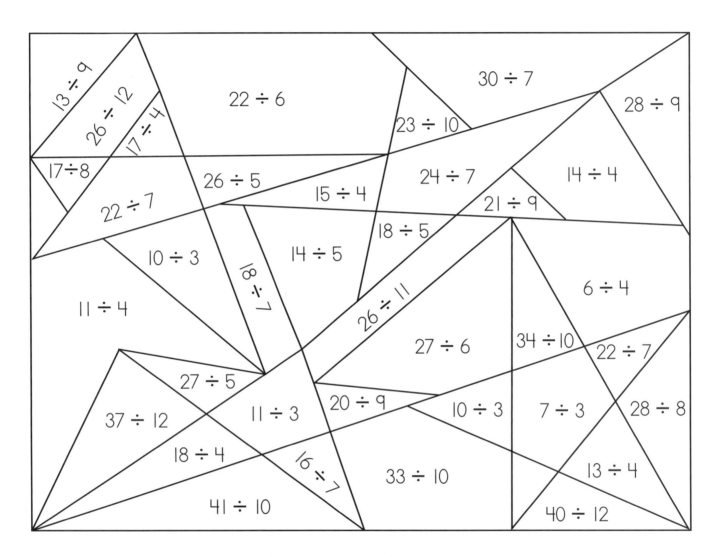

Blue—remainder of 1   Green—remainder of 3

Red—remainder of 2   Yellow—remainder of 4

How many whole five-pointed stars did you color in? _____

Parts and Parts

Complete each division problem, noting the remainder when appropriate.

1. $52 \div 5 =$ _____ $72 \div 7 =$ _____ $94 \div 8 =$ _____

2. $26 \div 5 =$ _____ $25 \div 8 =$ _____ $98 \div 7 =$ _____

3. $24 \div 6 =$ _____ $54 \div 5 =$ _____ $80 \div 9 =$ _____

4. $54 \div 9 =$ _____ $98 \div 9 =$ _____ $14 \div 5 =$ _____

5. $62 \div 8 =$ _____ $67 \div 8 =$ _____ $52 \div 4 =$ _____

6. $70 \div 9 =$ _____ $72 \div 9 =$ _____ $96 \div 7 =$ _____

7. $81 \div 9 =$ _____ $84 \div 2 =$ _____ $18 \div 6 =$ _____

8. $48 \div 5 =$ _____ $96 \div 5 =$ _____ $49 \div 5 =$ _____

9. $64 \div 8 =$ _____ $72 \div 4 =$ _____ $51 \div 8 =$ _____

10. $68 \div 9 =$ _____ $61 \div 3 =$ _____ $49 \div 7 =$ _____

Demonstrate division with remainders using single-digit divisors

Leftovers

Complete each of the following division problems, noting the remainder when appropriate.

1. $4\overline{)24}$ $8\overline{)62}$ $8\overline{)27}$ $9\overline{)70}$

2. $2\overline{)15}$ $5\overline{)49}$ $6\overline{)42}$ $8\overline{)15}$

3. $7\overline{)25}$ $6\overline{)35}$ $8\overline{)29}$ $4\overline{)65}$

4. $4\overline{)32}$ $4\overline{)20}$ $2\overline{)23}$ $9\overline{)97}$

5. $5\overline{)84}$ $9\overline{)58}$ $5\overline{)81}$ $6\overline{)85}$

6. $3\overline{)15}$ $8\overline{)29}$ $3\overline{)29}$ $4\overline{)29}$

7. $7\overline{)26}$ $4\overline{)25}$ $4\overline{)19}$ $4\overline{)33}$

8. $9\overline{)54}$ $9\overline{)81}$ $6\overline{)36}$ $6\overline{)50}$

Demonstrate division with remainders using single-digit divisors

     EMC 3018 • Basic Math Skills, Grade 5 • ©2003 by Evan-Moor Corp.

Shares and Extras

Solve each problem.

1. Timothy has 94 cookies that he would like to share with his 8 friends.
   If he divides them evenly among his friends (including himself), how many
   cookies will each get? If there are extras, what should he do with them?

   _____

2. Sharise is counting the measures in the piano music she is memorizing.
   She figures that there are 95 measures in the entire song. She also figures
   that she can memorize 8 measures in one day. How many days will it take
   her to memorize the entire song?

   _____

3. Marisol has 50 pencils and she wants to share them with the 6 other
   students in her math group. If she shares them among the students
   (including herself), how many pencils will each student get? What should
   she do with any extras if there are any?

   _____

4. Juanita has 74 fish that she is putting into 9 fish tanks. Dividing them
   evenly among the 9 fish tanks, how many fish should she put in each?
   What should she do with any extras if there are any?

   _____

5. Raul is learning to play the guitar. His teacher tells him that there are
   48 chords to learn during the year, and Raul wants to learn them as quickly
   as possible. If he learns 5 new chords every day, how many days will it take
   him to learn all 48 chords?

   _____

Demonstrate division with remainders using single-digit divisors

What's My Number?

Name _____

Find the number that satisfies each set of clues.

1. Guess what my number is, given the following clues:
   - If divided by 7, the remainder is 3.
   - If divided by 4, the remainder is 0.
   - It is less than 30.

   _____

2. Guess what my number is, given the following clues:
   - If divided by 6, the remainder is 1.
   - If divided by 5, the remainder is also 1.
   - If divided by 10, the remainder is still 1.
   - It is less than 50.

   _____

3. Guess what my number is, given the following clues:
   - If divided by 7, the remainder is 0.
   - If divided by 8, the remainder is 2.
   - If divided by 12, the remainder is 6.
   - It is less than 50.

   _____

4. Guess what my number is, given the following clues:
   - If divided by 5, the remainder is 4.
   - If divided by 4, the remainder is 1.
   - It is more than 20.
   - It is less than 50.

   What are TWO possible numbers so far?   _____

   Write a clue to narrow it down to just one of the numbers.

   _____

   _____

   _____

Demonstrate division with remainders using single-digit divisors

EMC 3018 • Basic Math Skills, Grade 5 • ©2003 by Evan-Moor Corp.

Math Test

Name _____

Fill in the circle next to the correct answer.

1. 36 ÷ 5 = _____

  Ⓐ 5 R1   Ⓒ 6 R1

  Ⓑ 5   Ⓓ 7 R1

2. 52 ÷ 10 = _____

  Ⓐ 5 R2   Ⓒ 5 R4

  Ⓑ 2 R5   Ⓓ 10 R5

3. 7)‾40

  Ⓐ 6   Ⓒ 5 R6

  Ⓑ 6 R2   Ⓓ 5 R5

4. 2)‾15

  Ⓐ 7   Ⓒ 7 R1

  Ⓑ 8   Ⓓ 8 R1

5. Which of the following has a remainder of 4?

  Ⓐ 45 ÷ 5   Ⓒ 51 ÷ 10

  Ⓑ 36 ÷ 8   Ⓓ none of the above

6. Which of the following has a remainder of 2?

  Ⓐ 42 ÷ 8   Ⓒ 27 ÷ 9

  Ⓑ 26 ÷ 5   Ⓓ none of the above

7. Which of the following does NOT have a remainder of 5?

  Ⓐ 25 ÷ 10

  Ⓑ 41 ÷ 6

  Ⓒ 48 ÷ 7

  Ⓓ All of the above have a remainder of 5.

8. Which of the following does NOT have a remainder of 1?

  Ⓐ 7 ÷ 2

  Ⓑ 25 ÷ 2

  Ⓒ 33 ÷ 8

  Ⓓ All of the above have a remainder of 1.

9. Juan is dividing his 60 pieces of hard candy among his 7 friends and himself. How many pieces of candy will each get? Are there any extras? What would be a good thing for him to do with the extras if any exist?

_____

10. Lucille has 59 cookies that she wants to share with her six brothers and sisters (including herself). How many cookies should each person get? Are there any extras? What would be a good thing for her to do with the extras if any exist?

_____

_____

_____

Demonstrate division with remainders using single-digit divisors

Tongue Twister #3

Name _____

Complete each division problem below and keep track of the remainder. Look at the key and find the corresponding letter. Write the letter on the line in front of the problem. The letters will spell out a tongue twister when read from the top to the bottom. Once you have the tongue twister completed, try to say it fast three times. Good luck!

_F_   219 ÷ 24 = _____

_____   211 ÷ 34 = _____

_____   154 ÷ 17 = _____

_____   105 ÷ 26 = _____

_____   248 ÷ 35 = _____

_____   110 ÷ 21 = _____

_____   248 ÷ 62 = _____

_____   64 ÷ 15 = _____

remainder of 0	A
remainder of 1	E
remainder of 2	D
remainder of 3	F
remainder of 4	G
remainder of 5	L
remainder of 6	M
remainder of 7	R
remainder of 8	T

Demonstrate division with remainders using two-digit divisors

EMC 3018 • Basic Math Skills, Grade 5 • ©2003 by Evan-Moor Corp.

What Happened at the Milking Competition?

Name_____

Complete each division problem below and keep track of the remainder. Look at the key and find the corresponding letter. Write the letter on the line in front of the problem. The letters will spell out the solution to the riddle when read from top to bottom.

__U__ $321 \div 52 =$ ___6 R9___

_____ $259 \div 64 =$ _____

_____ $111 \div 18 =$ _____

_____ $151 \div 49 =$ _____

_____ $182 \div 25 =$ _____

_____ $84 \div 41 =$ _____

_____ $340 \div 67 =$ _____

_____ $638 \div 91 =$ _____

_____ $153 \div 21 =$ _____

_____ $212 \div 34 =$ _____

remainder of 1	**A**
remainder of 2	**C**
remainder of 3	**D**
remainder of 4	**E**
remainder of 5	**H**
remainder of 6	**O**
remainder of 7	**R**
remainder of 8	**S**
remainder of 9	**U**

Demonstrate division with remainders using two-digit divisors

What's Left Over?

Name _____

Complete each of the following division problems. If there is a remainder, include
that information in your answer.

1. 180 ÷ 25 = _____ 7 R5 _____

2. 429 ÷ 52 = _____

3. 429 ÷ 16 = _____

4. 816 ÷ 14 = _____

5. 589 ÷ 12 = _____

6. 849 ÷ 26 = _____

7. 719 ÷ 43 = _____

8. 815 ÷ 15 = _____

9. 6,421 ÷ 40 = _____

10. 9,428 ÷ 72 = _____

Demonstrate division with remainders using two-digit divisors

Number & Operations

EMC 3018 • Basic Math Skills, Grade 5 • ©2003 by Evan-Moor Corp.

What's Left Over II?

Name _____

Complete each of the following division problems. If there is a remainder, include that information in your answer.

1. $24\overline{)491}$ $43\overline{)619}$ $25\overline{)6,429}$

2. $15\overline{)267}$ $19\overline{)826}$ $82\overline{)4,290}$

3. $43\overline{)915}$ $21\overline{)726}$ $37\overline{)3,000}$

4. $51\overline{)924}$ $18\overline{)4,921}$ $68\overline{)4,380}$

Demonstrate division with remainders using two-digit divisors

Number & Operations

Books and More Books

Name_____

Solve each problem.

1. Shirley's teacher was just given 429 books for the students in her class. There are 27 students including Shirley. If they divide the books evenly, how many books should each student get?

   _____

2. There are 953 books in Tom's library. He can put an average of 48 books on each shelf. How many shelves does he need to put all the books away?

   _____

3. Katrina has 492 books and her sister Julia has 524 books. They would like to give all of these books away to needy children. If they combine their books and then put them in bundles of 24, how many bundles will they make? Are there any extras? What would be a good thing for them to do with the extras if there are any?

   _____

4. Kenny and Kathy are twins. They have a total collection of 960 baseball cards organized in three different books. They want to give them to the 24 other students in their class. How many cards will each student receive? Are there any extras? What would be a good thing for them to do with the extras if there are any?

   _____

5. Liam is reading a book that has 638 pages. He figures that he can read 22 pages in an hour, and he is wondering how many hours it will take him to read the book. How many hours will it take Liam to read the book?

   _____

Demonstrate division with remainders using two-digit divisors

EMC 3018 • Basic Math Skills, Grade 5 • ©2003 by Evan-Moor Corp.

Snow

Solve each problem.

1. For every inch of snow, it takes Jimmy 17 minutes to shovel the driveway
    and sidewalk. If it takes him 3 minutes less than 6 hours to shovel the snow,
    how many inches of snow were on the ground for Jimmy to shovel?

    _____

2. Derek and his 18 classmates packed 492 snowballs. They are getting
    ready for a snowball pass and they want to divide them evenly among the
    19 of them. How many snowballs should each person get? Are there any
    extras? What would be a good thing for them to do with the extras if there
    are any?

    _____

3. For the last snowstorm in Greeley, the snowplow could plow 18 blocks in
    one-half hour. If there were 490 blocks to be plowed, how long did it take?

    _____

4. Teachers at Scott School marked off the field for students to make snow
    angels. They marked off 42 inches for each student. If the field was 200 feet
    across, how many spaces did they mark off for snow angels?

    _____

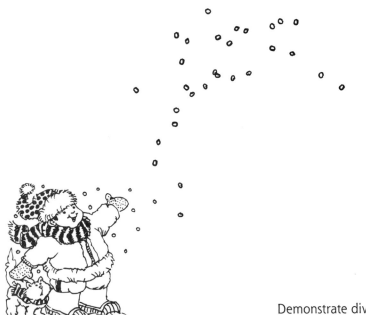

Demonstrate division with remainders using two-digit divisors

Number & Operations

Math Test

Name _____

Fill in the circle next to the correct answer.

1. 82 ÷ 16 = _____

  Ⓐ 5
  Ⓑ 5 R1
  Ⓒ 5 R2
  Ⓓ 5 R4

2. 94 ÷ 5 = _____

  Ⓐ 18 R4
  Ⓑ 16 R3
  Ⓒ 16 R2
  Ⓓ 6

3. 194 ÷ 4 = _____

  Ⓐ 49
  Ⓑ 43 R6
  Ⓒ 47 R2
  Ⓓ 48 R2

4. 429 ÷ 49 = _____

  Ⓐ 37 R8
  Ⓑ 8 R37
  Ⓒ 7 R86
  Ⓓ 6 R8

5. 23⟌528

  Ⓐ 22
  Ⓑ 22 R20
  Ⓒ 22 R22
  Ⓓ 22 R21

6. 42⟌964

  Ⓐ 22 R40
  Ⓑ 40 R22
  Ⓒ 22 R22
  Ⓓ 22 R20

7. 51⟌942

  Ⓐ 18 R24
  Ⓑ 18 R20
  Ⓒ 24 R18
  Ⓓ 20 R18

8. 42⟌9,428

  Ⓐ 220 R24
  Ⓑ 20 R224
  Ⓒ 224
  Ⓓ 224 R20

9. Sally has 529 pennies that she is rolling into rolls each with 50 pennies. How many rolls can she make? Are there any extras? What would be a good thing for her to do with the extras if there are any?

_____

10. Justin has 802 bolts that he is boxing up in packages of 25. How many packages can he create? Are there any extras? What would be a good thing for him to do with the extras if there are any?

_____

_____

_____

Demonstrate division with remainders using two-digit divisors

EMC 3018 • Basic Math Skills, Grade 5 • ©2003 by Evan-Moor Corp.

Race to the Finish Line

Name _____

Help the race car get to the finish line. Draw a path through the maze. At each number, decide if the number is odd or even, and then continue down the path in that direction.

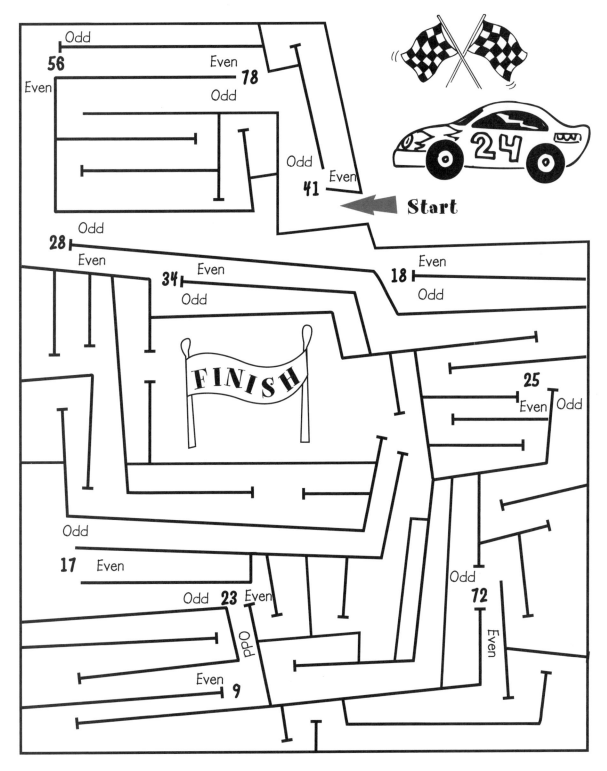

All Primed Out

Name _____

Use the following hundreds table as you follow these directions:

1. In black, cross out the number **1** since it is neither prime nor composite.
2. Use a red crayon to circle the next smallest number, the **2**. This number is the first prime number.
3. Because **2** goes into all even numbers, go through the table and cross out all the even numbers with a blue crayon.
4. Now, back to the red crayon, circle the next smallest number, the **3**. This is the next smallest prime number.
5. Use the blue crayon to cross out all multiples of 3 that have not already been marked out.
6. Continue alternating between the red and blue crayon, following steps 4 and 5, until all the numbers on the chart have either been crossed out or circled.

1	2	3	4	5	6	7	8	9	10
11	12	13	14	15	16	17	18	19	20
21	22	23	24	25	26	27	28	29	30
31	32	33	34	35	36	37	38	39	40
41	42	43	44	45	46	47	48	49	50
51	52	53	54	55	56	57	58	59	60
61	62	63	64	65	66	67	68	69	70
71	72	73	74	75	76	77	78	79	80
81	82	83	84	85	86	87	88	89	90
91	92	93	94	95	96	97	98	99	100

All prime numbers have been circled in red. List all the prime numbers between 1 and 100 below.

_____

_____

Identify any number as odd or even, and numbers less than 100 as prime or composite

EMC 3018 • Basic Math Skills, Grade 5 • ©2003 by Evan-Moor Corp.

Are You Odd?

Next to each number below, write *odd* if the number is odd and *even* if the number is even.

1. 26 _____   19 _____   518 _____

2. 49 _____   87 _____   492 _____

3. 51 _____   491 _____   828 _____

4. 82 _____   627 _____   672 _____

5. 15 _____   198 _____   1,625 _____

6. 16 _____   600 _____   5,298 _____

7. 54 _____   504 _____   7,222 _____

8. 90 _____   555 _____   9,999 _____

9. 28 _____   942 _____   4,261 _____

10. 16 _____   618 _____   8,210 _____

Identify any number as odd or even, and numbers less than 100 as prime or composite

Primed for Life

Name _____

Next to each number below, identify each number as *prime* or *composite*.

1. 26 _____   9 _____   6 _____

2. 81 _____   41 _____   47 _____

3. 19 _____   17 _____   13 _____

4. 54 _____   38 _____   63 _____

5. 69 _____   5 _____   23 _____

6. 11 _____   82 _____   4 _____

7. 8 _____   10 _____   7 _____

8. 12 _____   2 _____   79 _____

9. 3 _____   69 _____   75 _____

10. 37 _____   31 _____   29 _____

Identify any number as odd or even, and numbers less than 100 as prime or composite

EMC 3018 • Basic Math Skills, Grade 5 • ©2003 by Evan-Moor Corp.

Carpet World

Name _____

Solve each problem.

1. Tommy is helping his dad at their carpet store. They have several stacks of carpet squares that they would like to arrange into rectangles, and they need your help. The stacks are 26 of dusty rose, 17 of navy blue, 29 of taupe, and 39 of emerald green. Some of the stacks can be arranged into rectangles, while others can just be laid out in a straight line. Which can be laid out into rectangles other than just a straight line of them? (You must use all of the carpet pieces, and you cannot lay them on top of each other.)

   _____

2. Tommy has 69 tiles that are each 1 foot long. Can he divide them evenly so that they can be placed along the two edges of a hallway?

   _____

3. Daryl is buying 19 bathroom tiles and he would like to lay them out in a rectangle other than a 1 by 19 rectangle. Is this possible? What are the dimensions of the rectangle? If he can't, write a note to him explaining why he can't make this into a rectangle.

   _____

4. Suzanne has collected 44 carpet squares she and would like to place them side by side going down the hallway, creating two columns of carpets. Will the columns each have the same number of carpet squares?

   _____

Identify any number as odd or even, and numbers less than 100 as prime or composite

The Quilt Affair

Solve each problem.

1. Sam and his mom are making a quilt. They have created 37 squares and are now attempting to lay them out into a rectangle that is close to a square shape. They keep running into problems where they have a few left over. Can you write them a note giving them some hints about their dilemma?

   _____

2. Georgia has made a wonderful quilt and wants to add some squares along two sides of the quilt to finish it off. She has 34 squares. Can she divide them evenly between the two sides?

   _____

3. Beth and Don have been working really hard in their classroom to create a quilt that has 48 squares. They want to lay the squares out in a rectangle, and because 48 is a composite number, they have discovered that there are many different ways they could lay them out. What dimensions would you use to lay out the 48 squares to create a shape that is closest to a square?

   _____

4. Tristan and Julie have 49 strips of fabric that they want to divide evenly between the top and bottom of their quilt pattern. Can they divide the strips evenly?

   _____

Identify any number as odd or even, and numbers less than 100 as prime or composite

Math Test

Fill in the circle next to the correct answer.

1. Which of the following numbers is even?
   - Ⓐ 45
   - Ⓑ 76
   - Ⓒ 29
   - Ⓓ 11

2. Which of the following numbers is even?
   - Ⓐ 834
   - Ⓑ 635
   - Ⓒ 533
   - Ⓓ 637

3. Which of the following numbers is odd?
   - Ⓐ 26
   - Ⓑ 12
   - Ⓒ 90
   - Ⓓ 69

4. Which of the following numbers is odd?
   - Ⓐ 174
   - Ⓑ 377
   - Ⓒ 144
   - Ⓓ 286

5. Which of the following numbers is prime?
   - Ⓐ 16
   - Ⓑ 39
   - Ⓒ 33
   - Ⓓ 43

6. Which of the following numbers is composite?
   - Ⓐ 37
   - Ⓑ 29
   - Ⓒ 27
   - Ⓓ 47

7. Which of the following numbers is prime?
   - Ⓐ 35
   - Ⓑ 62
   - Ⓒ 57
   - Ⓓ All are composite.

8. Which of the following numbers is composite?
   - Ⓐ 67
   - Ⓑ 41
   - Ⓒ 83
   - Ⓓ All are prime.

9. List all the prime numbers between 20 and 50.

   _____

10. Write a sentence to explain why 14 is an even number.

   _____

   _____

   _____

Identify any number as odd or even, and numbers less than 100 as prime or composite

Riddle

Name _____

To answer the riddle, draw a straight line between each number on the left and all the corresponding numbers on the right that are factors of the given number. Since the number 1 is a factor of all numbers, it is not included in the right column of this puzzle. Nor is the number itself listed on the right, even though it is also a factor. Look for all the other factors of each number and draw a line for each appropriate factor.

Each line you draw will go through a small number. Write the letter in front of the number on the numbered line at the bottom of the page. The letters will spell out the solution to the riddle.

What's furry, has whiskers, and chases outlaws?

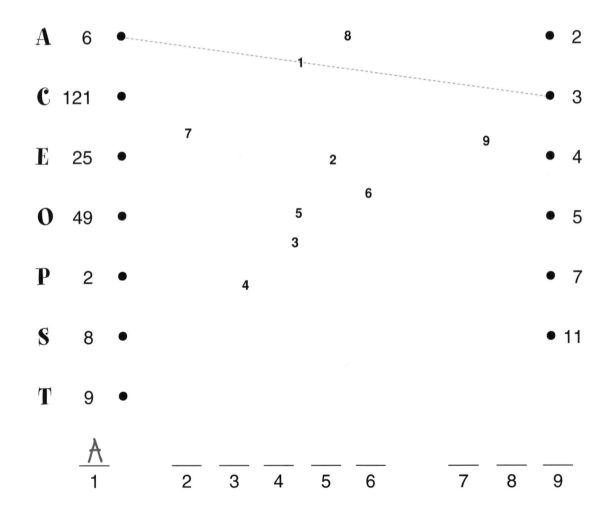

$$
\underset{1}{\underline{\text{A}}}\quad \underset{2}{\underline{}}\ \underset{3}{\underline{}}\ \underset{4}{\underline{}}\ \underset{5}{\underline{}}\ \underset{6}{\underline{}}\qquad \underset{7}{\underline{}}\ \underset{8}{\underline{}}\ \underset{9}{\underline{}}
$$

Identify factors of numbers less than 150, and multiples of single-digit numbers

Color My World

Name _____

Use the key below and color each region the appropriate color.

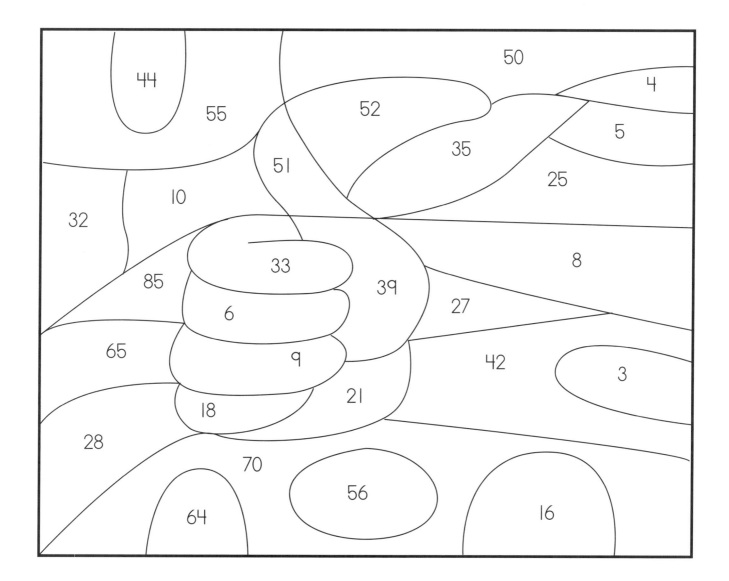

Red–multiples of **3**

Blue–multiples of **4**

Green–multiples of **5**

Identify factors of numbers less than 150, and multiples of single-digit numbers

Whatcha Factoring?

Next to each number below, write all the factors of the given number.

1. 24 _____

2. 64 _____

3. 32 _____

4. 25 _____

5. 90 _____

6. 48 _____

7. 18 _____

8. 83 _____

9. 99 _____

10. 125 _____

Identify factors of numbers less than 150, and multiples of single-digit numbers

My Multiples

Name _____

Next to each number below, list the first eight multiples.

1. 1 _____

2. 2 _____

3. 3 _____

4. 4 _____

5. 5 _____

6. 6 _____

7. 7 _____

8. 8 _____

9. 9 _____

10. 10 _____

Identify factors of numbers less than 150, and multiples of single-digit numbers

Number & Operations

City Grocery

Name _____

Solve each problem.

1. Cliff is looking at donuts that are packaged in groups of three. He is thinking to himself, "If I buy 1 package, then I get 3 donuts; if I buy 2 packages, then I get 6 donuts, ..." Help Cliff list the number of donuts he will get if he buys 1 package all the way to 10 packages of donuts.

_____

2. Mike has 24 boxes of cereal to use to create a design within the display area. He wants to set the boxes in a rectangle. What are all the possible dimensions of that rectangle?

_____

3. Kendra has a similar situation in which she is creating a display with a certain number of boxes. She has figured that she can arrange them with the following numbers as possibilities for the width of her rectangle: 1, 9, 27, or 3. How many boxes of cereal does she have to create her design with? Justify your response.

_____

4. Tate started with 150 bags of chips. He had them arranged in a nice rectangle, but then decided that he wanted to eat one bag of chips, which left 149 bags. Can he still arrange them into a rectangle, or should he eat another bag of chips in order to get to a number that is composite?

_____

5. Lesley is stacking six-packs of soda, one on top of the other. She is thinking about the number of bottles as she goes. First there are 6 bottles, and then there are 12 bottles, etc. If she has a total of 10 six-packs, how many bottles will she have in all?

_____

Identify factors of numbers less than 150, and multiples of single-digit numbers

EMC 3018 • Basic Math Skills, Grade 5 • ©2003 by Evan-Moor Corp.

My Number Is...

Solve each problem.

1. Julia is thinking of a number that has 7 and 4 as factors, and is larger than 30. What is the smallest number that Julia could be thinking of?

   _____

2. Mark is thinking of a number that has 2, 3, and 5 as factors. His number is smaller than 50. What is Mark's number?

   _____

3. Samantha is thinking of a number that is a multiple of 3, 5, and 7. What is the smallest number that Samantha could be thinking of?

   _____

4. Bryce is thinking of a number that is a multiple of 8 and 5, and is larger than 100. What is the smallest number that Bryce could be thinking of?

   _____

5. George is thinking of a number that is a multiple of 2, 3, 4, and 5. His number is also greater than 100. What is the smallest number that George could be thinking of?

   _____

Identify factors of numbers less than 150, and multiples of single-digit numbers

Math Test

Name _____

Fill in the circle next to the correct answer.

1. Which set of numbers lists all the factors of 12?

   Ⓐ 2, 3, 4, and 6
   Ⓑ 2, 3, 4, 6, and 12
   Ⓒ 3 and 4
   Ⓓ 1, 2, 3, 4, 6, and 12

2. Which set of numbers lists all the factors of 17?

   Ⓐ 1, 2, 3, 5, and 17
   Ⓑ 1 and 17
   Ⓒ 17
   Ⓓ 2 and 8

3. Which of the following is a factor of 135?

   Ⓐ 3   Ⓒ 11
   Ⓑ 7   Ⓓ all of the above

4. Which of the following is a factor of 147?

   Ⓐ 7   Ⓒ 3
   Ⓑ 49   Ⓓ all of the above

5. Which of the following numbers is a multiple of 5?
   Ⓐ 52   Ⓒ 85
   Ⓑ 69   Ⓓ 42

6. Which of the following numbers is a multiple of 9?
   Ⓐ 81   Ⓒ 69
   Ⓑ 29   Ⓓ 24

7. Which list of numbers contains only multiples of 4?

   Ⓐ 24, 36, 58, 68, 120
   Ⓑ 16, 32, 72, 82, 116
   Ⓒ 24, 32, 64, 124, 128
   Ⓓ 12, 24, 28, 36, 95

8. Which list of numbers contains only multiples of 3?

   Ⓐ 15, 24, 33, 54, 102
   Ⓑ 18, 21, 35, 42, 99
   Ⓒ 24, 36, 41, 45, 81
   Ⓓ 33, 39, 43, 54, 63

9. List all the factors of 18.

   _____

10. List five multiples of 4 between 40 and 80.

   _____

   _____

Identify factors of numbers less than 150, and multiples of single-digit numbers

Golfers' Socks

Name _____

Why do golfers take an extra pair of socks with them when they play golf?

To solve the riddle, find the answer for each problem in the box. Then write the corresponding letters on the lines above the answers.

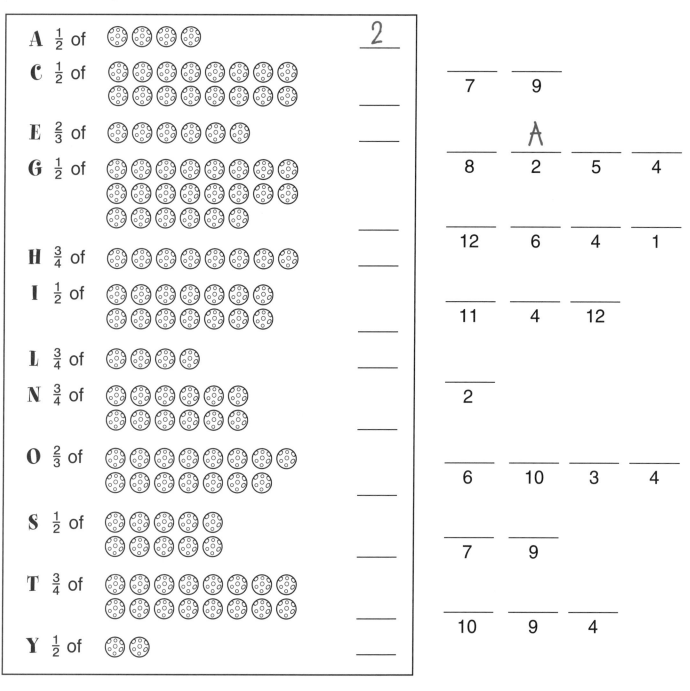

A ½ of ⊙⊙⊙⊙   __2__

C ½ of ⊙⊙⊙⊙⊙⊙⊙⊙
⊙⊙⊙⊙⊙⊙⊙⊙   ____

E ⅔ of ⊙⊙⊙⊙⊙⊙   ____

G ½ of ⊙⊙⊙⊙⊙⊙⊙⊙
⊙⊙⊙⊙⊙⊙⊙⊙
⊙⊙⊙⊙⊙⊙   ____

H ¾ of ⊙⊙⊙⊙⊙⊙⊙⊙   ____

I ½ of ⊙⊙⊙⊙⊙⊙⊙
⊙⊙⊙⊙⊙⊙⊙   ____

L ¾ of ⊙⊙⊙⊙   ____

N ¾ of ⊙⊙⊙⊙
⊙⊙⊙⊙   ____

O ⅔ of ⊙⊙⊙⊙⊙⊙⊙⊙
⊙⊙⊙⊙⊙⊙⊙   ____

S ½ of ⊙⊙⊙⊙
⊙⊙⊙⊙   ____

T ¾ of ⊙⊙⊙⊙⊙⊙⊙⊙
⊙⊙⊙⊙⊙⊙⊙⊙   ____

Y ½ of ⊙⊙   ____

___ ___
7   9

___ A ___ ___
8   2   5   4

___ ___ ___ ___
12   6   4   1

___ ___ ___
11   4   12

___
2

___ ___ ___ ___
6   10   3   4

___ ___
7   9

___ ___ ___
10   9   4

Identify halves, thirds, fourths, fifths, sixths, and eighths of sets

Number & Operations

What Does a Car Wear When It's Cold?

Name _____

To solve the riddle, find the answer for each problem in the box. Then write the corresponding letters on the lines above the answers.

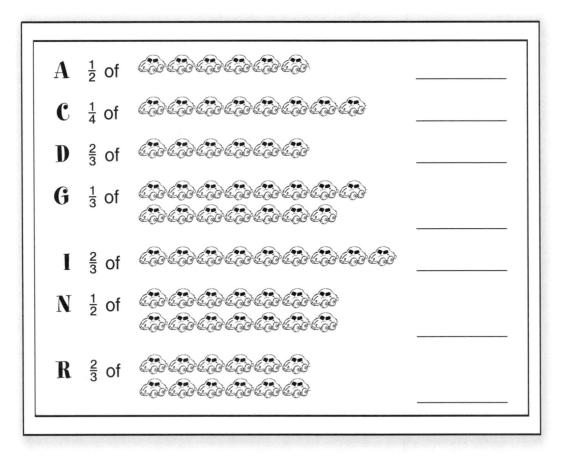

A $\frac{1}{2}$ of _____   _____

C $\frac{1}{4}$ of _____   _____

D $\frac{2}{3}$ of _____   _____

G $\frac{1}{3}$ of _____   _____

I $\frac{2}{3}$ of _____   _____

N $\frac{1}{2}$ of _____   _____

R $\frac{2}{3}$ of _____   _____

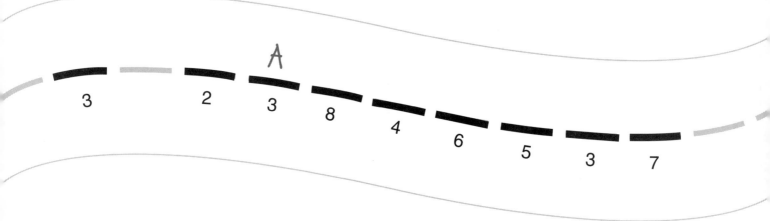

A

3   2   3   8   4   6   5   3   7

Identify halves, thirds, fourths, fifths, sixths, and eighths of sets

Number & Operations   EMC 3018 • Basic Math Skills, Grade 5 • ©2003 by Evan-Moor Corp.

In the Bag

Name _____

For each question, draw the answer in the bag.

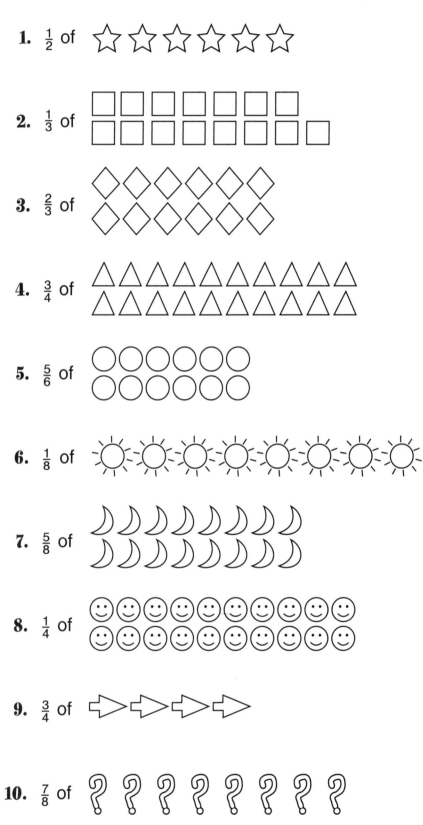

1. $\frac{1}{2}$ of

2. $\frac{1}{3}$ of

3. $\frac{2}{3}$ of

4. $\frac{3}{4}$ of

5. $\frac{5}{6}$ of

6. $\frac{1}{8}$ of

7. $\frac{5}{8}$ of

8. $\frac{1}{4}$ of

9. $\frac{3}{4}$ of

10. $\frac{7}{8}$ of

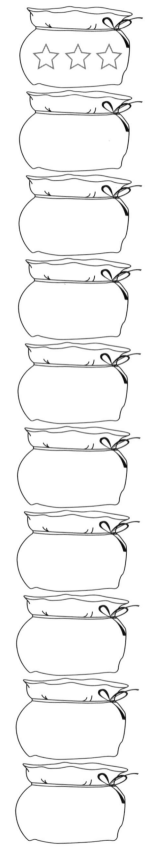

Identify halves, thirds, fourths, fifths, sixths, and eighths of sets

In the Bag II

Name _____

For each question, draw the answer in the bag.

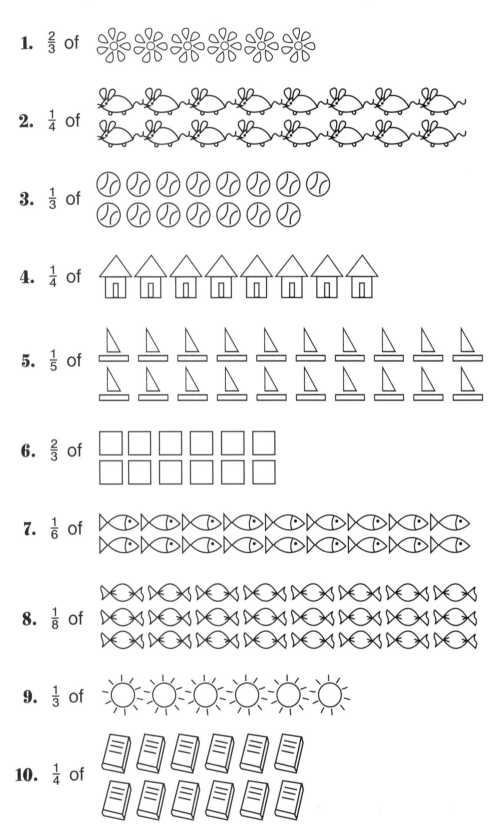

1. $\frac{2}{3}$ of

2. $\frac{1}{4}$ of

3. $\frac{1}{3}$ of

4. $\frac{1}{4}$ of

5. $\frac{1}{5}$ of

6. $\frac{2}{3}$ of

7. $\frac{1}{6}$ of

8. $\frac{1}{8}$ of

9. $\frac{1}{3}$ of

10. $\frac{1}{4}$ of

Identify halves, thirds, fourths, fifths, sixths, and eighths of sets

Number & Operations

EMC 3018 • Basic Math Skills, Grade 5 • ©2003 by Evan-Moor Corp.

Collections

Name_____ 65

Solve each problem.

1. Danny has 48 baseball cards in his collection. He would like to give $\frac{3}{4}$ of them to his little brother. How many should he give to his brother?

_____

2. Mary Anne has 60 trolls in her bedroom. Her parents have asked her to put $\frac{2}{3}$ of them away in storage because her room is too messy. How many does she need to put into storage?

_____

3. Miguel is collecting stamps and has 120 pages in his book. If $\frac{3}{5}$ of the pages are filled with stamps, how many blank pages are there in Miguel's book?

_____

4. Brendan has a rock collection that weighs 200 pounds. His dad tried to lift it and realized it was too heavy. He was only able to lift $\frac{5}{8}$ of the collection at once. How many pounds of rocks was Brendan's dad able to lift?

_____

5. Amy Beth is collecting decks of cards from each place that she visits. She has a collection of 36 decks. She has a box that holds $\frac{5}{6}$ of the decks. How many decks of cards do NOT fit inside the box?

_____

Identify halves, thirds, fourths, fifths, sixths, and eighths of sets

Gardening

Name _____

Solve each problem.

1. Jimmy's family bought a big bag of tulip bulbs to split evenly among his family and the neighbors on both sides of his house. The bag contains 120 bulbs. How many bulbs should Jimmy's family keep?

   _____

2. Juan and his mother bought 18 potato plants for their garden. They used only $\frac{5}{6}$ of the plants. Juan's aunt asked if she could have their leftover plants. How many plants could they give to Juan's aunt?

   _____

3. Nancy had a bag containing 40 pumpkin seeds. She planted several hills, each with three seeds in them. If she used $\frac{3}{4}$ of the seeds, how many hills did she plant?

   _____

4. Kelly started with 100 strawberry plants. He planted one-half of them in the garden in his backyard. Of those that were left, he planted three-fifths at his grandmother's house. Of the ones that were left, he planted three-fourths at his uncle's house. How many plants does he have left?

   _____

Identify halves, thirds, fourths, fifths, sixths, and eighths of sets

Math Test

Name _____

Fill in the circle next to the correct answer.

1. What is $\frac{1}{3}$ of ○○○○○○ ?

Ⓐ 1   Ⓒ 2
Ⓑ 3   Ⓓ 6

2. What is $\frac{3}{5}$ of ☆☆☆☆☆ ?

Ⓐ 3   Ⓒ 5
Ⓑ 6   Ⓓ 8

3. What is $\frac{1}{2}$ of △△△△△△ ?

Ⓐ 1   Ⓒ 4
Ⓑ 2   Ⓓ 3

4. What is $\frac{3}{4}$ of ☼☼☼☼ ?

Ⓐ 6   Ⓒ 4
Ⓑ 3   Ⓓ 8

5. What is $\frac{1}{2}$ of 8?

Ⓐ 1   Ⓒ 6
Ⓑ 4   Ⓓ 8

6. What is $\frac{3}{4}$ of 20?

Ⓐ 3   Ⓒ 5
Ⓑ 8   Ⓓ 15

7. What is $\frac{2}{3}$ of 9?

Ⓐ 2   Ⓒ 9
Ⓑ 3   Ⓓ 6

8. What is $\frac{1}{6}$ of 12?

Ⓐ 2   Ⓒ 3
Ⓑ 6   Ⓓ 4

9. Draw a bag of 12 stars. Shade in $\frac{1}{3}$ of the stars.

10. Draw a bag of 15 triangles. Shade in $\frac{3}{5}$ of the 15 triangles. Draw a circle around $\frac{1}{3}$ of the 15 triangles.

Identify halves, thirds, fourths, fifths, sixths, and eighths of sets

Tongue Twister #4

Name _____

Solve each addition problem below. Then write the letter for each problem on the line above the answer at the bottom of the page. The letters will spell out a tongue twister. Try to say it fast three times.

A $\frac{1}{2} + 1\frac{1}{2}$ = _____

C $\frac{3}{4} + \frac{1}{4}$ = _____

E $\frac{4}{5} + \frac{2}{5}$ = _____

F $1\frac{3}{7} + 2\frac{4}{7}$ = _____

H $\frac{1}{3} + \frac{1}{3}$ = _____

I $2\frac{4}{7} + 1\frac{1}{7}$ = _____

L $\frac{1}{6} + 2\frac{2}{3}$ = _____

N $\frac{4}{9} + 3\frac{2}{3}$ = _____

R $\frac{1}{2} + 2\frac{5}{8}$ = _____

S $2\frac{2}{3} + 1\frac{1}{9}$ = _____

T $\frac{1}{5} + \frac{1}{2}$ = _____

| 4 | $3\frac{1}{8}$ | 2 | $4\frac{1}{9}$ | 1 | $3\frac{5}{7}$ | $3\frac{7}{9}$ |

F
| 4 | $3\frac{1}{8}$ | $3\frac{5}{7}$ | $1\frac{1}{5}$ | $3\frac{7}{9}$ |

| 4 | $3\frac{1}{8}$ | $1\frac{1}{5}$ | $3\frac{7}{9}$ | $\frac{2}{3}$ |

| 4 | $3\frac{5}{7}$ | $3\frac{7}{9}$ | $\frac{2}{3}$ |

| 4 | $3\frac{5}{7}$ | $2\frac{5}{6}$ | $2\frac{5}{6}$ | $1\frac{1}{5}$ | $\frac{7}{10}$ | $3\frac{7}{9}$ |

Demonstrate addition and subtraction of fractions (including mixed numbers and unlike denominators)

EMC 3018 • Basic Math Skills, Grade 5 • ©2003 by Evan-Moor Corp.

Name _____

What word starts with an "E," but usually only contains one letter?

Solve each subtraction problem below. Then write the corresponding letter for each answer on the line in front of the problem. The letters will spell out the answer to the riddle when read from top to bottom.

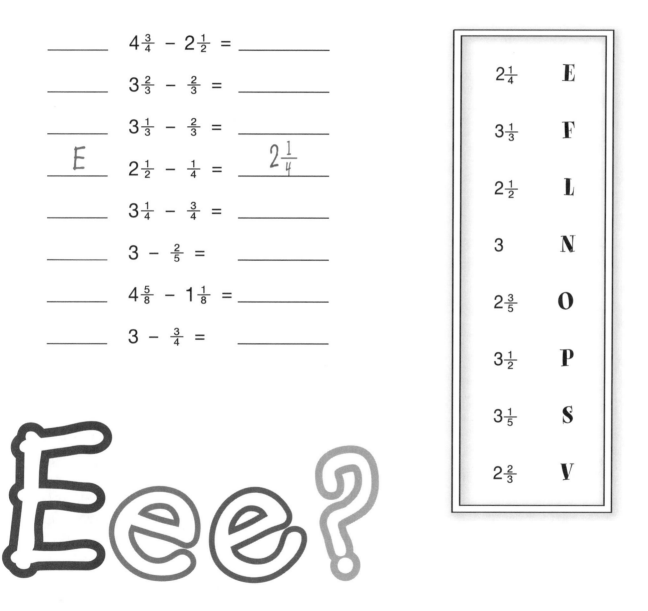

_____ $4\frac{3}{4} - 2\frac{1}{2} =$ _____

_____ $3\frac{2}{3} - \frac{2}{3} =$ _____

_____ $3\frac{1}{3} - \frac{2}{3} =$ _____

_E_ $2\frac{1}{2} - \frac{1}{4} =$ $2\frac{1}{4}$

_____ $3\frac{1}{4} - \frac{3}{4} =$ _____

_____ $3 - \frac{2}{5} =$ _____

_____ $4\frac{5}{8} - 1\frac{1}{8} =$ _____

_____ $3 - \frac{3}{4} =$ _____

$2\frac{1}{4}$	**E**
$3\frac{1}{3}$	**F**
$2\frac{1}{2}$	**L**
3	**N**
$2\frac{3}{5}$	**O**
$3\frac{1}{2}$	**P**
$3\frac{1}{5}$	**S**
$2\frac{2}{3}$	**V**

Demonstrate addition and subtraction of fractions (including mixed numbers and unlike denominators)

Sum Fraction Fun

Name _____

Complete each of the following addition problems.

1. $\frac{4}{5} + \frac{1}{5}$ = $\dfrac{5}{5} = 1$

2. $3\frac{1}{3} + 1\frac{2}{3}$ = _____

3. $3\frac{3}{4} + 1\frac{3}{4}$ = _____

4. $1\frac{1}{2} + \frac{1}{4}$ = _____

5. $2\frac{1}{5} + 3\frac{1}{2}$ = _____

6. $3\frac{4}{5} + 5\frac{1}{3}$ = _____

7. $2\frac{1}{3} + 2\frac{1}{2}$ = _____

8. $4\frac{6}{7} + 3$ = _____

9. $\frac{1}{5} + \frac{3}{8}$ = _____

10. $4\frac{2}{3} + 8\frac{5}{6}$ = _____

$\dfrac{1}{4}$

$\dfrac{3}{4}$

Demonstrate addition and subtraction of fractions (including mixed numbers and unlike denominators)

EMC 3018 • Basic Math Skills, Grade 5 • ©2003 by Evan-Moor Corp.

Can You Tell the Difference?

Complete each of the following subtraction problems.

1. $\frac{5}{8} - \frac{1}{8}$ = _____ $\frac{4}{8} = \frac{1}{2}$ _____

2. $5\frac{2}{3} - 2\frac{1}{3}$ = _____

3. $4 - \frac{1}{4}$ = _____

4. $3\frac{1}{3} - \frac{2}{3}$ = _____

5. $5\frac{1}{4} - 1\frac{3}{4}$ = _____

6. $4\frac{2}{5} - 1\frac{4}{5}$ = _____

7. $7\frac{7}{9} - \frac{2}{3}$ = _____

8. $5\frac{3}{4} - 2\frac{1}{2}$ = _____

9. $9\frac{1}{3} - 4\frac{5}{9}$ = _____

10. $3\frac{2}{5} - 1\frac{1}{2}$ = _____

Demonstrate addition and subtraction of fractions (including mixed numbers and unlike denominators)

Fabric World

Name _____

Solve each problem.

1. Samantha found a bolt of fabric that has $18\frac{1}{2}$ yards on it. She would like to buy $4\frac{1}{3}$ yards of fabric. How much will be left on the bolt after Samantha buys her fabric?

   _____

2. George found this cool ribbon for a costume he is making. The spool originally had 80 yards of ribbon. He noticed that they write on the spool each time someone buys some ribbon. The first person bought 15 yards. The second person bought $5\frac{1}{2}$ yards. The third person bought $4\frac{3}{4}$ yards. The last person bought $7\frac{1}{2}$ yards. George is wondering if there is enough left to buy 36 yards of it. Help him out by determining how much ribbon is actually left on the spool.

   _____

3. Alex found that there are $12\frac{2}{3}$ yards of fabric on one bolt and $3\frac{1}{2}$ yards of identical fabric on another bolt. If he buys both bolts of fabric, how much will he have?

   _____

4. Naomi is sewing a new pillow for her bedroom. She started out with $8\frac{1}{4}$ yards of fabric and used $5\frac{2}{3}$ yards. How much fabric does she have left?

   _____

5. Velda is collecting odd remnants of fabric to make a quilt. She needs 8 yards of fabric to create the quilt. The pieces that she has collected so far measure $2\frac{1}{4}$ yards, $3\frac{2}{3}$ yards, and $1\frac{1}{2}$ yards. Does she have enough fabric to complete her quilt? Justify your answer.

   _____

Demonstrate addition and subtraction of fractions (including mixed numbers and unlike denominators)

Number & Operations
EMC 3018 • Basic Math Skills, Grade 5 • ©2003 by Evan-Moor Corp.

Pizza Parlor

Name _____

Solve each problem.

1. Sam's family went to the Pizza Parlor for dinner. They started with 4 pizzas. Sam's parents ate $\frac{1}{2}$ of a pizza. Sam and his brothers ate $2\frac{1}{3}$ pizzas, while his sisters ate only $\frac{3}{4}$ of a pizza. How much pizza was left?

_____

2. Mike, Tim, and Tina went out for pizza. They ordered several of the mini pizzas and ate most of what they ordered. Mike ate $4\frac{2}{3}$ pizzas, Tim ate $5\frac{1}{2}$ pizzas, and Tina ate $7\frac{3}{4}$ pizzas. When they put the leftover pizza together, it was less than a whole pizza. How many pizzas did they order to start with?

_____

3. Suzanne and her friends went out to order an extra large pizza. They requested that pepperoni be placed on one-third of the pizza and sausage be placed on one-fourth of the pizza and to leave the rest of the pizza just plain cheese. How much of the pizza had just cheese?

_____

4. When the Pizza Parlor opened their doors at 4:00 Thursday afternoon, there were 200 empty pizza boxes ready to use that night. They used 50 boxes in the first half-hour and then were completely out of boxes one and one-third hours later. At what time did they run out of boxes?

_____

5. Trina and her two sisters went out for pizza while her oldest sister was home from college. They each ate $\frac{2}{3}$ of a pizza, and they started with 2 pizzas. How much of the pizza was left?

_____

Demonstrate addition and subtraction of fractions (including mixed numbers and unlike denominators)

Math Test

Name _____

Fill in the circle next to the correct answer.

1. $\frac{3}{4} + 1\frac{3}{4} =$ _____

    Ⓐ $1\frac{1}{2}$ Ⓒ $1\frac{6}{8}$

    Ⓑ $1\frac{3}{4}$ Ⓓ $2\frac{1}{2}$

2. $\frac{5}{7} + \frac{3}{7} =$ _____

    Ⓐ $1\frac{1}{7}$ Ⓒ $\frac{4}{7}$

    Ⓑ $\frac{8}{14}$ Ⓓ $\frac{7}{8}$

3. $3\frac{2}{5} + 4\frac{3}{5} =$ _____

    Ⓐ 7 Ⓒ $7\frac{3}{5}$

    Ⓑ $7\frac{2}{5}$ Ⓓ 8

4. $4\frac{3}{5} + 2\frac{1}{4} =$ _____

    Ⓐ $6\frac{4}{9}$ Ⓒ $6\frac{4}{20}$

    Ⓑ $6\frac{3}{5}$ Ⓓ $6\frac{17}{20}$

5. $\frac{9}{11} - \frac{5}{11} =$ _____

    Ⓐ 4 Ⓒ $\frac{4}{11}$

    Ⓑ 5 Ⓓ $\frac{5}{11}$

6. $3\frac{1}{3} - \frac{2}{3} =$ _____

    Ⓐ $3\frac{2}{3}$ Ⓒ $2\frac{2}{3}$

    Ⓑ $\frac{2}{3}$ Ⓓ 3

7. $5\frac{1}{4} - 2\frac{3}{4} =$ _____

    Ⓐ $2\frac{1}{2}$ Ⓒ $3\frac{2}{4}$

    Ⓑ 3 Ⓓ 2

8. $4\frac{1}{3} - 1\frac{1}{2} =$ _____

    Ⓐ 3 Ⓒ $5\frac{5}{6}$

    Ⓑ $3\frac{1}{6}$ Ⓓ $2\frac{5}{6}$

9. Simon has completed the following math problem:

$$\frac{1}{3} + \frac{1}{2} = \frac{2}{5}$$

Simon says that 1 + 1 = 2, so the numerator is 2, and similarly that 3 + 2 = 5, so the denominator is 5. Write a note to Simon agreeing with him if he has the correct answer. If he has made a mistake, explain in your note the mistake he made and what he should do differently.

_____

_____

_____

10. Cheryl has a piece of fabric that is $3\frac{1}{3}$ yards long. She wants to cut off a piece of fabric that is $1\frac{1}{2}$ yards long to sew a pillow. How much fabric will she have left?

_____

Demonstrate addition and subtraction of fractions (including mixed numbers and unlike denominators)

Number & Operations

EMC 3018 • Basic Math Skills, Grade 5 • ©2003 by Evan-Moor Corp.

What Has Six Feet and Can't Move?

Name _____

To solve this riddle, solve each of the multiplication problems below. Then write the letter corresponding to the correct answer on the line. Read the answer from top to bottom.

_____ $\frac{1}{4} \times \frac{3}{5} =$ _____

_____ $\frac{2}{7} \times \frac{5}{9} =$ _____

_____ $\frac{2}{3} \times \frac{5}{7} =$ _____

_____ $\frac{3}{5} \times \frac{2}{5} =$ _____

_____ $\frac{1}{6} \times \frac{5}{6} =$ _____

R _____ $\frac{1}{2} \times \frac{7}{8} =$ _____ $\frac{7}{16}$ _____

_____ $\frac{4}{5} \times \frac{1}{7} =$ _____

_____ $\frac{3}{7} \times \frac{4}{5} =$ _____

$\frac{5}{36}$	**A**
$\frac{4}{35}$	**D**
$\frac{5}{12}$	**L**
$\frac{3}{16}$	**M**
$\frac{10}{21}$	**O**
$\frac{7}{16}$	**R**
$\frac{12}{35}$	**S**
$\frac{3}{20}$	**T**
$\frac{10}{63}$	**W**
$\frac{6}{25}$	**Y**

Demonstrate multiplication with fractions (without the need to reduce)

Number & Operations

Tongue Twister #5

Solve each multiplication problem below. Write the letter next to each problem above the answer at the bottom of the page. The letters will spell out a tongue twister. Try to say it fast three times.

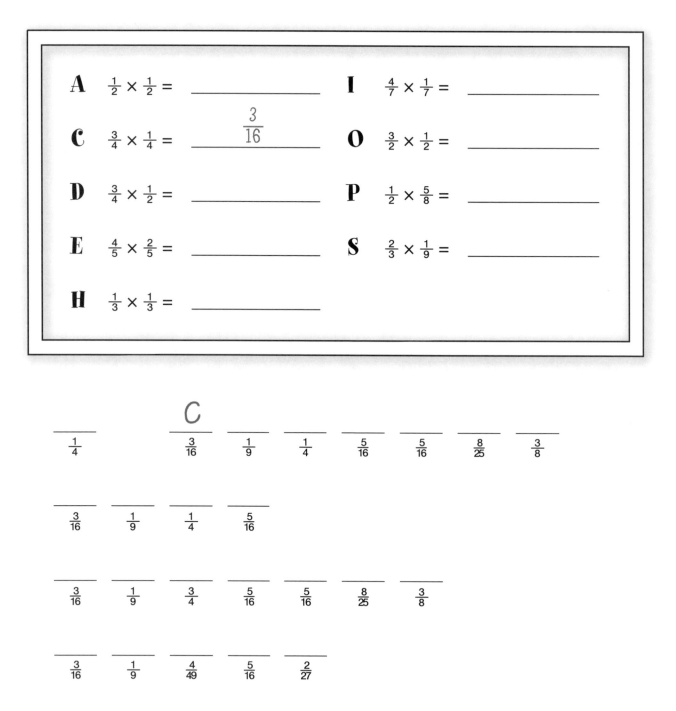

A $\frac{1}{2} \times \frac{1}{2} =$ _____

C $\frac{3}{4} \times \frac{1}{4} =$ _____$\frac{3}{16}$_____

D $\frac{3}{4} \times \frac{1}{2} =$ _____

E $\frac{4}{5} \times \frac{2}{5} =$ _____

H $\frac{1}{3} \times \frac{1}{3} =$ _____

I $\frac{4}{7} \times \frac{1}{7} =$ _____

O $\frac{3}{2} \times \frac{1}{2} =$ _____

P $\frac{1}{2} \times \frac{5}{8} =$ _____

S $\frac{2}{3} \times \frac{1}{9} =$ _____

$\underset{\frac{1}{4}}{\rule{2cm}{0.4pt}}$ $\overset{C}{\underset{\frac{3}{16}}{\rule{2cm}{0.4pt}}}$ $\underset{\frac{1}{9}}{\rule{2cm}{0.4pt}}$ $\underset{\frac{1}{4}}{\rule{2cm}{0.4pt}}$ $\underset{\frac{5}{16}}{\rule{2cm}{0.4pt}}$ $\underset{\frac{5}{16}}{\rule{2cm}{0.4pt}}$ $\underset{\frac{8}{25}}{\rule{2cm}{0.4pt}}$ $\underset{\frac{3}{8}}{\rule{2cm}{0.4pt}}$

$\underset{\frac{3}{16}}{\rule{2cm}{0.4pt}}$ $\underset{\frac{1}{9}}{\rule{2cm}{0.4pt}}$ $\underset{\frac{1}{4}}{\rule{2cm}{0.4pt}}$ $\underset{\frac{5}{16}}{\rule{2cm}{0.4pt}}$

$\underset{\frac{3}{16}}{\rule{2cm}{0.4pt}}$ $\underset{\frac{1}{9}}{\rule{2cm}{0.4pt}}$ $\underset{\frac{3}{4}}{\rule{2cm}{0.4pt}}$ $\underset{\frac{5}{16}}{\rule{2cm}{0.4pt}}$ $\underset{\frac{5}{16}}{\rule{2cm}{0.4pt}}$ $\underset{\frac{8}{25}}{\rule{2cm}{0.4pt}}$ $\underset{\frac{3}{8}}{\rule{2cm}{0.4pt}}$

$\underset{\frac{3}{16}}{\rule{2cm}{0.4pt}}$ $\underset{\frac{1}{9}}{\rule{2cm}{0.4pt}}$ $\underset{\frac{4}{49}}{\rule{2cm}{0.4pt}}$ $\underset{\frac{5}{16}}{\rule{2cm}{0.4pt}}$ $\underset{\frac{2}{27}}{\rule{2cm}{0.4pt}}$

Demonstrate multiplication with fractions (without the need to reduce)

Fraction Products

Name _____

Complete each problem below by finding the product.

1. $\frac{3}{4} \times \frac{1}{2} =$ _____$\frac{3}{8}$_____

2. $\frac{2}{5} \times \frac{1}{3} =$ _____

3. $\frac{4}{7} \times \frac{1}{3} =$ _____

4. $\frac{2}{5} \times \frac{4}{5} =$ _____

5. $\frac{1}{2} \times \frac{1}{6} =$ _____

6. $\frac{3}{4} \times \frac{1}{5} =$ _____

7. $\frac{5}{6} \times \frac{5}{7} =$ _____

8. $\frac{1}{5} \times \frac{2}{3} =$ _____

9. $\frac{4}{7} \times \frac{1}{9} =$ _____

10. $\frac{5}{9} \times \frac{4}{7} =$ _____

Demonstrate multiplication with fractions (without the need to reduce)

Number & Operations

Find the Products

Name_____

Solve each multiplication problem.

1. $\frac{1}{3} \times \frac{2}{5} =$ _____ $\frac{2}{15}$ _____

2. $\frac{7}{8} \times \frac{3}{5} =$ _____

3. $\frac{1}{8} \times \frac{3}{8} =$ _____

4. $\frac{5}{9} \times \frac{4}{7} =$ _____

5. $\frac{1}{2} \times \frac{5}{9} =$ _____

6. $\frac{2}{5} \times \frac{3}{7} =$ _____

7. $\frac{7}{9} \times \frac{10}{11} =$ _____

8. $\frac{1}{3} \times \frac{10}{13} =$ _____

9. $\frac{2}{7} \times \frac{6}{7} =$ _____

10. $\frac{1}{8} \times \frac{3}{7} =$ _____

Demonstrate multiplication with fractions (without the need to reduce)

Number & Operations   EMC 3018 • Basic Math Skills, Grade 5 • ©2003 by Evan-Moor Corp.

Tim's Confused

Solve each problem.

1. Tim was working on two different problems and got stuck. The first problem was $\frac{1}{7} \times \frac{2}{3}$ and the second problem was $\frac{2}{7} \times \frac{1}{3}$. He is confused because he keeps getting the same answer even though the problems are different. Write a note to Tim explaining your solution to each problem. If the answers are the same, explain why in your note.

   _____

   _____

2. Tim had another problem that was $\frac{1}{2} \times \frac{1}{3}$. His third-grade teacher told him that when you multiply, your answer is larger. But when he multiplies these two fractions, he gets the answer of $\frac{1}{6}$, which is smaller than both of the fractions he started with. Write another note to him explaining why his solution is correct and why his answer is smaller than the two original fractions.

   _____

   _____

3. Tim is starting to think ahead of his class and reasons that $2 \times \frac{1}{3}$ is the same as $1 \times \frac{1}{3}$ plus another $1 \times \frac{1}{3}$, so he thinks the answer is $\frac{2}{3}$. Do you agree with his reasoning? Why or why not?

   _____

   _____

Demonstrate multiplication with fractions (without the need to reduce)

What's the Story?

Look at each multiplication problem below. Write a word problem that could use the multiplication problem to solve it. Then write the answer to each problem.

1. $\frac{1}{2} \times 8 =$

_____

_____

2. $\frac{1}{4} \times 5 =$

_____

_____

_____

3. $\frac{1}{2} \times \frac{1}{4} =$

_____

_____

_____

4. $\frac{1}{5} \times 5\frac{1}{2} =$

_____

_____

_____

Demonstrate multiplication with fractions (without the need to reduce)

EMC 3018 • Basic Math Skills, Grade 5 • ©2003 by Evan-Moor Corp.

Math Test

Fill in the circle next to the correct answer.

1. $\frac{1}{2} \times \frac{3}{5} =$ _____

    Ⓐ $\frac{3}{10}$ Ⓒ $\frac{3}{5}$

    Ⓑ $\frac{4}{7}$ Ⓓ $\frac{3}{2}$

2. $\frac{3}{7} \times \frac{5}{8} =$ _____

    Ⓐ $\frac{3}{56}$ Ⓒ $\frac{15}{56}$

    Ⓑ $\frac{15}{7}$ Ⓓ $\frac{15}{8}$

3. $\frac{1}{3} \times \frac{2}{9} =$ _____

    Ⓐ $\frac{2}{3}$ Ⓒ $\frac{1}{27}$

    Ⓑ $\frac{2}{9}$ Ⓓ $\frac{2}{27}$

4. $\frac{6}{7} \times \frac{2}{7} =$ _____

    Ⓐ $\frac{12}{49}$ Ⓒ $\frac{1}{49}$

    Ⓑ $\frac{12}{7}$ Ⓓ $\frac{6}{49}$

5. $\frac{2}{5} \times \frac{9}{11} =$ _____

    Ⓐ $\frac{2}{55}$ Ⓒ $\frac{9}{11}$

    Ⓑ $\frac{18}{55}$ Ⓓ $\frac{2}{11}$

6. $\frac{3}{5} \times \frac{7}{13} =$ _____

    Ⓐ $\frac{21}{65}$ Ⓒ $\frac{21}{13}$

    Ⓑ $\frac{3}{13}$ Ⓓ $\frac{21}{45}$

7. $\frac{11}{12} \times \frac{5}{7} =$ _____

    Ⓐ $\frac{11}{70}$ Ⓒ $\frac{55}{70}$

    Ⓑ $\frac{55}{64}$ Ⓓ $\frac{55}{84}$

8. $\frac{4}{15} \times \frac{2}{7} =$ _____

    Ⓐ $\frac{4}{105}$ Ⓒ $\frac{8}{105}$

    Ⓑ $\frac{8}{15}$ Ⓓ $\frac{8}{7}$

9. Write a story problem in which you would have to multiply $\frac{1}{2} \times 5$.

_____

_____

_____

10. Write a story problem in which you would have to multiply $\frac{1}{4} \times \frac{1}{2}$.

_____

_____

_____

Demonstrate multiplication with fractions (without the need to reduce)

Number & Operations

Trivia #1

Name _____

Solve each problem below. (Remember to line up your decimals when you add or subtract.) After completing each problem, look for the solution and write the corresponding letter on the line in front of the problem. The letters will spell out a piece of trivia when read from top to bottom.

_____ 1.5 + 1.02 = _____

_____ 4.0 + 0.06 = _____

_____ 2.0 − 0.75 = _____

_____ 2.16 + 0.65 = _____

_____ 2.26 + 2.54 = _____

_____ 1.23 + 3.35 = _____

_____ 3.6 − 1.08 = _____

_____ 5.2 − 1.14 = _____

__F__ 2.54 − 1.23 = _1.31_

_____ 6.42 − 1.87 = _____

_____ 4.59 − 1.78 = _____

_____ 1.2 + 1.1 = _____

_____ 2.0 − 0.65 = _____

_____ 5.2 − 0.65 = _____

_____ 5.13 − 1.07 = _____

_____ 3.0 + 1.1 = _____

_____ 2.49 + 1.57 = _____

2.52	**A**
4.1	**E**
1.31	**F**
4.8	**G**
4.58	**H**
1.25	**L**
1.35	**N**
4.55	**O**
2.3	**R**
4.06	**S**
2.81	**U**

Demonstrate addition and subtraction with decimals to the thousandths

Number & Operations   EMC 3018 • Basic Math Skills, Grade 5 • ©2003 by Evan-Moor Corp.

Where Do Cats Like to Swim?

Name _____

To solve the riddle, complete each problem below. Then write the corresponding letter on the line in front of the problem. The letters will spell out the solution to the riddle when read from top to bottom.

_____ 1.0 + 1.49 = _____

_____ 1.4 + 0.41 = _____

__T__ 7.0 − 0.46 = 6.54

_____ 5.6 − 1.8 = _____

_____ 2.64 + 2.31 = _____

_____ 1.49 + 1.77 = _____

_____ 9.62 − 5.01 = _____

_____ 6.1 − 4.0 = _____

_____ 1.94 + 0.16 = _____

_____ 3.4 − 0.91 = _____

_____ 1.4 + 0.99 = _____

_____ 5.16 − 2.67 = _____

_____ 6.49 − 2.93 = _____

2.52	A
3.56	C
4.95	E
2.39	F
3.8	H
2.49	I
1.81	N
3.26	P
2.1	S
6.54	T
4.61	U

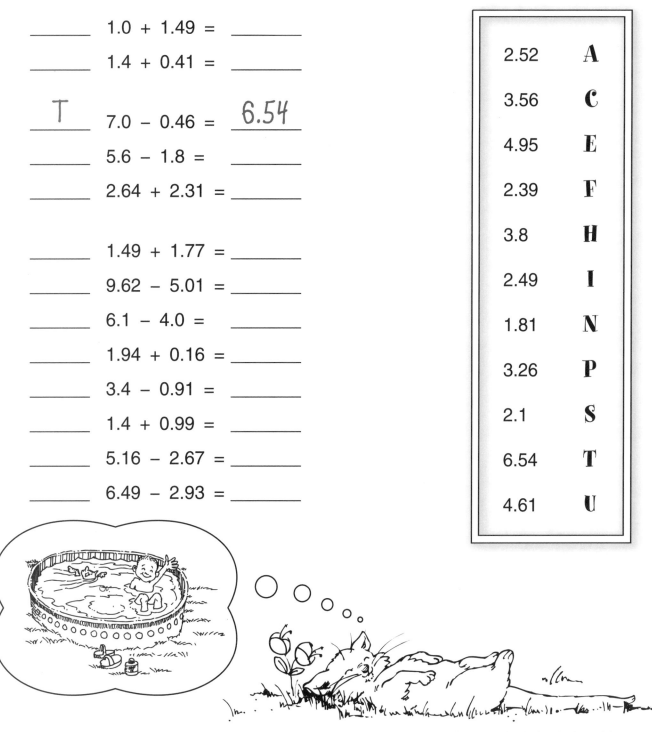

Demonstrate addition and subtraction with decimals to the thousandths

Number & Operations

Some Sums

Complete each of the following addition problems.

1.	2.5 + 6.4	**2.**	1.2 + 6.7	**3.**	4.29 + 4.31	**4.**	92.5 + 43.8	**5.**	91.64 + 15.28

6.	24.9 + 6.52	**7.**	15.3 + 5.915	**8.**	12.5 + 2.9	**9.**	51.6 + 4.0	**10.**	21.951 + 5.319

11. 15.3 + 84.6 = _____

12. 49.2 + 6.5 = _____

13. 15.0 + 6.4 = _____

14. 4.23 + 6.51 = _____

15. 4.29 + 93.34 = _____

16. 6.294 + 5.2 = _____

17. 9.264 + 842.26 = _____

18. 925.2 + 6.295 = _____

19. 5.492 + 6.0 = _____

20. 4.529 + 4.391 = _____

Demonstrate addition and subtraction with decimals to the thousandths

 EMC 3018 • Basic Math Skills, Grade 5 • ©2003 by Evan-Moor Corp.

What's the Difference?

Name _____

Complete each of the following subtraction problems.

1. 61.2
   − 60.1

2.   5.9
   − 2.3

3.   4.1
   − 3.9

4. 12.9
   − 9.2

5. 15.9
   − 7.8

6. 12.1
   − 5.8

7. 15.26
   − 5.49

8.   4.59
   − 2.0

9. 83.49
   − 2.95

10.   8.0
    − 5.12

11. 51.2 − 14.1 = _____

12. 96.0 − 4.8 = _____

13. 49.2 − 15.9 = _____

14. 91.0 − 2.5 = _____

15. 16.29 − 5.49 = _____

16. 4.0 − 1.12 = _____

17. 19.5 − 13.04 = _____

18. 16.0 − 0.84 = _____

19. 19.8 − 2.192 = _____

20. 8.5 − 4.111 = _____

Demonstrate addition and subtraction with decimals to the thousandths

Number & Operations

85

Dollar World

Name _____

Solve each problem.

1. Jimmy bought a CD for $15.95. If he paid the clerk $20, how much change did he receive?

   _____

2. Carlos bought two puzzles. Each one cost $4.95 and he paid $0.59 in tax. How much was his total bill?

   _____

3. Jennifer bought two music videos on sale. She paid $20 and received $3.90 back in change. The tax on the bill was $0.76. If each video cost the same amount of money, how much did one cost before tax?

   _____

4. Sky bought a new poster for his room. The poster was originally $14.50, but the sale price was $2.35 less. If he paid the clerk $15, how much change did he get back?

   _____

5. Akiko wanted to buy a CD for $14.95 and a new poster for $23.95. She had $40.00 with her. Was that enough to buy both the CD and the poster?

   _____

Demonstrate addition and subtraction with decimals to the thousandths

EMC 3018 • Basic Math Skills, Grade 5 • ©2003 by Evan-Moor Corp.

Pet Shop

Name _____

Solve each problem.

1. Shirley bought four fish for $12.95 and some fish food for $4.90. The tax on the two items was $1.08. What is the fewest bills and coins that Shirley could have used to pay the clerk the exact amount due?

   _____

2. Fluffy, one of the pets at the pet store, has been sick. The owners have been watching the animal's weight pretty closely to see if it is gaining or losing weight. Last Friday, Fluffy weighed 1.492 pounds. One week later, Fluffy weighed 1.489 pounds. Has Fluffy gained or lost weight? How much?

   _____

3. The vet at the store was weighing a mother animal and found that its weight was 3.820 pounds. When he added the baby animal onto the scale with it's mom, the scale read 4.209 pounds. How much did the baby weigh by itself?

   _____

4. The clerk opened a new bag of feed this morning that had a starting weight of 5 pounds. If the store used 0.725 pounds of feed today, how much is left in the bag?

   _____

5. The snake that is for sale was 0.872 meters long two months ago. Today, it is 0.902 meters long. How much has it grown over the last two months?

   _____

Demonstrate addition and subtraction with decimals to the thousandths

Math Test

Name _____

Fill in the circle next to the correct answer.

1. $5 + 1.2 =$ _____

   Ⓐ 6.0   Ⓒ 8.0

   Ⓑ 5.2   Ⓓ 6.2

2. $4.3 + 2.5 =$ _____

   Ⓐ 6.3   Ⓒ 6.5

   Ⓑ 6.8   Ⓓ 6.7

3. $4.99 + 5.32 =$ _____

   Ⓐ 10.31   Ⓒ 9.131

   Ⓑ 9.31   Ⓓ 9.99

4. $15.3 + 2.85 =$ _____

   Ⓐ 17.115   Ⓒ 18.15

   Ⓑ 17.85   Ⓓ 17.3

5. $1.932 + 4.92 =$ _____

   Ⓐ 5.852   Ⓒ 8.1852

   Ⓑ 6.852   Ⓓ 5.1852

6. $6.0 - 2.5 =$ _____

   Ⓐ 3.5   Ⓒ 2.5

   Ⓑ 4.5   Ⓓ 4.0

7. $7.5 - 2.6 =$ _____

   Ⓐ 5.1   Ⓒ 4.1

   Ⓑ 4.9   Ⓓ 5.9

8. $6.2 - 1.492 =$ _____

   Ⓐ 5.708   Ⓒ 5.2

   Ⓑ 5.292   Ⓓ 4.708

9. Samuel has been saving his allowance for quite a while, and he currently has $95.72. If he buys a new CD for $14.82, how much will he have left?

_____

_____

_____

10. Write a story problem in which you would have to do the following math problem to solve it.

$$5.2 + 3.86 =$$

_____

_____

_____

Demonstrate addition and subtraction with decimals to the thousandths

Number & Operations   EMC 3018 • Basic Math Skills, Grade 5 • ©2003 by Evan-Moor Corp.

Tongue Twister #6

Name _____

Solve each problem below. Write the letter next to each problem above the answer at the bottom of the page. The letters will spell out a tongue twister. Try to say it fast three times.

A $2.0 \times 0.5 =$ _____ **I** $2.0 \times 0.9 =$ _____

D $5.0 \times 0.6 =$ _____ **R** $5.2 \times 1.1 =$ _____

E $4.0 \times 0.9 =$ _____ **S** $1.9 \times 0.5 =$ _____

G $0.2 \times 0.6 =$ _____ **T** $0.25 \times 5.0 =$ _____

H $1.2 \times 5.0 =$ _____ **Y** $6.24 \times 0.1 =$ _____

___   ___   _G_   ___   ___   ___   ___   ___
3.6   3.0   0.12 1.0   5.72   1.0   1.25 3.6

___   ___   ___   ___   ___   ___   ___   ___   ___
3.6   1.8   0.12 6.0   1.25   3.6   0.12 0.12 0.95

            ___   ___   ___   ___
            1.0   3.0   1.0   0.624

Demonstrate multiplication with decimals to the hundredths

How Do You Know That a Clock Is Hungry?

Name _____

To solve the riddle, complete each of the multiplication problems. Then write the letter for each problem on the line above the answer at the bottom of the page. The letters will spell out the solution to the riddle.

A 2.0 × 0.3 = _____	**I** 2.1 × 5.0 = _____
B 3.0 × 0.7 = _____	**K** 5.1 × 7.2 = _____
C 5.0 × 0.2 = _____	**N** 4.8 × 9.1 = _____
D 4.0 × 0.5 = _____	**O** 4.7 × 1.4 = _____
E 2.0 × 0.9 = _____	**R** 5.9 × 1.5 = _____
F 0.5 × 5.0 = _____	**S** 1.3 × 6.2 = _____
G 0.6 × 0.6 = _____	**T** 0.2 × 6.8 = _____

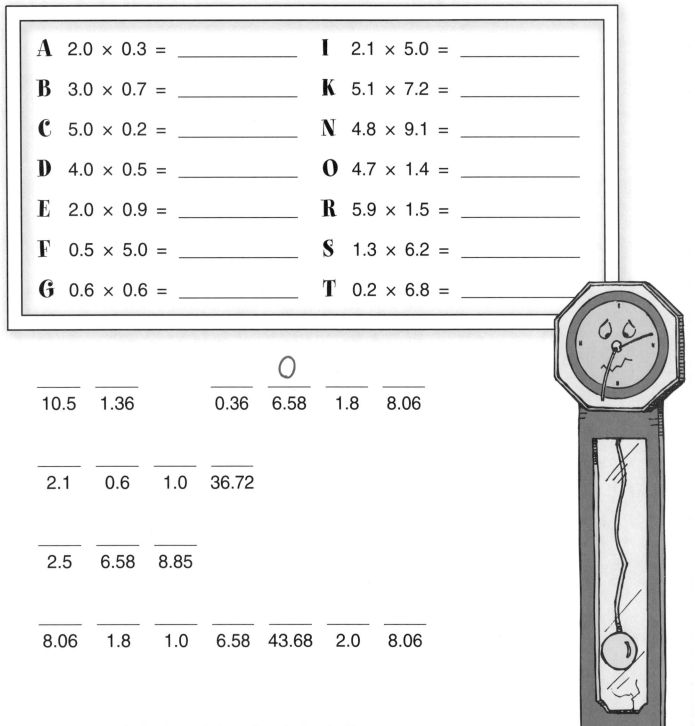

_____ _____   _O_ _____ _____ _____
10.5 1.36   0.36 6.58 1.8 8.06

_____ _____ _____ _____
2.1   0.6   1.0   36.72

_____ _____ _____
2.5   6.58 8.85

_____ _____ _____ _____ _____ _____ _____
8.06 1.8   1.0   6.58 43.68 2.0 8.06

Demonstrate multiplication with decimals to the hundredths

EMC 3018 • Basic Math Skills, Grade 5 • ©2003 by Evan-Moor Corp.

What Are Your Products?

Complete each of the following multiplication problems. If you get stuck on any of these, think of them in terms of money.

1. 2.0 × 0.1 = _____

2. 4.0 × 0.5 = _____

3. 8.0 × 0.25 = _____

4. 5.0 × 0.5 = _____

5. 1.0 × 0.75 = _____

6. 3.0 × 0.25 = _____

7. 2.0 × 0.04 = _____

8. 5.0 × 0.8 = _____

9. 4.0 × 0.95 = _____

10. 2.0 × 0.87 = _____

Demonstrate multiplication with decimals to the hundredths

Number & Operations

What Are Your Products II?

Complete each of the following multiplication problems.

1. 4.0 × 0.27 = _____

2. 0.5 × 0.2 = _____

3. 0.6 × 8.0 = _____

4. 3.2 × 8.0 = _____

5. 0.6 × 0.7 = _____

6. 0.21 × 0.5 = _____

7. 0.02 × 0.19 = _____

8. 4.2 × 7.5 = _____

9. 0.29 × 3.1 = _____

10. 4.29 × 3.05 = _____

0.29

0.05

Demonstrate multiplication with decimals to the hundredths

Number & Operations

EMC 3018 • Basic Math Skills, Grade 5 • ©2003 by Evan-Moor Corp.

City Music Hall

Name _____

Solve each problem.

1. Jimmy was looking at the concert hall and realized there were 120 seats on the top balcony alone. Then he started to think, if each person paid $4.50 to get into the concert, how much money was collected just from the people in the top balcony. How much was collected from the 120 people?

   _____

2. Four people came to the concert late. They said they were eating dinner and had run into some difficulty paying their bill. Each person ordered a dinner that was $4.75, and the tax on the whole bill was the total times 0.06 (or 6% sales tax). How much was their total bill for all four dinners including the tax?

   _____

3. The cleaning crew said they would clean up the concert hall after the concert for $0.03 per seat. There are 690 seats in the concert hall. How much would it cost to pay the cleaning crew to clean up around all 690 seats?

   _____

4. The programs that were printed cost $0.23 each. For the upcoming concert, they printed 700 programs. How much was the total bill (without tax)?

   _____

5. The floor for the dancers is 8.3 meters by 9.2 meters. The owners need to resurface that rectangle of floor and need to know what the area is. How many square meters is this dance floor?

   _____

Demonstrate multiplication with decimals to the hundredths

Benjamin's Circus

Name_____

Solve each problem.

1. For the first night of the circus, 225 tickets were sold for $0.35 each.
   How much money was collected just from the tickets?

   _____

2. There are 5 elephants in the circus and they weigh an average of
   5.38 tons. What is the total weight of all the elephants?

   _____

3. The circus has 4 lions and each lion cage is 56.9 square feet in size.
   What is the total area of all the cages?

   _____

4. The smallest animal in Benjamin's Circus is fed only 0.72 ounces of food
   at each meal. If the trainer feeds it three times a day, how much does it eat
   in a day? Think about that amount of food and guess what type of an animal
   it might be.

   _____

5. The spacing between the poles for the high stunts is 18.5 feet. If there are
   5 poles in a straight line, what is the total distance from the first pole to the
   last pole?

   _____

Demonstrate multiplication with decimals to the hundredths

EMC 3018 • Basic Math Skills, Grade 5 • ©2003 by Evan-Moor Corp.

Math Test

Fill in the circle next to the correct answer.

1. $5.0 \times 0.5 =$ _____

 Ⓐ 25.0   Ⓒ 2.5

 Ⓑ 0.25   Ⓓ 0.025

2. $6.0 \times 0.25 =$ _____

 Ⓐ 0.15   Ⓒ 15.0

 Ⓑ 1.5   Ⓓ 150.0

3. $1.5 \times 4.0 =$ _____

 Ⓐ 6.0   Ⓒ 0.6

 Ⓑ 60.0   Ⓓ 0.06

4. $2.5 \times 1.3 =$ _____

 Ⓐ 325.0   Ⓒ 3.25

 Ⓑ 32.5   Ⓓ 0.325

5. $2.58 \times 4.5 =$ _____

 Ⓐ 1161.0   Ⓒ 1.161

 Ⓑ 11.61   Ⓓ 116.1

6. $2.47 \times 8.31 =$ _____

 Ⓐ 205.257   Ⓒ 2.05257

 Ⓑ 2052.57   Ⓓ 20.5257

7. $2.1 \times 8.02 =$ _____

 Ⓐ 16.842   Ⓒ 1.6842

 Ⓑ 168.42   Ⓓ 0.16842

8. $8.0 \times 1.05 =$ _____

 Ⓐ 0.84   Ⓒ 8.4

 Ⓑ 0.084   Ⓓ 84.0

9. Jimmy has worked the following multiplication problem. Write a note to Jimmy telling him of any mistakes he made or if he did it perfectly.

$$\begin{array}{r} 1.5 \\ \times\ 26.0 \\ \hline 0\ 0 \\ 90 \\ 30 \\ \hline 120.0 \end{array}$$

_____

_____

_____

10. Write a story problem in which you would have to use 0.7×2.56 to solve the problem. Write the solution to the problem.

_____

_____

_____

Demonstrate multiplication with decimals to the hundredths

Trivia #2

Name _____

Answer each question below. Then look for the answer in the box and write the corresponding letter in front of the question. The letters will spell out a piece of trivia when read from **bottom to top.**

_____ What is the decimal form of 30%? _____

_____ What is the fraction form of 25%? _____

_____ What is the percent form of $\frac{1}{10}$? _____

_____ What is the decimal form of $\frac{3}{5}$? _____

_____ What is the fraction form of 0.75? _____

_____ What is the percent form of 0.1? _____

_____ What is the decimal form of 25%? _____

_____ What is the decimal form of $\frac{3}{10}$? _____

__A__ What is the decimal form of 50%? _0.5_

_____ What is the decimal form of $\frac{1}{5}$? _____

_____ What is the fraction form of 10%? _____

_____ What is the percent form of $\frac{1}{10}$? _____

_____ What is the decimal form of $\frac{1}{4}$? _____

_____ What is the decimal form of 30%? _____

_____ What is the percent form of $\frac{1}{4}$? _____

_____ What is the fraction form of 0.9? _____

_____ What is the decimal form of 60%? _____

_____ What is the decimal form of $\frac{1}{2}$? _____

0.5	A
25%	B
10%	E
$\frac{1}{4}$	G
0.2	H
0.6	L
$\frac{3}{4}$	N
$\frac{9}{10}$	O
$\frac{1}{10}$	R
0.3	S
0.25	T

Calculate equivalent fractions, decimals, and percents

Number & Operations
EMC 3018 • Basic Math Skills, Grade 5 • ©2003 by Evan-Moor Corp.

Riddle

What do you get when you cross a lighthouse and a hen house?

To find the answer to the riddle, answer each question below. Then look for the answer in the box and write the corresponding letter in front of the question. The letters will spell out the solution when read from **bottom to top.**

_____ What is the decimal form of 80%? _____

_____ What is the fraction form of 20%? _____

_____ What is the fraction form of 0.2? _____

_____ What is the percent form of 0.5? _____

_____ What is the decimal form of 60%? _____

_____ What is the fraction form of 50%? _____

_____ What is the decimal form of $\frac{1}{4}$? _____

_____ What is the fraction form of 0.5? _____

_____ What is the fraction form of 60%? _____

_____ What is the decimal form of $\frac{2}{5}$? _____

_____ What is the decimal form of 25%? _____

_____ What is the percent form of $\frac{1}{2}$? _____

_____ What is the percent form of $\frac{1}{10}$? _____

0.25	**A**
10%	**B**
0.4	**C**
0.6	**D**
50%	**E**
$\frac{1}{5}$	**G**
$\frac{1}{2}$	**N**
$\frac{3}{5}$	**O**
0.8	**S**

Calculate equivalent fractions, decimals, and percents

Number & Operations

That's the Same

Name _____

Complete the table below so that each row shows three representations of the same value.

Problem Number	Fraction	Decimal	Percent
1	$\frac{1}{4}$	0.25	25%
2		0.5	50%
3	$\frac{1}{3}$		
4			75%
5	$\frac{4}{5}$	0.8	
6	$\frac{3}{8}$		
7		0.125	
8			10%
9	$\frac{9}{10}$		
10			62.5%

Calculate equivalent fractions, decimals, and percents

EMC 3018 • Basic Math Skills, Grade 5 • ©2003 by Evan-Moor Corp.

That's the Same II

Name _____

Complete the table below so that each row shows three representations of the same value.

Problem Number	Fraction	Decimal	Percent
1	$\frac{3}{4}$	0.75	75%
2		0.25	
3	$\frac{1}{2}$		
4			30%
5		0.6	
6	$\frac{1}{10}$		
7		0.8	
8			40%
9	$\frac{9}{10}$		
10			100%

Calculate equivalent fractions, decimals, and percents

Number & Operations

On Sale

Solve each problem.

1. James was shopping and found a jacket that had an original price of $75.00. The discount for the sale is 30%. In order for him to find out how much money to take off the price of the jacket, he has to change the percent into a decimal. What is 30% as a decimal?

   _____

2. The tax for the sale is calculated at 6%. Martha was asked to change 6% into a decimal. She claims that the answer is 0.6. Write a note to her either agreeing or helping her to understand what the answer should be.

   _____

   _____

3. Kirk saw a sports jersey on sale for $\frac{1}{5}$ off. What percent discount is that?

   _____

4. Julia saw a sweater on sale. The sale price was $45 and the original price was $60. How could you use this information to figure out the percent of the discount? Explain your steps and reasoning as you give your answer.

   _____

   _____

5. A set of CDs was originally priced at $90 and the sale price was $45. What percent was the discount?

   _____

Calculate equivalent fractions, decimals, and percents

Spelling Tests

Solve each problem.

1. Mark got 15 out of 20 correct on his spelling test. What percent did he get correct?

   _____

2. Julianne got 18 out of 20 correct. What was her percent?

   _____

3. Timothy got 30 out of 30 correct. What was his percent?

   _____

4. Tate got 6 out of 30 correct on his test. What percent grade did he receive?

   _____

5. Beth couldn't remember how many she got right out of 30. But she did remember that she received a 90% grade. How many did she get correct on the test?

   _____

Calculate equivalent fractions, decimals, and percents

Math Test

Name_____

Fill in the circle next to the correct answer.

1. What fraction is equivalent to 50%?

Ⓐ $\frac{1}{5}$ Ⓒ $\frac{2}{5}$

Ⓑ $\frac{1}{2}$ Ⓓ $\frac{3}{4}$

2. What decimal is equivalent to $\frac{3}{4}$?

Ⓐ 0.25 Ⓒ 0.75

Ⓑ 0.5 Ⓓ 0.34

3. What percent is equivalent to $\frac{1}{10}$?

Ⓐ 110% Ⓒ 5%

Ⓑ 1% Ⓓ 10%

4. What fraction is equivalent to 0.25?

Ⓐ $\frac{1}{3}$ Ⓒ $\frac{1}{25}$

Ⓑ $\frac{1}{2}$ Ⓓ $\frac{1}{4}$

5. What decimal is equivalent to 45%?

Ⓐ 4.5 Ⓒ 0.45

Ⓑ 5.4 Ⓓ 0.54

6. What percent is equivalent to 0.2?

Ⓐ 80% Ⓒ 2.0%

Ⓑ 20% Ⓓ 0.2%

7. Which of the following is equivalent to 0.8?

Ⓐ 80% Ⓒ $\frac{4}{5}$

Ⓑ $\frac{8}{10}$ Ⓓ all of the above

8. Which of the following is equivalent to $\frac{1}{8}$?

Ⓐ 0.125 Ⓒ 0.18

Ⓑ 1.25 Ⓓ all of the above

9. Miguel has been asked to write two other representations for the value of 25%. Help Miguel by writing a fraction and a decimal that are equivalent to 25%.

_____

10. Draw a picture to demonstrate that $\frac{1}{2}$ is the same as 0.5.

Calculate equivalent fractions, decimals, and percents

  EMC 3018 • Basic Math Skills, Grade 5 • ©2003 by Evan-Moor Corp.

What Kind of Car Does an Electrician Drive?

Name _____

To solve the riddle, draw a straight line between each math sentence on the left and the appropriate symbol that would complete the sentence on the right. Each line will go through one or two small numbers. These numbers refer to the spaces at the bottom of the page. Write the corresponding letter in front of the math sentence on each of these lines. The letters will spell out the solution to the riddle.

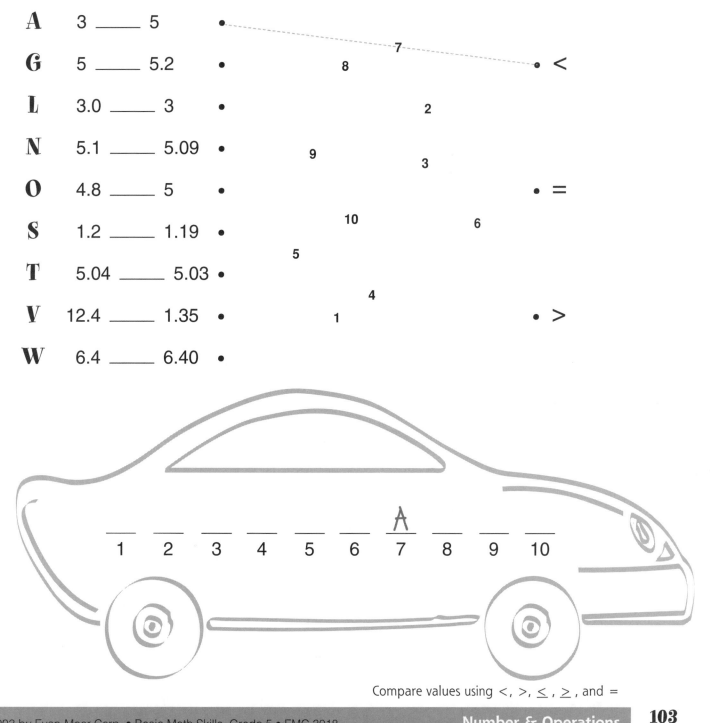

A   3 _____ 5

G   5 _____ 5.2

L   3.0 _____ 3

N   5.1 _____ 5.09

O   4.8 _____ 5

S   1.2 _____ 1.19

T   5.04 _____ 5.03

V   12.4 _____ 1.35

W   6.4 _____ 6.40

7   8   2   9   3   <   =   10   6   5   4   1   >

A
___ ___ ___ ___ ___ ___ A ___ ___ ___
 1   2   3   4   5   6   7   8   9   10

Compare values using <, >, ≤, ≥, and =

Which Way?

Help Randy find the way to the Skateboard Park. Decide if each inequality is true (T) or false (F). Then go in the direction of the correct arrow. Continue through the maze until you come to the Skateboard Park.

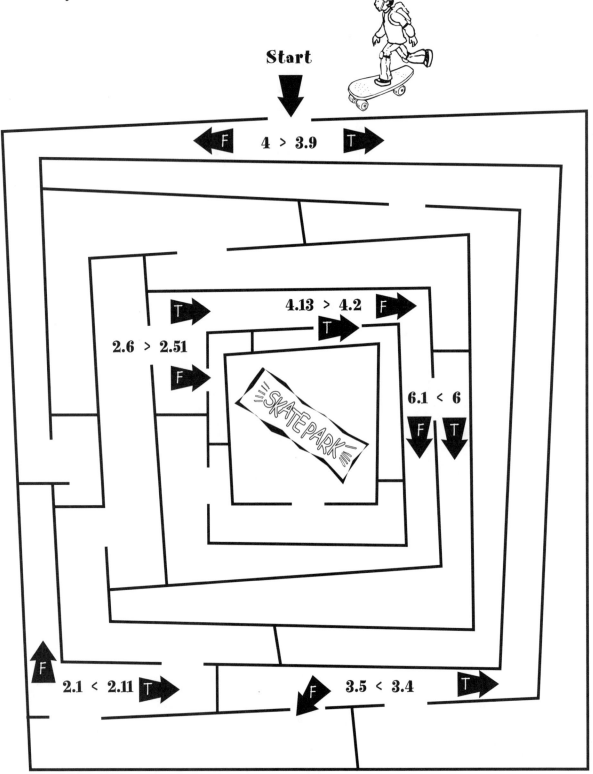

Compare values using $<$, $>$, $\le$, $\ge$, and $=$

True or False?

Write *True* or *False* next to each math sentence below.

1. 6.2 < 6.21 _____

2. 4.5 ≤ 4.51 _____

3. 4.2 > 4.4 _____

4. 2.1 ≥ 2.5 _____

5. 5.3 > 4.98 _____

6. 2.3 ≤ 2.30 _____

7. 2.1 < 2.18 _____

8. 4.0 = 4 _____

9. 4.2 ≥ 4.18 _____

10. 5.6 > 5.1 _____

Compare values using <, >, ≤, ≥, and =

True or False? Again

Name_____

Write *True* or *False* next to each math sentence below.

1. 4 < 8   _____

2. 6.3 ≤ 6.35   _____

3. 4.0 = 4   _____

4. 2.7 ≥ 2.70   _____

5. 5.29 > 5.5   _____

6. 7.83 < 7.99   _____

7. 4.02 ≥ 4.4   _____

8. 9.4 > 8.99   _____

9. 3.10 ≤ 3.12   _____

10. 8.41 > 8.401 _____

True?

False?

Compare values using <, >, ≤, ≥, and =

Number & Operations

EMC 3018 • Basic Math Skills, Grade 5 • ©2003 by Evan-Moor Corp.

The Signs

Solve each problem.

1. Jody is really confused about the signs. She understood that 7.5 is bigger than 7.48, but she can't remember which symbol goes in the sentence 7.5 ___ 7.48. Help Jody by completing the math sentence. Then give Jody a way to remember which symbol to use and what each symbol means.

   _____

   _____

   _____

2. Ken and Stacy were arguing about the math sentence 7 ___ 7.0. Ken says that the = sign is the only symbol that works to make it a true sentence. Stacy, however, believes that there are other symbols that could be used to also make a true sentence. Do you agree or disagree with Stacy? Write a note to Stacy explaining why you agree or disagree.

   _____

   _____

   _____

3. Daryl couldn't figure out the following math sentence: 4.2 ___ 4.29. The teacher asked him to pick out two different symbols that could be used to complete this sentence. Help Daryl by identifying the two symbols that would work to make a true math sentence.

   _____

Compare values using $<$, $>$, $\leq$, $\geq$, and $=$

Symbols and Symbols

Name _____

Solve each problem.

1. Jennifer can't remember what the difference is between these two symbols: < and ≤. Write a note to Jennifer explaining the difference between these two symbols and what each symbol represents.

_____

_____

_____

2. Stephanie is working on this problem: 2.03 ____ 2.30. She can't figure out what to put in the blank to make it a true math sentence. Help her figure out what symbol to use and tell why you selected that symbol.

_____

_____

_____

3. Matthew is working on this problem: 4.9 ____ 4.89. He thinks that since 49 is so much smaller than 489, that the < symbol has to be the one to make it a true sentence. However, his teacher tells him that he is mistaken. Write a note to Matthew explaining the error in his thinking and help him understand what symbol should be used to make a true sentence.

_____

_____

_____

Compare values using <, >, ≤, ≥, and =

EMC 3018 • Basic Math Skills, Grade 5 • ©2003 by Evan-Moor Corp.

Math Test

Name _____

Fill in the circle next to the correct answer.

1. Which of the following math sentences is true?

   Ⓐ 7.0 = 7   Ⓒ 6.1 = 6.11

   Ⓑ 2.5 = 25   Ⓓ 6.4 = 4.6

2. Which of the following math sentences is true?

   Ⓐ 1.5 > 1.9   Ⓒ 2.4 < 2.45

   Ⓑ 2.9 < 2.89   Ⓓ 4.7 > 4.8

3. Which of the following math sentences is true?

   Ⓐ 8.8 < 8.78   Ⓒ 9.0 < 9

   Ⓑ 3.2 > 3.28   Ⓓ 4.5 > 4.29

4. Which symbol makes this number sentence true?

   6.2 ___ 6.49

   Ⓐ ≤   Ⓒ =

   Ⓑ ≥   Ⓓ any of the above

5. Which symbol makes this number sentence true?

   4.6 ___ 4.60

   Ⓐ ≤   Ⓒ =

   Ⓑ ≥   Ⓓ any of the above

6. Which symbol makes this number sentence true?

   5.5 ___ 5.38

   Ⓐ ≤   Ⓒ =

   Ⓑ ≥   Ⓓ any of the above

7. Which of the following is NOT true?

   Ⓐ 7 < 7.01   Ⓒ 7.9 < 8.1

   Ⓑ 6.4 > 5.9   Ⓓ 5.4 > 5.40

8. Which of the following is NOT true?

   Ⓐ 6.9 > 5.9   Ⓒ 9.3 > 9.29

   Ⓑ 4.2 = 42   Ⓓ 7 = 7.0

9. Use the numbers 4.9 and 5.4 and the > symbol to write a true math sentence.

   _____

10. Use the numbers 2.9 and 7.4 and the ≤ symbol to write a true math sentence.

   _____

Compare values using <, >, ≤, ≥, and =

Algebra

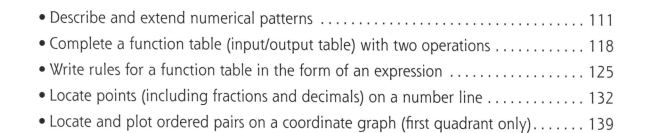

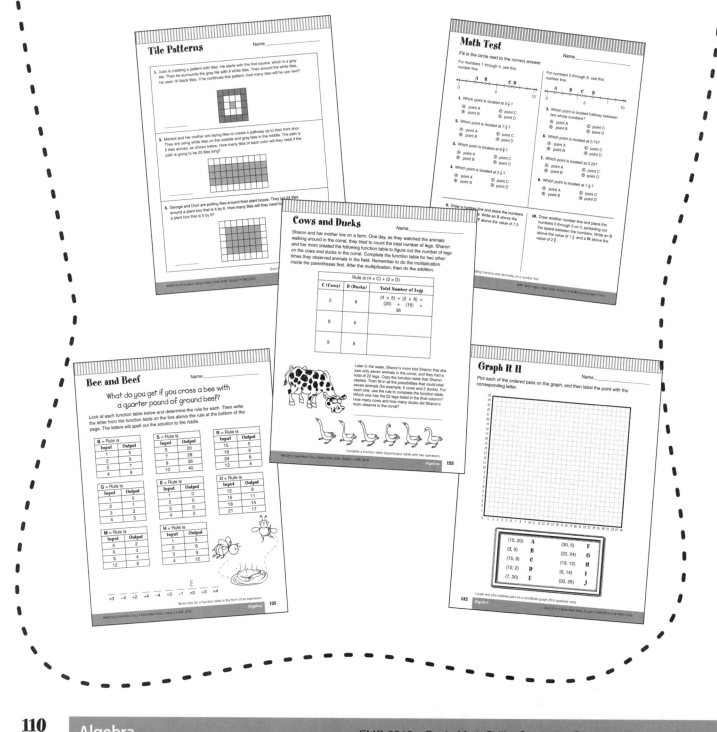

EMC 3018 • Basic Math Skills, Grade 5 • ©2003 by Evan-Moor Corp.

What's a Lazy Shoe Called?

Name _____

Look at each pattern in the box below and write the next number in the pattern.
Then write the letter from in front of the pattern on the line above the answer.
The letters will spell out the solution to the riddle.

A 1, 2, 3, 4, 5, _____

A 2, 4, 6, 8, 10, _____

E 5, 8, 11, 14, 17, _____

F 2, 8, 14, 20, _____

L 50, 45, 40, 35, _____

O 1, 2, 4, 8, 16, _____

R 1, 3, 9, 27, _____

$$\overline{} \quad \overline{} \ \overline{} \ \overset{A}{\overline{}} \ \overline{} \ \overline{} \ \overline{}$$

12   30   32   6   26   20   81

Describe and extend numerical patterns

What Vegetable Would You Least Want on a Ship?

Look at each pattern below and write the next number in the pattern. Then write the corresponding letter on the line in front of the pattern. The letters will spell out the solution to the riddle when read from top to bottom.

Name _____

99	A
49	B
81	E
36	K
62	L
48	M
50	S
56	T

_____ 15, 36, 57, 78, _____

_____ 90, 83, 76, 69, _____

_E_ 1, 3, 9, 27, _81_

_____ 25, 36, 49, 64, _____

_____ 6, 12, 18, 24, 30, _____

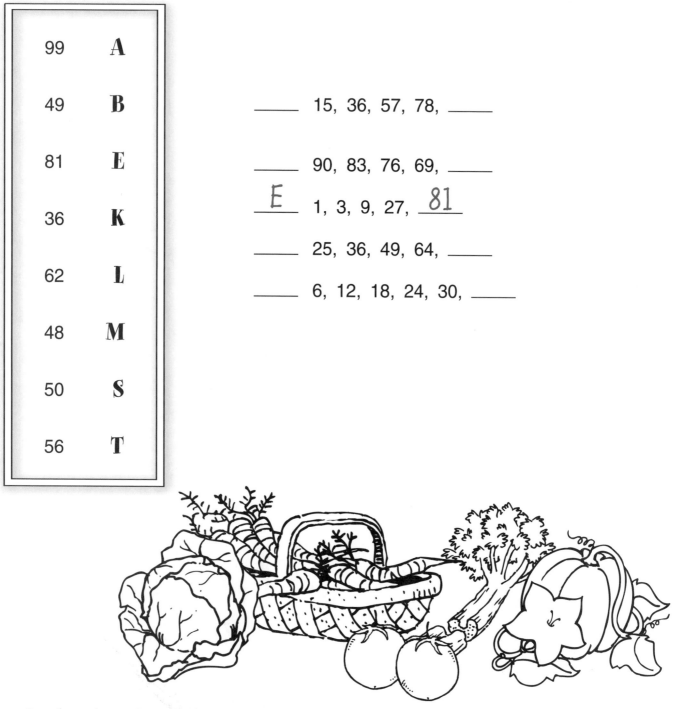

Describe and extend numerical patterns

EMC 3018 • Basic Math Skills, Grade 5 • ©2003 by Evan-Moor Corp.

Pattern Chains

Name_____

Describe how you would get the next number in each of the following patterns.

1. 2, 4, 6, 8, …

_____

2. 11, 13, 15, 17, …

_____

3. 35, 40, 45, 50, 55, …

_____

4. 6, 10, 14, 18, 22, …

_____

5. 90, 82, 74, 66, 58, …

_____

6. 5, 10, 20, 40, …

_____

7. 81, 27, 9, 3, …

_____

8. 42, 61, 80, 99, 118, …

_____

Describe and extend numerical patterns

What's Next?

What number comes next in each of the following patterns?

1. 1, 3, 5, 7, 9, ...

_____

2. 1, 4, 9, 16, 25, ...

_____

3. 6, 11, 16, 21, 26, ...

_____

4. 15, 24, 33, 42, 51, ...

_____

5. 80, 69, 58, 47, 36, ...

_____

6. 3, 3, 3, 3, 3, ...

_____

7. 10, 8, 6, 4, 2, 0, ...

_____

8. 2, 6, 18, 54, 162, ...

_____

Describe and extend numerical patterns

Tile Patterns

Name_____

1. Juan is creating a pattern with tiles. He starts with the first square, which is a gray tile. Then he surrounds the gray tile with 8 white tiles. Then around the white tiles, he uses 16 black tiles. If he continues this pattern, how many tiles will he use next?

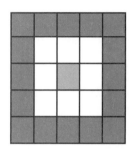

_____

2. Marisol and her mother are laying tiles to create a pathway up to their front door. They are using white tiles on the outside and gray tiles in the middle. The path is 5 tiles across, as shown below. How many tiles of each color will they need if the path is going to be 25 tiles long?

_____

3. George and Doni are putting tiles around their planter boxes. They put 24 tiles around a planter box that is 4 by 6. How many tiles will they need to surround a planter box that is 5 by 8?

_____

Describe and extend numerical patterns

Horse Corrals

Name _____

Solve each problem.

1. Jed and his father are putting up fence posts for a new corral. They realize that for 8 feet of fence they need 3 railings and 2 poles. For 16 feet of fence, they need 6 railings and 3 poles. For 24 feet of fence, they need 9 railings and 4 poles. How many railings and poles do they need for a straight fence that is 96 feet long?

_____

2. Fritz's Farm has several corrals for horses. They figure that for one horse, they need 120 feet along the side of the corral. For two horses, they need 160 feet along the side of the corral. For three horses, they need 200 feet along the side of the corral. How long should the side of the corral be if they have five horses?

_____

3. Jim is stacking bales of hay in a pyramid fashion. He wants 1 bale of hay on the very top. The second row down will have four bales. The third row will have nine bales. He wants to continue this pattern and have a total of eight rows. How many bales of hay in all does he need to create this pyramid?

_____

Describe and extend numerical patterns

EMC 3018 • Basic Math Skills, Grade 5 • ©2003 by Evan-Moor Corp.

Math Test

Name _____

Fill in the circle next to the correct answer.

What value comes next in each of the following patterns?

1. 1, 2, 3, 4, 5, _____

   Ⓐ 5   Ⓒ 7

   Ⓑ 6   Ⓓ 8

2. 2, 4, 6, 8, 10, _____

   Ⓐ 10   Ⓒ 12

   Ⓑ 11   Ⓓ 13

3. 5, 5, 5, 5, _____

   Ⓐ 0   Ⓒ 10

   Ⓑ 5   Ⓓ 15

4. 11, 17, 23, 29, 35, _____

   Ⓐ 36   Ⓒ 40

   Ⓑ 39   Ⓓ 41

5. 50, 47, 44, 41, 38, _____

   Ⓐ 35   Ⓒ 33

   Ⓑ 34   Ⓓ 32

6. 1, 2, 4, 8, 16, _____

   Ⓐ 18   Ⓒ 24

   Ⓑ 20   Ⓓ 32

7. 89, 78, 67, 56, _____

   Ⓐ 45   Ⓒ 44

   Ⓑ 55   Ⓓ 40

8. 81, 27, 9, 3, 1, _____

   Ⓐ 3   Ⓒ 0

   Ⓑ 1   Ⓓ $\frac{1}{3}$

9. Describe how you would get the next value in the following pattern:

$$28, 22, 16, 10, 4, \ldots$$

_____

_____

_____

10. Describe how you would get the next value in the following pattern:

$$81, 64, 49, 36, 25, 16, \ldots$$

_____

_____

_____

Describe and extend numerical patterns

What Has Twelve Legs, Is Gray, and Can't See?

Name _____

Use the rule at the top of each function table to write the output. Write the letter next to each output on the line above the corresponding number. The letters will spell out the solution to the riddle.

Rule is ×2 +1		
Input	**Output**	
1	3	
2	5	H
3		E
4		R
5		T

Rule is ×4 ÷2		
Input	**Output**	
1	2	
2		B
3		D
6		I
9		L
10		N

Rule is ×5 −2		
Input	**Output**	
1	3	
2		C
5		E
7		I
9		M

	H													
11	5	9	7	7		4	18	12	20	6		43	33	8	23

Complete a function table (input/output table) with two operations

Algebra

EMC 3018 • Basic Math Skills, Grade 5 • ©2003 by Evan-Moor Corp.

Tongue Twister #7

Name _____

Use the rule that is listed at the top of each function table to complete the table.
Write the letter next to each output on the line above the corresponding number.
The letters will spell out a tongue twister. Try to say it fast three times.

Rule is ×3 +1	
Input	**Output**
1	4
2	
3	
4	

D
E
G

Rule is ×6 −3	
Input	**Output**
4	21
8	
5	
9	
10	

N
R
T
U

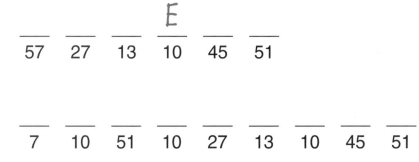

E			
___	___	___	___ ___ ___
57	27	13	10 45 51

___ ___ ___ ___ ___ ___ ___ ___ ___
7 10 51 10 27 13 10 45 51

Complete a function table (input/output table) with two operations

Algebra

Function Machines

Name _____

Use the rule listed at the top of each function table to help you complete each table.

1.

Rule is ×3 +1	
Input	**Output**
1	
2	
4	
	22
	25
	37

2.

Rule is ×6 ÷3	
Input	**Output**
1	
2	
3	
	12
	8
	10

3.

Rule is ×4 −3	
Input	**Output**
1	
2	
4	
	17
	9
	29

4.

Rule is +5 −3	
Input	**Output**
1	
3	
8	
	6
	9
	15

Complete a function table (input/output table) with two operations

EMC 3018 • Basic Math Skills, Grade 5 • ©2003 by Evan-Moor Corp.

Function Machines II

Name _____

Use the rule listed at the top of each function table to help you complete each table.

1.

Rule is ×2 +3	
Input	**Output**
1	
2	
7	
	13
	19
	37

2.

Rule is ×9 ÷3	
Input	**Output**
1	
	15
8	
	21
12	
	45

3.

Rule is ×5 −6	
Input	**Output**
2	
5	
	14
9	
	44
1	

4.

Rule is +9 −2	
Input	**Output**
5	
	26
36	
	15
81	
	92

Complete a function table (input/output table) with two operations

Algebra

Swimming Pools

Name _____

Fred and his dad are putting in a swimming pool in their backyard. They want to put a border of decorative tiles around their swimming pool. They realize that if their pool is 4 by 6, for example, they would need 24 decorative tiles as shown below.

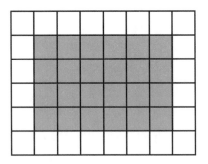

Fred and his dad created the function table below to help them determine the number of decorative tiles they will need for different dimensions of a pool. The rule they used is shown at the top. The **W** in the rule represents the width and the **L** represents the length of the pool. The first row has been completed for you. Remember to do the multiplication inside the parentheses first. After the multiplication, then do the addition. Complete the function table for the other two pool dimensions.

Rule is (2 × W) + (2 × L) + 4		
W (width)	**L (length)**	**Number of Decorative Tiles**
4	6	(2 × 4) + (2 × 6) + 4 = (8) + (12) + 4 = 20 + 4 = 24
8	10	
10	12	

Complete a function table (input/output table) with two operations

EMC 3018 • Basic Math Skills, Grade 5 • ©2003 by Evan-Moor Corp.

Cows and Ducks

Name _____

Sharon and her mother live on a farm. One day, as they watched the animals walking around in the corral, they tried to count the total number of legs. Sharon and her mom created the following function table to figure out the number of legs on the cows and ducks in the corral. Complete the function table for two other times they observed animals in the field. Remember to do the multiplication inside the parentheses first. After the multiplication, then do the addition.

Rule is $(4 \times C) + (2 \times D)$		
C (Cows)	**D (Ducks)**	**Total Number of Legs**
5	8	$(4 \times 5) + (2 \times 8) =$ $(20) \ + \ (16) \ =$ 36
8	6	
9	8	

Later in the week, Sharon's mom told Sharon that she saw only seven animals in the corral, and they had a total of 22 legs. Copy the function table that Sharon started. Then fill in all the possibilities that could total seven animals (for example, 5 cows and 2 ducks). For each one, use the rule to complete the function table. Which one has the 22 legs listed in the final column? How many cows and how many ducks did Sharon's mom observe in the corral?

_____

Complete a function table (input/output table) with two operations

Math Test

Name _____

Fill in the circle next to the correct answer.

For Numbers 1 through 4, use this function table.

Rule is ×2 −3	
Input	Output
2	1
1. 4	
2. 5	
3.	11
4.	17

For Numbers 5 through 8, use this function table.

Rule is ÷2 +3	
Input	Output
5. 4	
6. 6	
7.	8
8.	12

1. What is the output, if the input is 4?

   Ⓐ 5   Ⓒ 7
   Ⓑ 1   Ⓓ 3

2. What is the output, if the input is 5?

   Ⓐ 5   Ⓒ 7
   Ⓑ 6   Ⓓ 8

3. What is the input, if the output is 11?

   Ⓐ 4   Ⓒ 6
   Ⓑ 5   Ⓓ 7

4. What is the input, if the output is 17?

   Ⓐ 9   Ⓒ 11
   Ⓑ 10   Ⓓ 12

5. What is the output, if the input is 4?

   Ⓐ 3   Ⓒ 5
   Ⓑ 4   Ⓓ 6

6. What is the output, if the input is 6?

   Ⓐ 3   Ⓒ 5
   Ⓑ 4   Ⓓ 6

7. What is the input, if the output is 8?

   Ⓐ 8   Ⓒ 12
   Ⓑ 10   Ⓓ 14

8. What is the input, if the output is 12?

   Ⓐ 16   Ⓒ 18
   Ⓑ 17   Ⓓ 19

9. Draw a function table with five inputs and five outputs utilizing the rule ×3 −1.

10. Draw a function table with five inputs and five outputs utilizing the rule +3 −1.

Complete a function table (input/output table) with two operations

124 **Algebra**

Bee and Beef

What do you get if you cross a bee with a quarter pound of ground beef?

Look at each function table below and determine the rule for each. Then write the letter from the function table on the line above the rule at the bottom of the page. The letters will spell out the solution to the riddle.

B = Rule is

Input	Output
1	5
2	6
3	7
4	8

S = Rule is

Input	Output
5	20
7	28
9	36
10	40

R = Rule is

Input	Output
15	5
18	6
24	8
12	4

G = Rule is

Input	Output
1	0
2	1
3	2
4	3

E = Rule is

Input	Output
1	0
2	0
3	0
4	0

U = Rule is

Input	Output
12	8
15	11
18	14
21	17

M = Rule is

Input	Output
4	2
6	3
8	4
12	6

H = Rule is

Input	Output
1	3
2	6
3	9
4	12

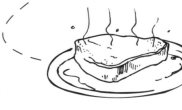

$$\frac{}{\times 3} \quad \frac{}{-4} \quad \frac{}{\div 2} \quad \frac{}{+4} \quad \frac{}{-4} \quad \frac{}{\div 3} \quad \frac{}{-1} \quad \frac{}{\times 0} \quad \frac{E}{\div 3} \quad \frac{}{\times 4}$$

Write rules for a function table in the form of an expression

Algebra

Tongue Twister #8

Name _____

Look at each function table below and determine the rule for each. Then write the letter from the function table on the line above the rule at the bottom of the page. The letters will spell out a tongue twister. Try to say it fast three times.

A = Rule is	
Input	**Output**
1	3
6	8
3	5
4	6

C = Rule is	
Input	**Output**
4	2
8	6
5	3
9	7

E = Rule is	
Input	**Output**
1	2
2	4
5	10
7	14

H = Rule is	
Input	**Output**
2	1
8	4
10	5
12	6

I = Rule is	
Input	**Output**
1	5
3	7
8	12
10	14

P = Rule is	
Input	**Output**
1	0
3	2
8	7
10	9

T = Rule is	
Input	**Output**
6	2
9	3
12	4
3	1

U = Rule is	
Input	**Output**
5	0
2	0
4	0
9	0

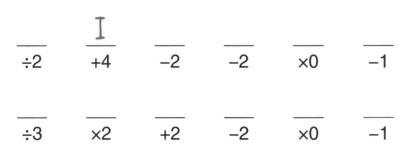

$$\overline{} \quad \overline{I} \quad \overline{} \quad \overline{} \quad \overline{} \quad \overline{}$$
$$\div 2 \quad\quad +4 \quad\quad -2 \quad\quad -2 \quad\quad \times 0 \quad\quad -1$$

$$\overline{} \quad \overline{} \quad \overline{} \quad \overline{} \quad \overline{} \quad \overline{}$$
$$\div 3 \quad\quad \times 2 \quad\quad +2 \quad\quad -2 \quad\quad \times 0 \quad\quad -1$$

Write rules for a function table in the form of an expression

Algebra

EMC 3018 • Basic Math Skills, Grade 5 • ©2003 by Evan-Moor Corp.

What's My Rule?

Look at each function table and determine a rule that works for each input and output pair of numbers. Write the rule at the top of each function table.

1.

Rule =	
Input	**Output**
1	3
2	4
3	5
4	6

2.

Rule =	
Input	**Output**
1	0
2	1
3	2
4	3

3.

Rule =	
Input	**Output**
1	2
2	4
3	6
4	8

4.

Rule =	
Input	**Output**
1	4
2	8
3	12
4	16

5.

Rule =	
Input	**Output**
2	1
4	2
6	3
8	4

6.

Rule =	
Input	**Output**
1	6
5	10
7	12
10	15

Write rules for a function table in the form of an expression

What's My Function?

Name _____

Look at each function table and determine a rule that works for each input and output pair of numbers. Write the rule at the top of each function table.

1.

Rule =	
Input	**Output**
1	0
3	2
8	7
12	11

2.

Rule =	
Input	**Output**
2	6
4	8
9	13
12	16

3.

Rule =	
Input	**Output**
3	1
15	5
18	6
27	9

4.

Rule =	
Input	**Output**
3	9
4	16
2	4
7	49

5.

Rule =	
Input	**Output**
4	2
26	13
18	9
14	7

6.

Rule =	
Input	**Output**
15	7
14	6
16	8
20	12

Write rules for a function table in the form of an expression

EMC 3018 • Basic Math Skills, Grade 5 • ©2003 by Evan-Moor Corp.

What Function Machine Am I Thinking Of?

Solve each problem.

1. Juanita is thinking of a function machine. She says that the output is 18 when the input is 4. What are two different rules that she could be thinking of?

   _____

2. Jeff is thinking of a function machine. He says that the output is 5 when the input is 4. What are two different rules that he could be thinking of?

   _____

3. Rob is thinking of a function machine. He says that the output is 2 when the input is 5. What are two different rules that he could be thinking of?

   _____

4. Larissa is thinking of a function machine. She says that the output is 26 when the input is 6. What are two different rules that she could be thinking of?

   _____

Write rules for a function table in the form of an expression

What Function Machine Am I Thinking Of II?

Name _____

Solve each problem.

1. Michelle is thinking of a function machine. She says that the output is 25 when the input is 10. What are two different rules that she could be thinking of?

_____

2. Raul is thinking of a function machine. He says that the output is 16 when the input is 5. What are two different rules that he could be thinking of?

_____

3. Scott is thinking of a function machine. He says that the output is 4 when the input is 6. What are two different rules that he could be thinking of?

_____

4. Rebecca is thinking of a function machine. She says that the output is 21 when the input is 9. What are two different rules that she could be thinking of?

_____

Write rules for a function table in the form of an expression

EMC 3018 • Basic Math Skills, Grade 5 • ©2003 by Evan-Moor Corp.

Math Test

Fill in the circle next to the correct answer.

For Numbers 1 through 4, use the following function table. The input stays the same, but the output is different for each problem.

	1	2	3	4
Input	**Output**	**Output**	**Output**	**Output**
2	4	1	3	4
4	6	2	7	5
6	8	3	11	6
8	10	4	15	7

1. What is the rule for the output in column #1?

   Ⓐ +2   Ⓒ +1

   Ⓑ ×2   Ⓓ +4

2. What is the rule for the output in column #2?

   Ⓐ −1   Ⓒ ÷2

   Ⓑ +1   Ⓓ ×1

3. What is the rule for the output in column #3?

   Ⓐ ×2 −1   Ⓒ ×3 −3

   Ⓑ +3   Ⓓ ÷2 ×3

4. What is the rule for the output in column #4?

   Ⓐ ÷2   Ⓒ ×2 −1

   Ⓑ ×2   Ⓓ ÷2 +3

For Numbers 5 through 8, use the following function table. The input stays the same, but the output is different for each problem.

	5	6	7	8
Input	**Output**	**Output**	**Output**	**Output**
3	1	2	3	2
6	2	8	3	3
9	3	14	3	4
12	4	20	3	5

5. What is the rule for the output in column #5?

   Ⓐ −2   Ⓒ ÷3

   Ⓑ −6   Ⓓ ÷2

6. What is the rule for the output in column #6?

   Ⓐ ×2 −4   Ⓒ +2

   Ⓑ −1   Ⓓ ×3 −7

7. What is the rule for the output in column #7?

   Ⓐ ×3   Ⓒ −3

   Ⓑ −0   Ⓓ ×0 +3

8. What is the rule for the output in column #8?

   Ⓐ −1   Ⓒ −3

   Ⓑ ÷3 +1   Ⓓ ÷3 +2

9. Julie is thinking of a function machine. She said that the output is 5 if the input is 10. What are two rules that she could be thinking of for her function machine?

_____

_____

10. Carlos is thinking of another function machine. He said that the output is 3 if the input is 2. What are two rules that he could be thinking of for his function machine?

_____

_____

Write rules for a function table in the form of an expression

Riddle

What's silvery, swims in shoals, and goes "Dot, Dot, Dash, Dash"?

To solve the riddle, look at each value below. Locate that point on the number line. Write the corresponding letter above the point line. The letters will spell out the solution to the riddle when read from left to right.

$7\frac{1}{3}$	**D**	$\frac{1}{2}$	**M**
1.25	**O**	3	**E**
$2\frac{1}{3}$	**S**	5.75	**C**
$6\frac{1}{2}$	**O**	$1\frac{3}{4}$	**R**

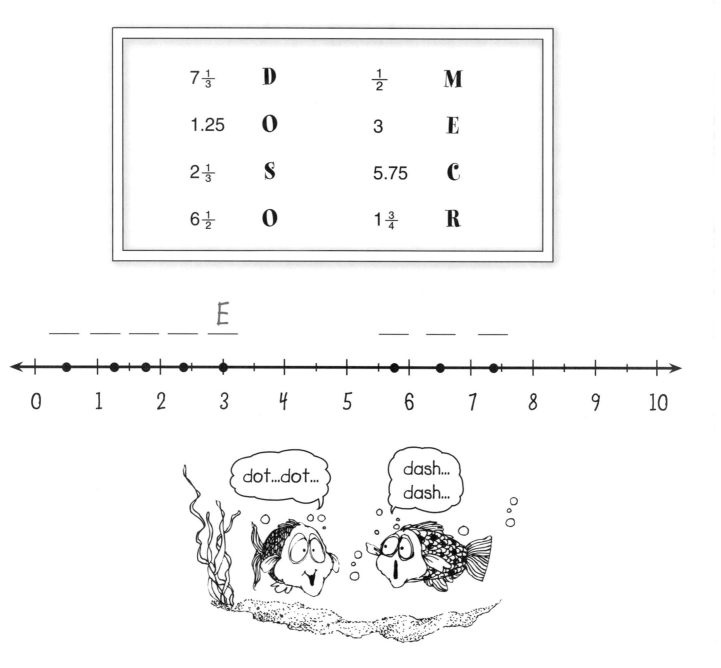

Locate points (including fractions and decimals) on a number line

What Does a Ghost Use to Go Hunting?

Name _____

To solve the riddle, look at each value in the box. Locate that point on the numberline. Write the corresponding letter above the point line. The letters will spell out the solution to the riddle when read from left to right.

$62\frac{1}{2}$	**O**
$37\frac{1}{2}$	**D**
58	**R**
15.5	**O**
34	**N**
$55\frac{1}{2}$	**R**
5	**A**
12	**B**
19	**O**
52	**A**
65	**W**
$30\frac{1}{2}$	**A**

A ___ ___ ___ ___   ___ ___ ___ ___   ___ ___ ___ ___

Locate points (including fractions and decimals) on a number line

Algebra

What's My Point?

Name _____

On the number line below, mark each value with a dot and then label the point with the appropriate letter.

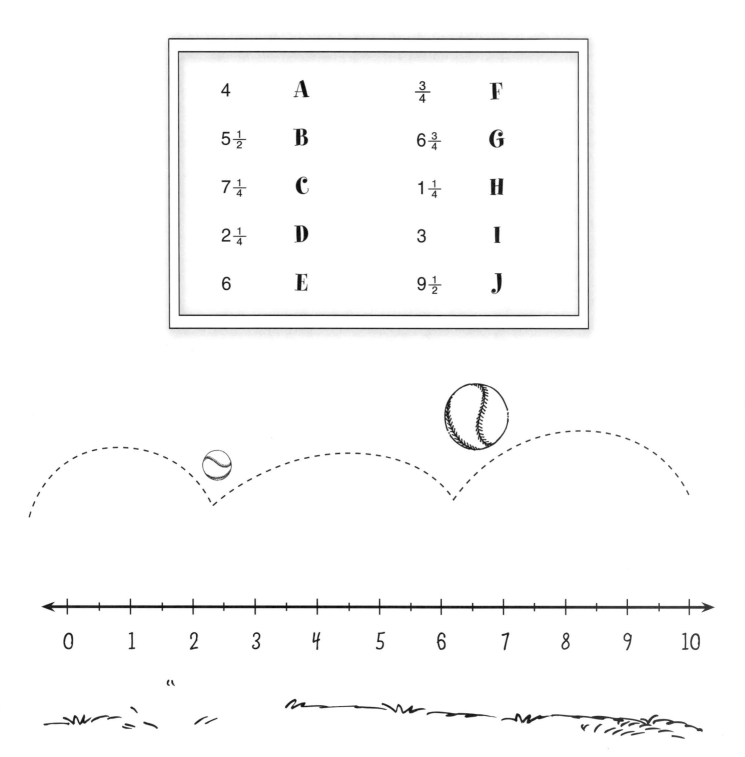

4	**A**	$\frac{3}{4}$	**F**
$5\frac{1}{2}$	**B**	$6\frac{3}{4}$	**G**
$7\frac{1}{4}$	**C**	$1\frac{1}{4}$	**H**
$2\frac{1}{4}$	**D**	3	**I**
6	**E**	$9\frac{1}{2}$	**J**

Locate points (including fractions and decimals) on a number line

What's My Point II?

Name _____

On the number line below, mark each value with a dot and then label the point with the appropriate letter.

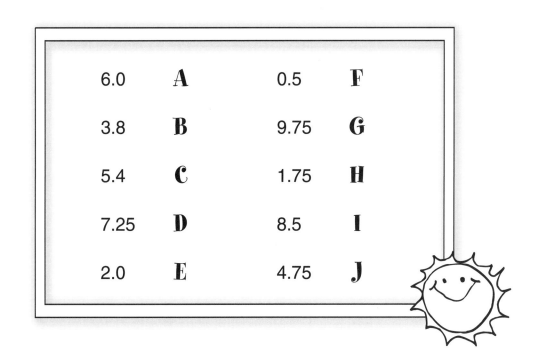

6.0	A	0.5	F
3.8	B	9.75	G
5.4	C	1.75	H
7.25	D	8.5	I
2.0	E	4.75	J

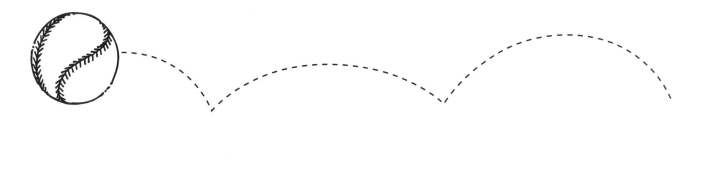

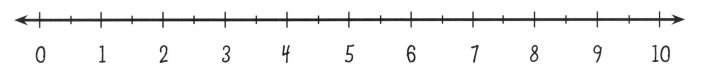

Locate points (including fractions and decimals) on a number line

Help Fred

Fred is having some problems with his assignments. Please correct Fred's work. Write a note to him for each problem. If he placed the numbers correctly, write a positive note, such as "good job." If he made a mistake, tell him what he should have done differently.

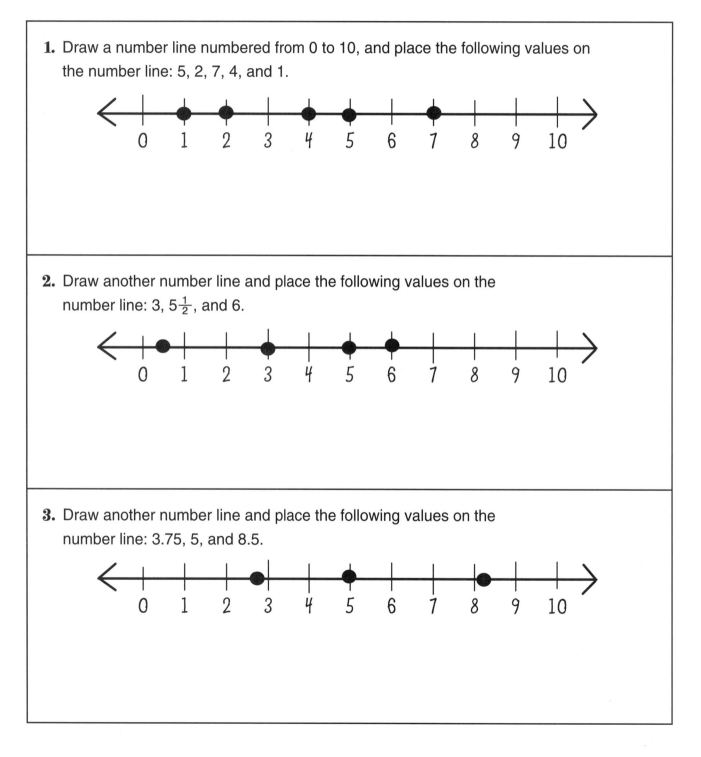

1. Draw a number line numbered from 0 to 10, and place the following values on the number line: 5, 2, 7, 4, and 1.

2. Draw another number line and place the following values on the number line: 3, $5\frac{1}{2}$, and 6.

3. Draw another number line and place the following values on the number line: 3.75, 5, and 8.5.

Locate points (including fractions and decimals) on a number line

EMC 3018 • Basic Math Skills, Grade 5 • ©2003 by Evan-Moor Corp.

Woodshop

1. Julie is helping her dad in their woodshop. They are building a new doghouse for their dog Buddy. The first board they are cutting needs to be $5\frac{1}{2}$ feet in length. Mark the board with a line where Julie's dad should cut it.

2. The next board needs to be cut in two places. They want one board that is 4 feet long and another one that is $3\frac{1}{4}$ feet long. Draw two marks on the board where Julie's dad can cut to give them the two pieces they need.

3. The last board that they need your help with is a 10-foot board. They need three boards that are the following lengths: $2\frac{2}{3}$ feet, $3\frac{1}{3}$ feet, and $2\frac{1}{2}$ feet. Draw three marks on the board where Julie's dad can cut, giving them the three pieces they need.

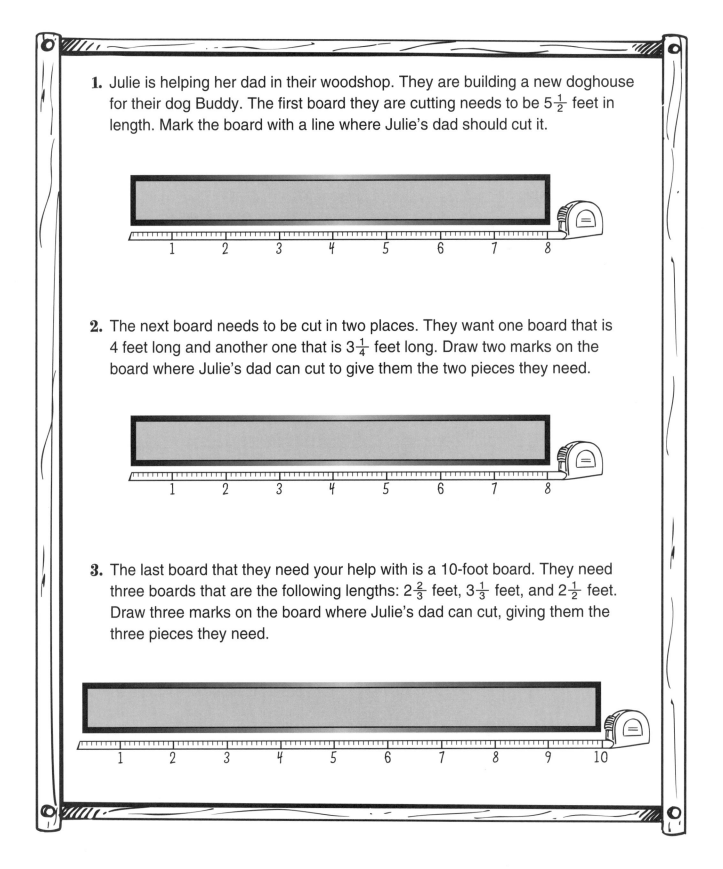

Locate points (including fractions and decimals) on a number line

Math Test

Name _____

Fill in the circle next to the correct answer.

For Numbers 1 through 4, use this number line.

A   B   C D

0   5   10

For Numbers 5 through 8, use this number line.

A   B   C   D

0   1   2

1. Which point is located at $3\frac{1}{2}$?

   (A) point A   (C) point C
   (B) point B   (D) point D

2. Which point is located at $7\frac{1}{3}$?

   (A) point A   (C) point C
   (B) point B   (D) point D

3. Which point is located at $6\frac{2}{3}$?

   (A) point A   (C) point C
   (B) point B   (D) point D

4. Which point is located at $2\frac{1}{4}$?

   (A) point A   (C) point C
   (B) point B   (D) point D

5. Which point is located halfway between two whole numbers?

   (A) point A   (C) point C
   (B) point B   (D) point D

6. Which point is located at 0.75?

   (A) point A   (C) point C
   (B) point B   (D) point D

7. Which point is located at 0.25?

   (A) point A   (C) point C
   (B) point B   (D) point D

8. Which point is located at $1\frac{1}{8}$?

   (A) point A   (C) point C
   (B) point B   (D) point D

9. Draw a number line and place the numbers 0 through 10 on it. Write an **X** above the value of 3 and a **Y** above the value of 7.5.

10. Draw another number line and place the numbers 0 through 3 on it, spreading out the space between the numbers. Write an **S** above the value of $1\frac{1}{3}$ and a **W** above the value of $2\frac{3}{4}$.

Locate points (including fractions and decimals) on a number line

EMC 3018 • Basic Math Skills, Grade 5 • ©2003 by Evan-Moor Corp.

Picture This

Start by numbering the x-axis and y-axis. Be sure to put the origin (0, 0) at the bottom left corner of the grid. Then plot the ordered pairs of numbers on the graph in the order they are listed and connect them with straight lines. Start each new set of points with a new line.

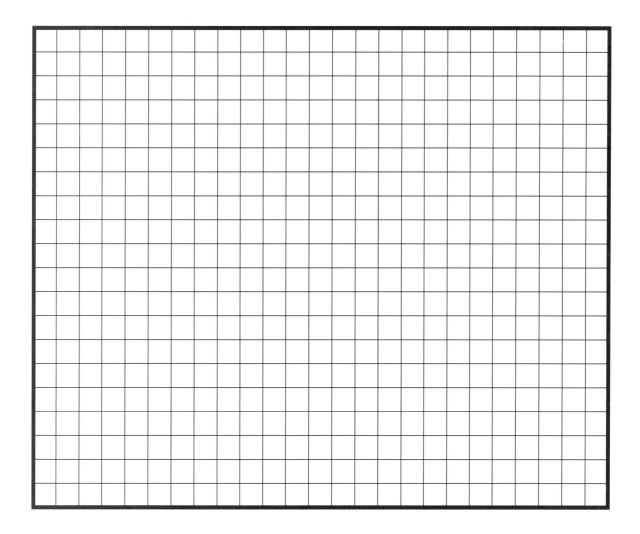

▶ (12, 8) (12, 10) (14, 10) (14, 8) (12, 8) line ends

▶ (5, 11) (5, 13) (8, 13) (8, 11) (5, 11) line ends

▶ (12, 6) (10, 8) (10, 10) (12, 12) (14, 12) (16, 10) (16, 8) (14, 6) (12, 6) line ends

▶ (4, 5) (4, 14) (20, 14) (20, 15) (21, 15) (21, 5) (4, 5) line ends

Locate and plot ordered pairs on a coordinate graph (first quadrant only)

Felines

Name _____

Plot the ordered pairs of numbers on the graph in the order they are listed and connect them with straight lines. Start each new set of points with a new line.

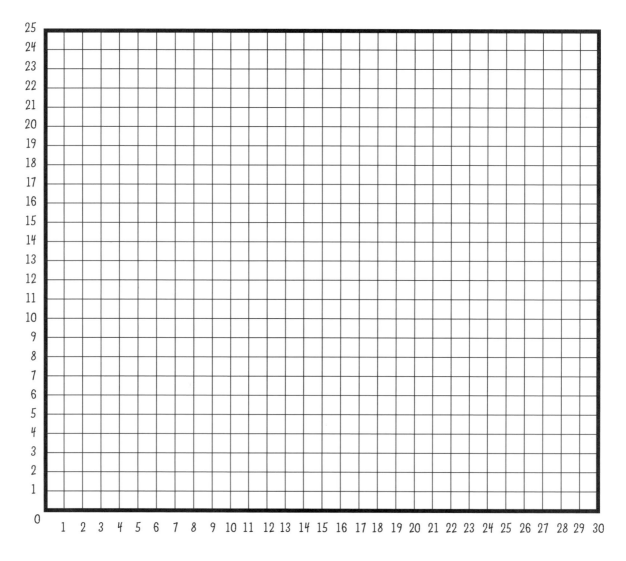

▶ (10, 10) (10, 5) (9, 5) (9, 4) (11, 4) (11, 10) (14, 9) (18, 9) (20, 10) (18, 5) (17, 5) (17, 4) (19, 4) (21, 9) line ends

▶ (4, 15) (10, 17) line ends

▶ (4, 17) (10, 15) line ends

▶ (4, 16) (10, 16) line ends

▶ (21, 10) (21, 5) (20, 5) (20, 4) (22, 4) (23, 10) (23, 14) (27, 14) (30, 17) (30, 20) (29, 21) (28, 20) (29, 19) (29, 18) (27, 15) (10, 15) (9, 16) (9, 18) (8, 19) (8, 21) (7, 19) (6, 21) (6, 19) (5, 18) (5, 16) (7, 14) (8, 14) (8, 9) (7, 5) (6, 5) (6, 4) (8, 4) (10, 9) line ends

▶ draw point at (6, 17)

▶ draw point at (8, 17)

Locate and plot ordered pairs on a coordinate graph (first quadrant only)

Algebra   EMC 3018 • Basic Math Skills, Grade 5 • ©2003 by Evan-Moor Corp.

Graph It

Name _____

Plot each of the ordered pairs on the graph, and then label the point with the corresponding letter.

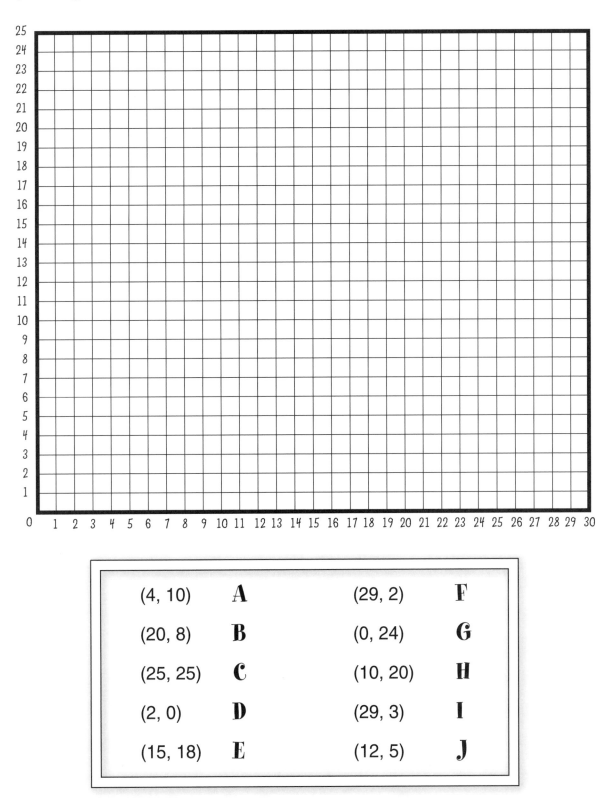

(4, 10)	**A**	(29, 2)	**F**
(20, 8)	**B**	(0, 24)	**G**
(25, 25)	**C**	(10, 20)	**H**
(2, 0)	**D**	(29, 3)	**I**
(15, 18)	**E**	(12, 5)	**J**

Locate and plot ordered pairs on a coordinate graph (first quadrant only)

Algebra

Graph It II

Plot each of the ordered pairs on the graph, and then label the point with the corresponding letter.

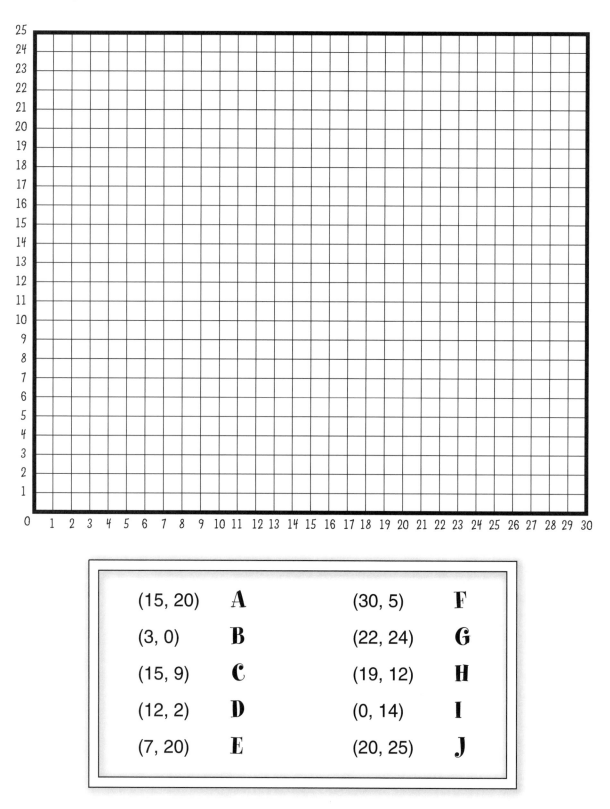

(15, 20)	**A**	(30, 5)	**F**
(3, 0)	**B**	(22, 24)	**G**
(15, 9)	**C**	(19, 12)	**H**
(12, 2)	**D**	(0, 14)	**I**
(7, 20)	**E**	(20, 25)	**J**

Locate and plot ordered pairs on a coordinate graph (first quadrant only)

Algebra

South Fork

Name _____

This is a map of South Fork. Use the map to answer the questions below.

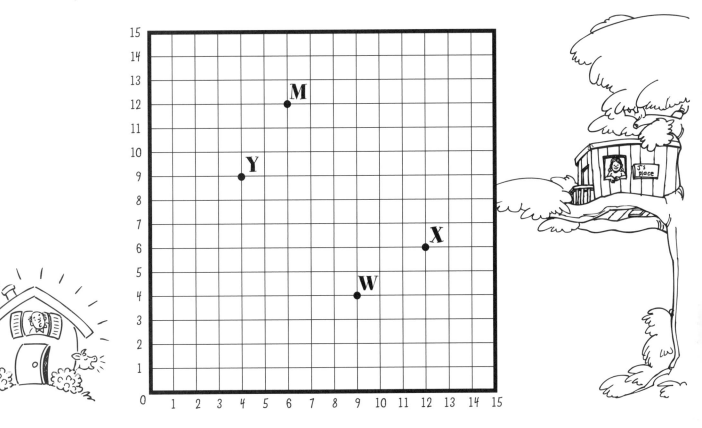

1. If the **X** is the town's general store, what is the ordered pair for that location? _____

2. The Laundry Mat is located at (9, 4) and the City Bank is located at (4, 9). What letters are represented for both businesses? _____

3. The **M** is the South Fork School. What is the ordered pair for that location? _____

4. Jeremy lives at the intersection of (4, 5) and Whitney lives at the intersection of (10, 12). Plot each of their homes on the map, making sure to label which is Jeremy's and which is Whitney's house.

5. How many blocks is it for Jeremy to walk to Whitney's house without cutting diagonally through a block? _____

Locate and plot ordered pairs on a coordinate graph (first quadrant only)

Jacksonville

Name _____

Here is a map of Jacksonville. Use the map to answer the questions below.

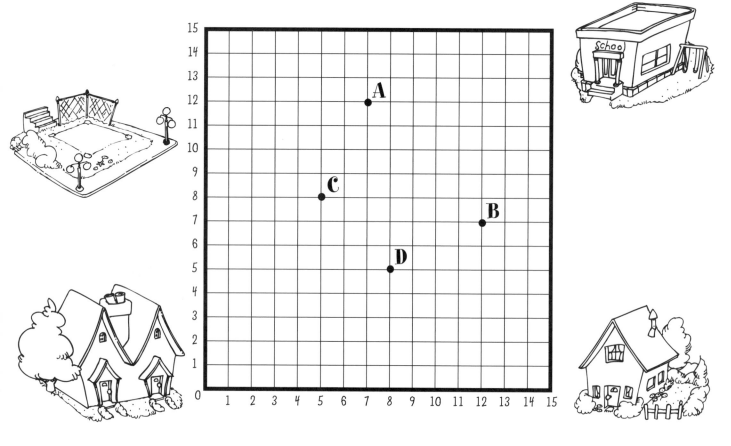

1. If the **A** is Jacksonville Elementary School, what is the ordered pair for its location? _____

2. The Clothing Store is located at (5, 8) and the Cloth World store is located at (8, 5). What letters are represented for both businesses? _____

3. The **B** is the Jacksonville High School. What is the ordered pair for that location? _____

4. Brendan lives at the intersection of (2, 10) and Leslie lives at the intersection of (9, 14). Plot each of their homes on the map, making sure to label which is Brendan's house and which is Leslie's house.

5. How many blocks is it for Leslie to walk to Brendan's house without cutting diagonally through a block? _____

Locate and plot ordered pairs on a coordinate graph (first quadrant only)

EMC 3018 • Basic Math Skills, Grade 5 • ©2003 by Evan-Moor Corp.

Math Test

Name _____

Fill in the circle next to the correct answer.

For Numbers 1 through 4, use the graph below.

1. Which point is located at (3, 6)?

   Ⓐ point A   Ⓒ point C

   Ⓑ point B   Ⓓ point D

2. Which point is located at (5, 3)?

   Ⓐ point A   Ⓒ point C

   Ⓑ point B   Ⓓ point D

3. Which point is located at (2, 2)?

   Ⓐ point A   Ⓒ point C

   Ⓑ point B   Ⓓ point D

4. Which point is located at (8, 5)?

   Ⓐ point A   Ⓒ point C

   Ⓑ point B   Ⓓ point D

For Numbers 5 through 8, use the graph below.

5. What is the ordered pair for point W?

   Ⓐ (2, 7)   Ⓒ (3, 5)

   Ⓑ (7, 2)   Ⓓ (5, 3)

6. What is the ordered pair for point Z?

   Ⓐ (2, 7)   Ⓒ (3, 5)

   Ⓑ (7, 2)   Ⓓ (5, 3)

7. What is the ordered pair for point Y?

   Ⓐ (2, 7)   Ⓒ (3, 5)

   Ⓑ (7, 2)   Ⓓ (5, 3)

8. What is the ordered pair for point X?

   Ⓐ (2, 7)   Ⓒ (3, 5)

   Ⓑ (7, 2)   Ⓓ (5, 3)

9. Draw a 10 by 10 grid. Number the grid, starting with the origin (0, 0) in the bottom left corner. Then place an **X** on point (5, 2) and a **Z** on point (7, 9).

10. Use the grid you created in Number 9 to answer this question: Sally is walking from the **X** to the **Z**. How many blocks will she walk if she has to stay on the streets and can NOT walk diagonally across a block?

Locate and plot ordered pairs on a coordinate graph (first quadrant only)

Algebra

Geometry

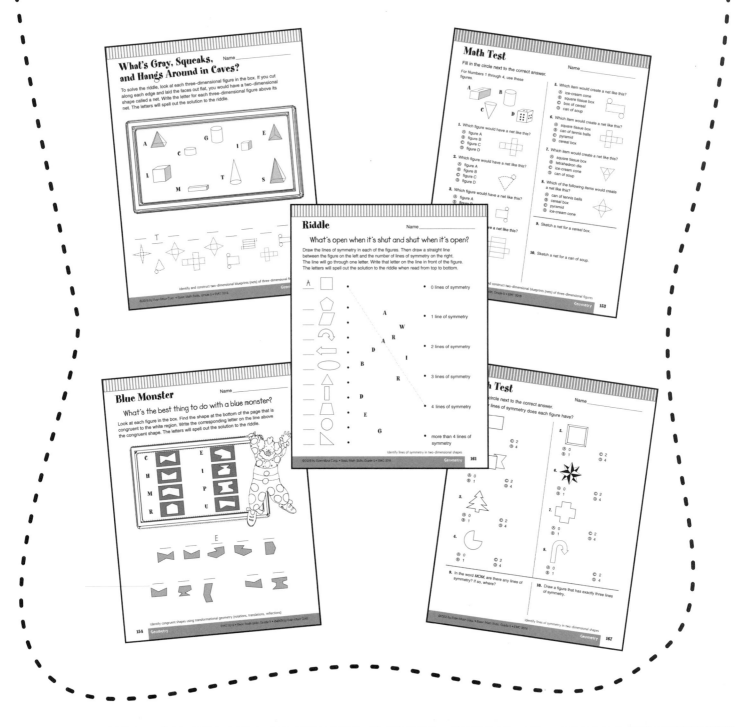

EMC 3018 • Basic Math Skills, Grade 5 • ©2003 by Evan-Moor Corp.

What's Gray, Squeaks, and Hangs Around in Caves?

Name_____

To solve the riddle, look at each three-dimensional figure in the box. If you cut along each edge and laid the faces out flat, you would have a two-dimensional shape called a net. Write the letter for each three-dimensional figure above its net. The letters will spell out the solution to the riddle.

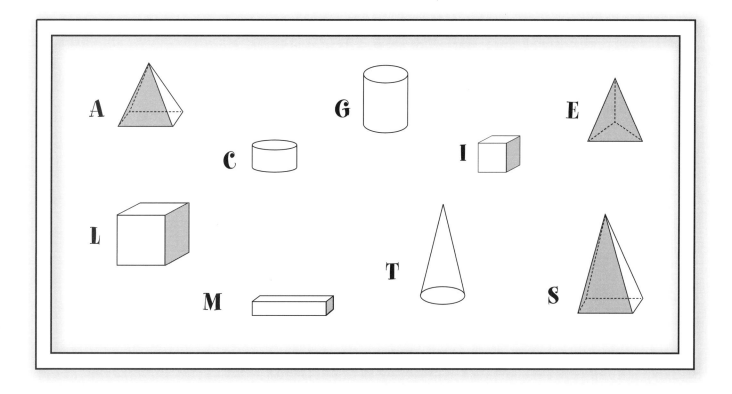

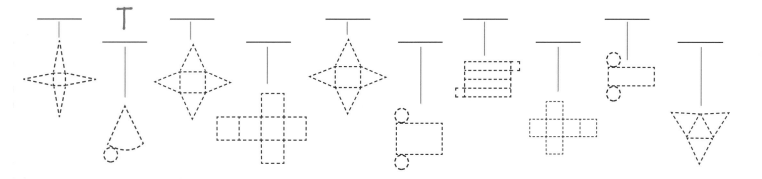

Identify and construct two-dimensional blueprints (nets) of three-dimensional figures

Geometry   **147**

Tongue Twister #9

Name_____

Look at each three-dimensional figure in the box. If you cut along each edge and laid the faces out flat, you would have a two-dimensional shape called a net. Write the letter for each three-dimensional figure above its net. The letters will spell out a tongue twister. Try to say it fast three times.

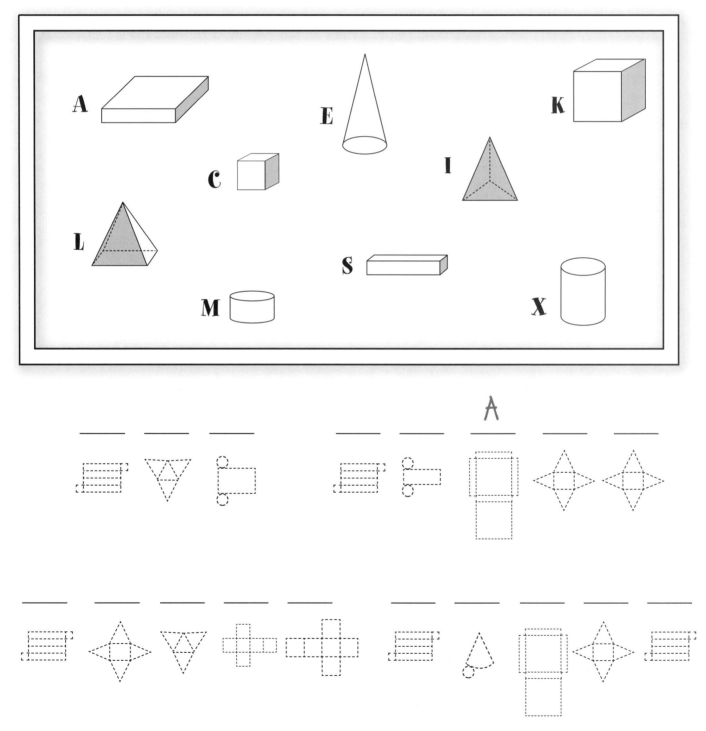

Identify and construct two-dimensional blueprints (nets) of three-dimensional figures

EMC 3018 • Basic Math Skills, Grade 5 • ©2003 by Evan-Moor Corp.

Nets

Name_____

Draw the two-dimensional blueprint (net) of each three-dimensional figure.

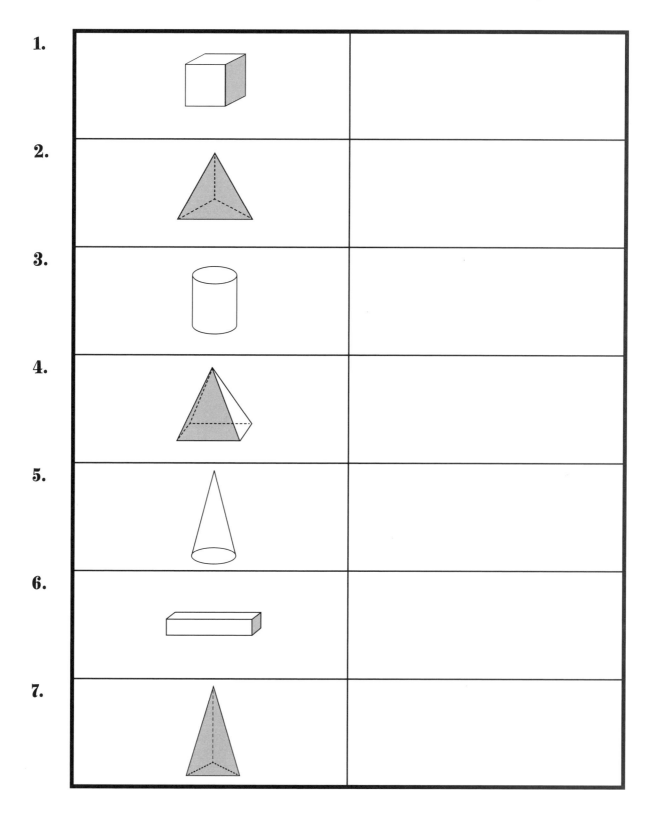

Identify and construct two-dimensional blueprints (nets) of three-dimensional figures

Nets II

Draw the two-dimensional blueprint (net) of each three-dimensional figure.

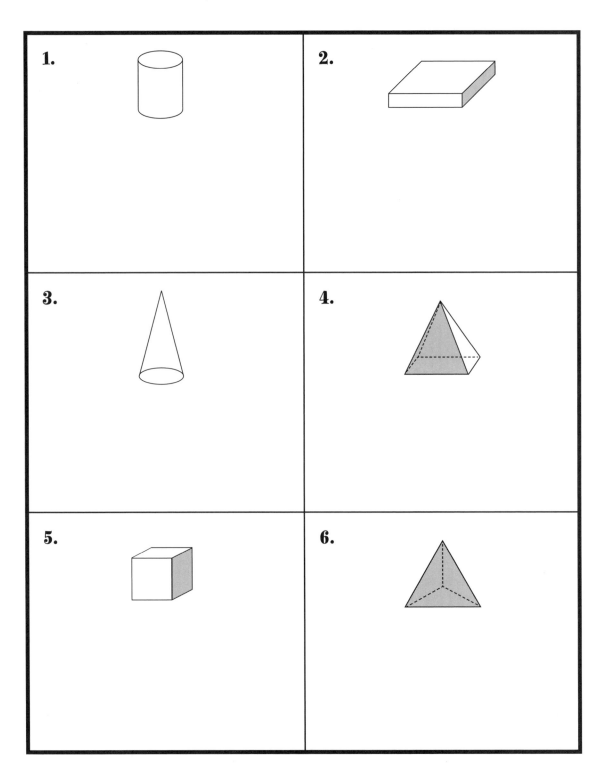

1.

2.

3.

4.

5.

6.

Identify and construct two-dimensional blueprints (nets) of three-dimensional figures

EMC 3018 • Basic Math Skills, Grade 5 • ©2003 by Evan-Moor Corp.

Boxes

1. Claudia was trying to wrap a present in a shoebox. She was trying to create a net that would cover all the sides of her shoebox. Sketch what her net might look like.

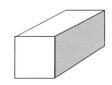

2. Jeremiah was cutting along the edges of a hatbox. The hatbox had a cylindrical shape to it. After he cut the edges, he laid them out flat, creating the net of the hatbox. What did his net look like?

3. Brandon had an empty tissue box. He wanted to see what the net would look like. He cut along all the edges and laid the box out flat. What shape was the net of the tissue box?

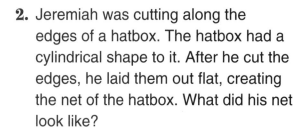

4. Gerald just got an ice-cream cone. He laid the wrapper out flat that was around the ice-cream cone. Sketch the net of the cone.

5. April cut along the edges of a cereal box. She laid out the faces, creating a flat net of the cereal box. Sketch what the net might have looked like.

Identify and construct two-dimensional blueprints (nets) of three-dimensional figures

The Speedy Warehouse

Name_____

Each of the following products is shipped out of the Speedy Warehouse. They need your help in creating the net for each item, so they can create the boxes with as little waste as possible. Next to each item, sketch the net.

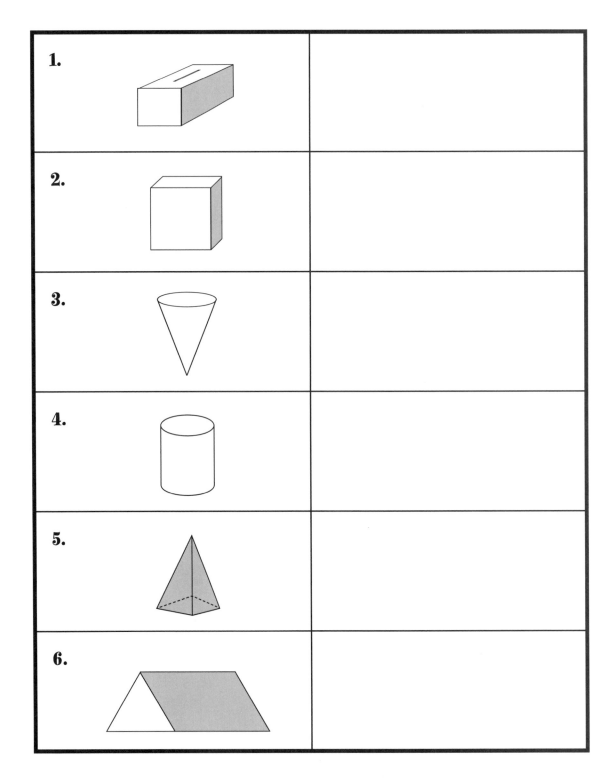

Identify and construct two-dimensional blueprints (nets) of three-dimensional figures

Math Test

Name _____

Fill in the circle next to the correct answer.

For Numbers 1 through 4, use these figures.

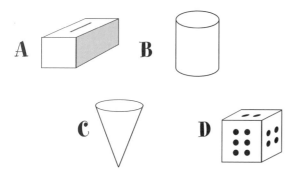

A   B   C   D

1. Which figure would have a net like this?

Ⓐ figure A
Ⓑ figure B
Ⓒ figure C
Ⓓ figure D

2. Which figure would have a net like this?

Ⓐ figure A
Ⓑ figure B
Ⓒ figure C
Ⓓ figure D

3. Which figure would have a net like this?

Ⓐ figure A
Ⓑ figure B
Ⓒ figure C
Ⓓ figure D

4. Which figure would have a net like this?

Ⓐ figure A
Ⓑ figure B
Ⓒ figure C
Ⓓ figure D

5. Which item would create a net like this?

Ⓐ ice-cream cone
Ⓑ square tissue box
Ⓒ box of cereal
Ⓓ can of soup

6. Which item would create a net like this?

Ⓐ square tissue box
Ⓑ can of tennis balls
Ⓒ pyramid
Ⓓ cereal box

7. Which item would create a net like this?

Ⓐ square tissue box
Ⓑ tetrahedron die
Ⓒ ice-cream cone
Ⓓ can of soup

8. Which of the following items would create a net like this?

Ⓐ can of tennis balls
Ⓑ cereal box
Ⓒ pyramid
Ⓓ ice-cream cone

9. Sketch a net for a cereal box.

10. Sketch a net for a can of soup.

Identify and construct two-dimensional blueprints (nets) of three-dimensional figures

Blue Monster

What's the best thing to do with a blue monster?

Look at each figure in the box. Find the shape at the bottom of the page that is congruent to the white region. Write the corresponding letter on the line above the congruent shape. The letters will spell out the solution to the riddle.

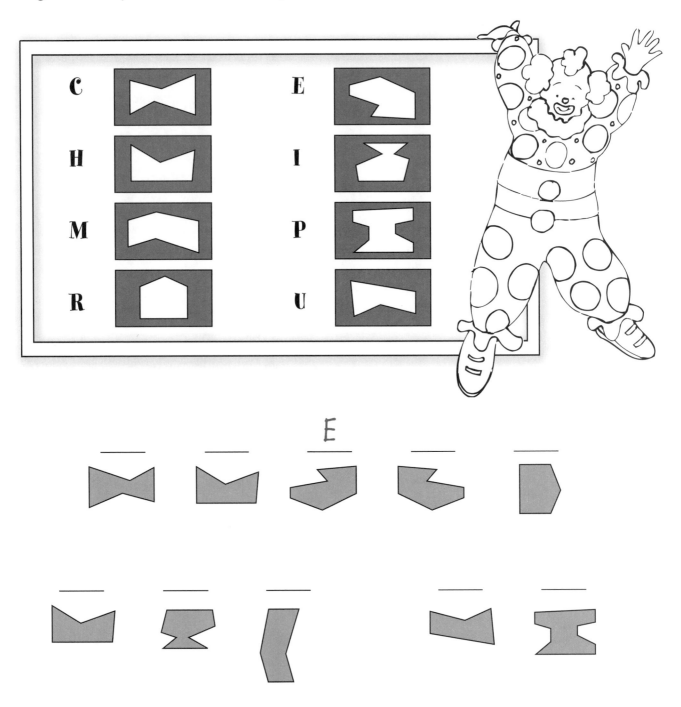

Identify congruent shapes using transformational geometry (rotations, translations, reflections)

    EMC 3018 • Basic Math Skills, Grade 5 • ©2003 by Evan-Moor Corp.

Tongue Twister #10

Look at each figure in the box. Find the shape at the bottom of the page that is congruent to the white region. Write the corresponding letter on the line above the congruent shape. The letters will spell out a tongue twister. Try to say it fast three times.

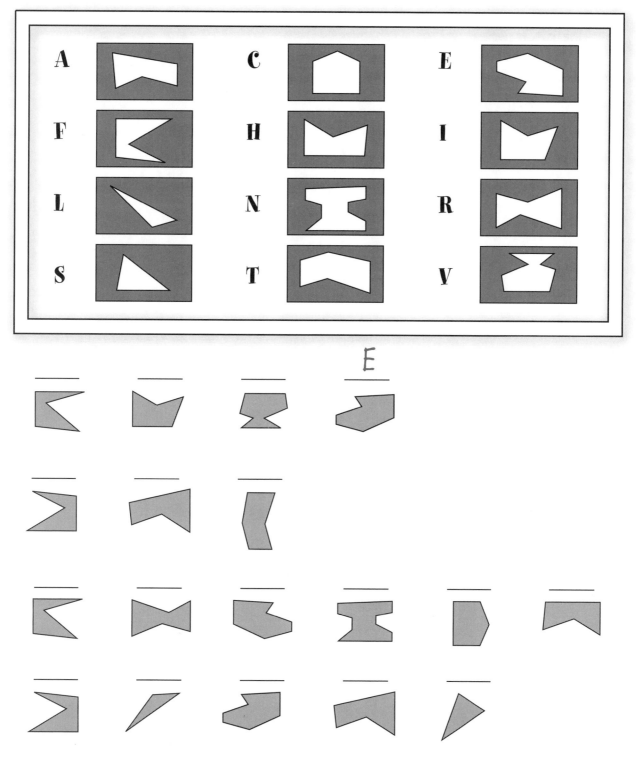

Identify congruent shapes using transformational geometry (rotations, translations, reflections)

Transformations

Name _____

Look at each pair of shapes. Determine how the shape is transformed from the one on the left to the one on the right. It could be a *turn* (rotation), *slide* (translation), or *flip* (reflection).

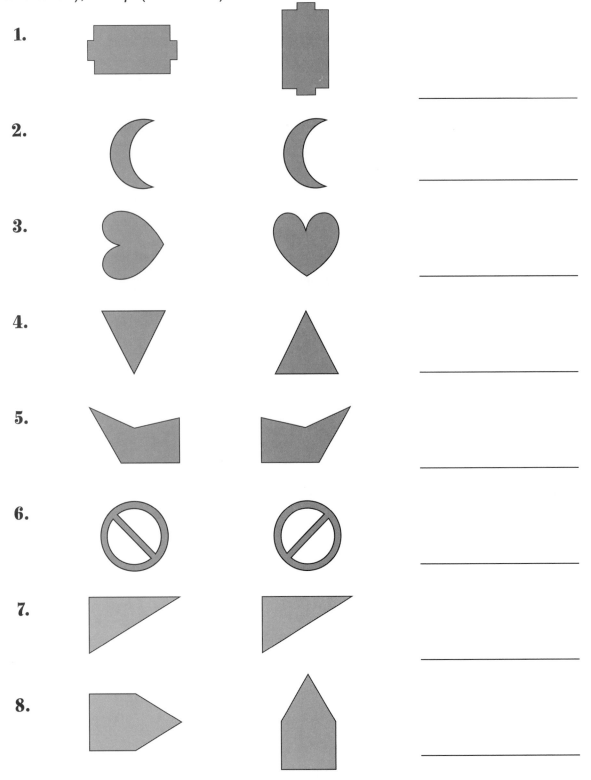

1. _____

2. _____

3. _____

4. _____

5. _____

6. _____

7. _____

8. _____

Identify congruent shapes using transformational geometry (rotations, translations, reflections)

EMC 3018 • Basic Math Skills, Grade 5 • ©2003 by Evan-Moor Corp.

Transformations II

Name_____

Look at each pair of shapes. Determine how the shape is transformed from the one on the left to the one on the right. It could be a *turn* (rotation), *slide* (translation), or *flip* (reflection).

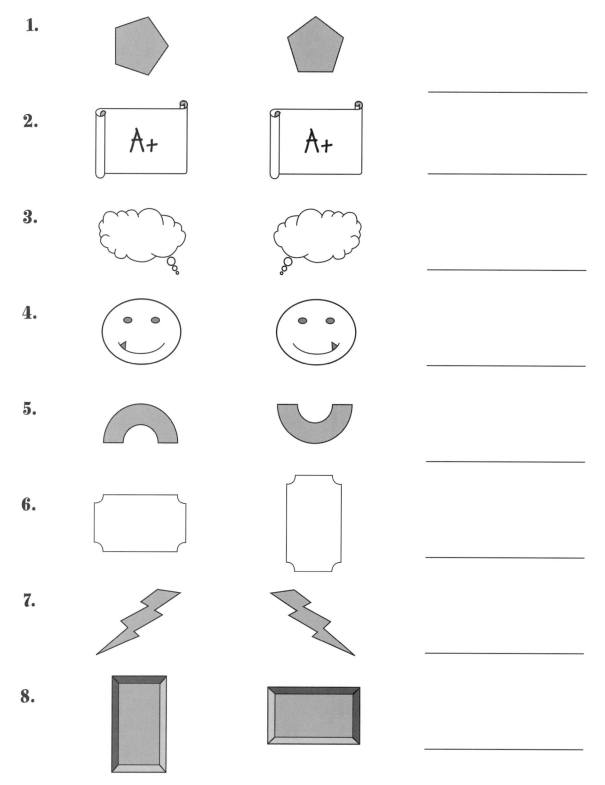

1. _____

2. _____

3. _____

4. _____

5. _____

6. _____

7. _____

8. _____

Identify congruent shapes using transformational geometry (rotations, translations, reflections)

Mirrors

Name _____

1. Sally is standing in front of a mirror, wearing a shirt with a picture of a horse on it. Draw what the reflection of her shirt looks like in the mirror.

2. Betty made the following design out of pattern blocks. She placed a mirror next to the design and looked at the reflection of the design. Sketch what the design looked like in the mirror.

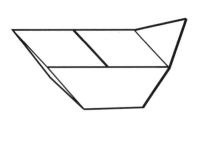 

3. Jimmy was trying to write a message for his sister. The trick was that he wanted her to read the message by holding it up to a mirror. Help Jimmy by reflecting (or flipping) his note.

Identify congruent shapes using transformational geometry (rotations, translations, reflections)

EMC 3018 • Basic Math Skills, Grade 5 • ©2003 by Evan-Moor Corp.

Pair Me Up

Find the shapes that are congruent to each other. Some congruent figures may be flipped or turned. Use a different color crayon to color each pair of figures.

How many pairs of congruent figures did you find? _____

Identify congruent shapes using transformational geometry (rotations, translations, reflections)

Math Test

Name _____

Fill in the circle next to the correct answer.

For Numbers 1 through 4, use these figures.

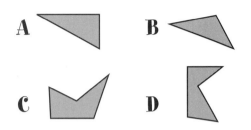

1. Which figure is congruent to the white region in this figure?

   Ⓐ figure A
   Ⓑ figure B
   Ⓒ figure C
   Ⓓ figure D

2. Which figure is congruent to the white region in this figure?

   Ⓐ figure A
   Ⓑ figure B
   Ⓒ figure C
   Ⓓ figure D

3. Which figure is congruent to the white region in this figure?

   Ⓐ figure A
   Ⓑ figure B
   Ⓒ figure C
   Ⓓ figure D

4. Which figure is congruent to the white region in this figure?

   Ⓐ figure A
   Ⓑ figure B
   Ⓒ figure C
   Ⓓ figure D

5. How is the figure on the left transformed to the one on the right?

   Ⓐ turned (rotated)
   Ⓑ flipped (reflected)
   Ⓒ slid (translated)
   Ⓓ turned and slid

6. How is the figure on the left transformed to the one on the right?

   Ⓐ turned (rotated)
   Ⓑ flipped (reflected)
   Ⓒ slid (translated)
   Ⓓ either turned or flipped

7. How is the figure on the left transformed to the one on the right?

   Ⓐ turned (rotated)
   Ⓑ flipped (reflected)
   Ⓒ slid (translated)
   Ⓓ flipped and slid

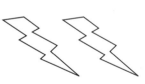

8. How is the figure on the left transformed to the one on the right?

   Ⓐ turned (rotated)
   Ⓑ flipped (reflected)
   Ⓒ slid (translated)
   Ⓓ turned and slid

9. Write your name. Then draw a line under it and write it under the line as if it were flipped over the line.

10. Draw a house. Then draw a line under the house. Sketch the house below the line with a vertical flip (reflection), where the top flips down to the bottom and the bottom flips up to become the top.

Identify congruent shapes using transformational geometry (rotations, translations, reflections)

EMC 3018 • Basic Math Skills, Grade 5 • ©2003 by Evan-Moor Corp.

Riddle

Name _____

What's open when it's shut and shut when it's open?

Draw the lines of symmetry in each of the figures. Then draw a straight line between the figure on the left and the number of lines of symmetry on the right. The line will go through one letter. Write that letter on the line in front of the figure. The letters will spell out the solution to the riddle when read from top to bottom.

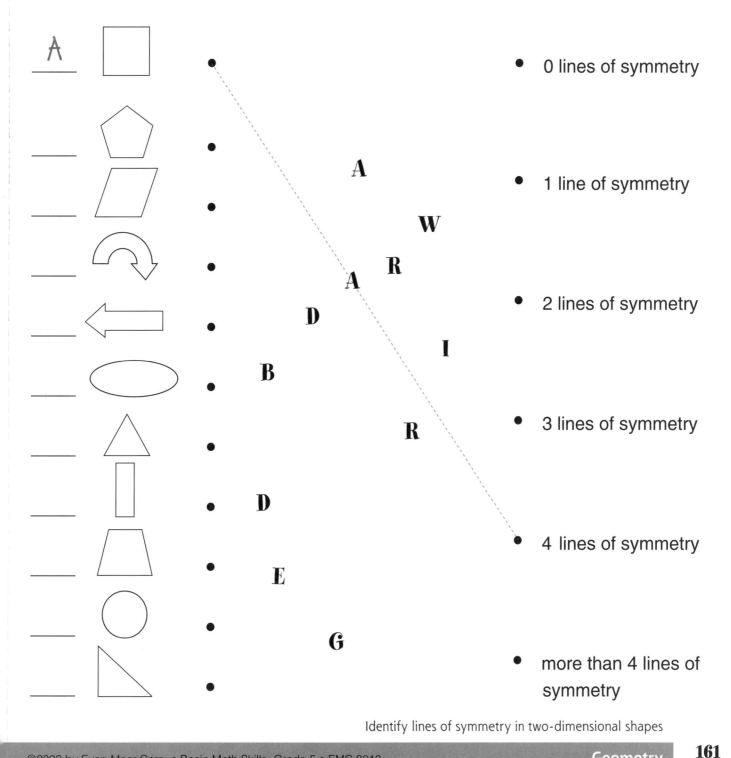

Identify lines of symmetry in two-dimensional shapes

What Is Dracula's Favorite Sport?

Name _____

Draw the lines of symmetry in each of the figures. Then draw a straight line between the figure on the left and the number of lines of symmetry on the right. The line will go through one letter. Write that letter on the line in front of the figure. The letters will spell out the solution to the riddle when read from top to bottom.

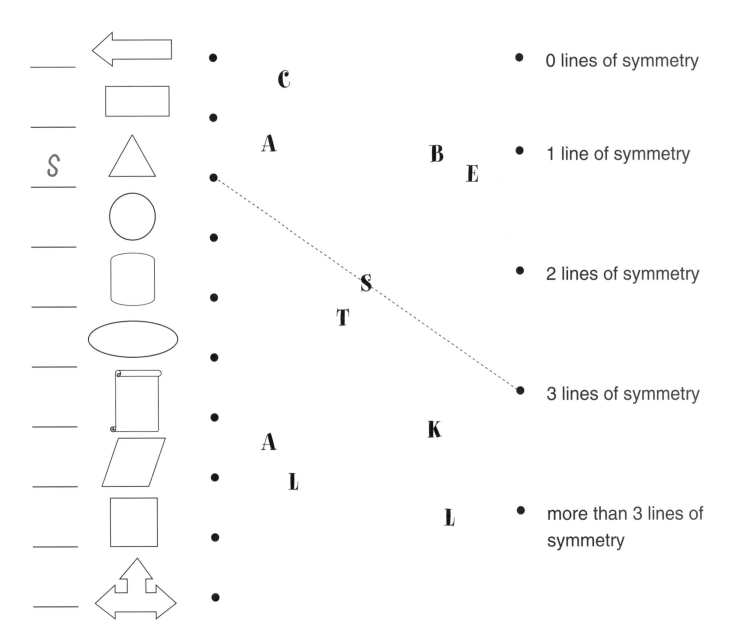

You Draw the Lines

Name _____

Draw all the lines of symmetry for each of the figures. Write the number of lines of symmetry next to each figure. If there are no lines of symmetry, write the word *none*.

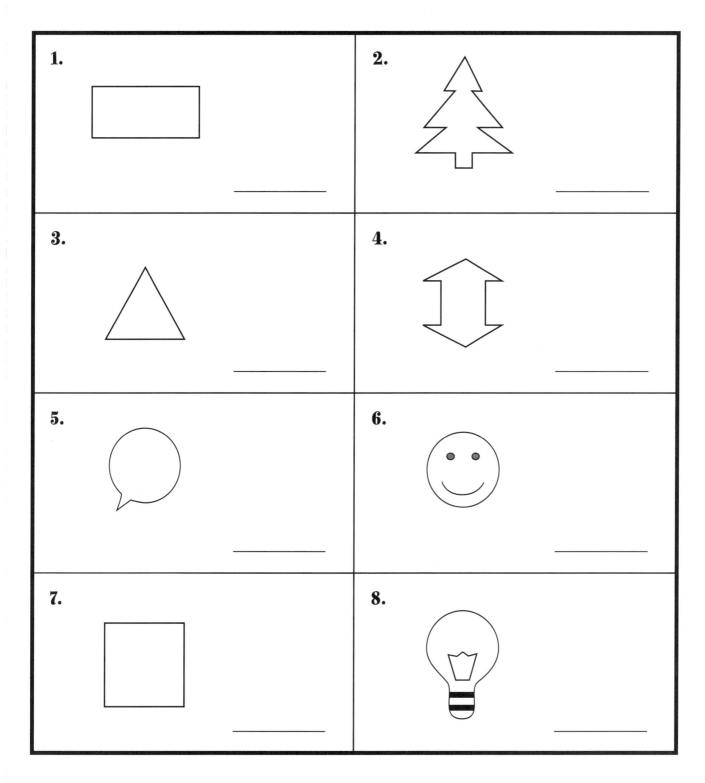

1. _____

2. _____

3. _____

4. _____

5. _____

6. _____

7. _____

8. _____

Identify lines of symmetry in two-dimensional shapes

You Draw the Lines II

Name _____

Draw all the lines of symmetry for each of the figures. Write the number of lines of symmetry next to each figure. If there are no lines of symmetry, write the word *none.*

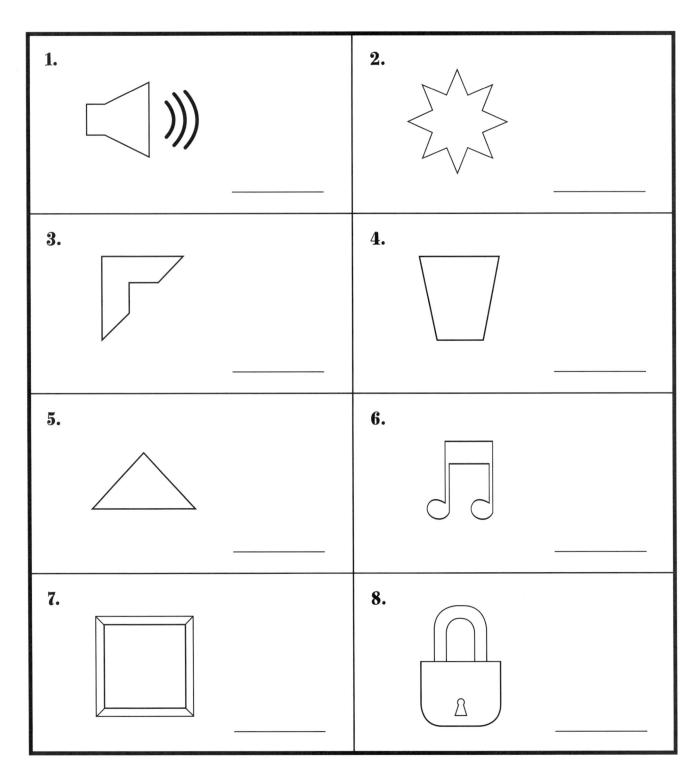

1. _____

2. _____

3. _____

4. _____

5. _____

6. _____

7. _____

8. _____

Identify lines of symmetry in two-dimensional shapes

EMC 3018 • Basic Math Skills, Grade 5 • ©2003 by Evan-Moor Corp.

Art Show

Name _____

1. Many artists include symmetry in their artwork. Look at the picture below and draw as many lines of symmetry as you can.

2. Here is a quilt design. Draw as many lines of symmetry as you can.

Identify lines of symmetry in two-dimensional shapes

Alphabet Letters

Name _____

The letters of the alphabet are shown below. Write the number of lines of symmetry each letter has. If a letter doesn't have any lines of symmetry, write *0*.

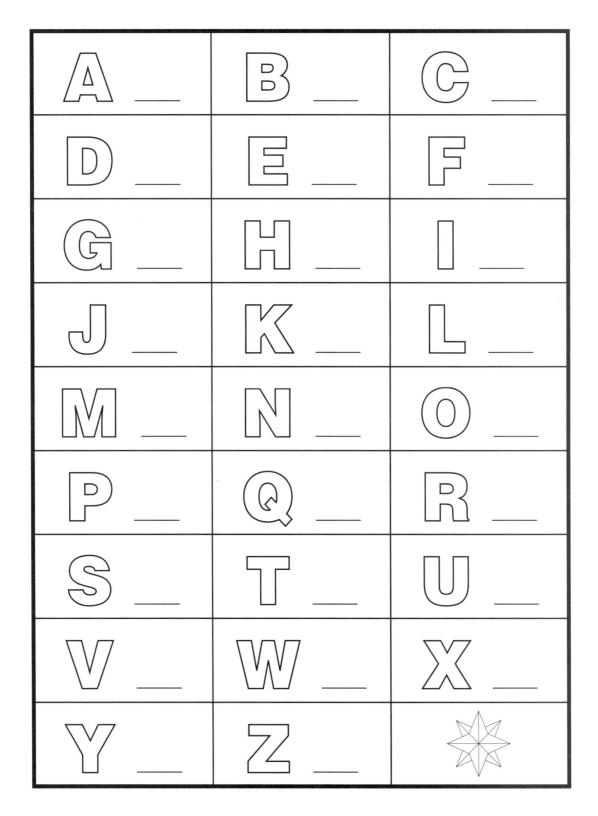

Identify lines of symmetry in two-dimensional shapes

Math Test

Name _____

Fill in the circle next to the correct answer.

How many lines of symmetry does each figure have?

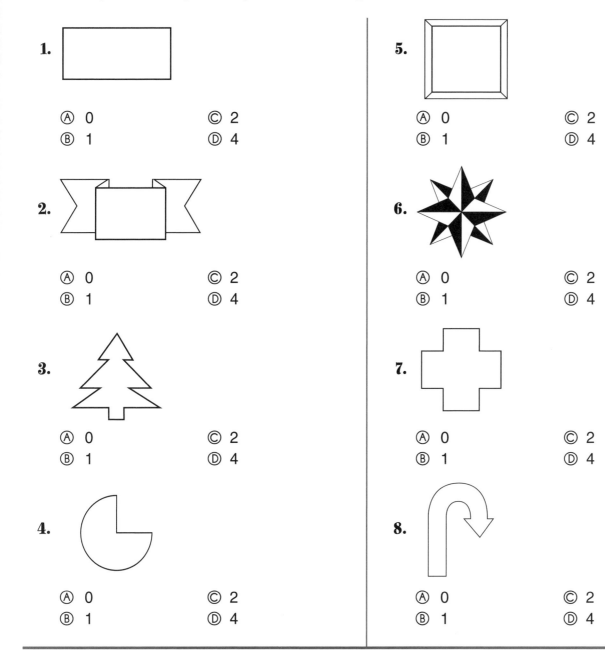

1.

Ⓐ 0   Ⓒ 2
Ⓑ 1   Ⓓ 4

2.

Ⓐ 0   Ⓒ 2
Ⓑ 1   Ⓓ 4

3.

Ⓐ 0   Ⓒ 2
Ⓑ 1   Ⓓ 4

4.

Ⓐ 0   Ⓒ 2
Ⓑ 1   Ⓓ 4

5.

Ⓐ 0   Ⓒ 2
Ⓑ 1   Ⓓ 4

6.

Ⓐ 0   Ⓒ 2
Ⓑ 1   Ⓓ 4

7.

Ⓐ 0   Ⓒ 2
Ⓑ 1   Ⓓ 4

8.

Ⓐ 0   Ⓒ 2
Ⓑ 1   Ⓓ 4

9. In the word *MOM,* are there any lines of symmetry? If so, where?

10. Draw a figure that has exactly three lines of symmetry.

Identify lines of symmetry in two-dimensional shapes

Measurement

Customary and Metric Measurement

Calendar and Temperature

Angles

Perimeter, Area, and Volume

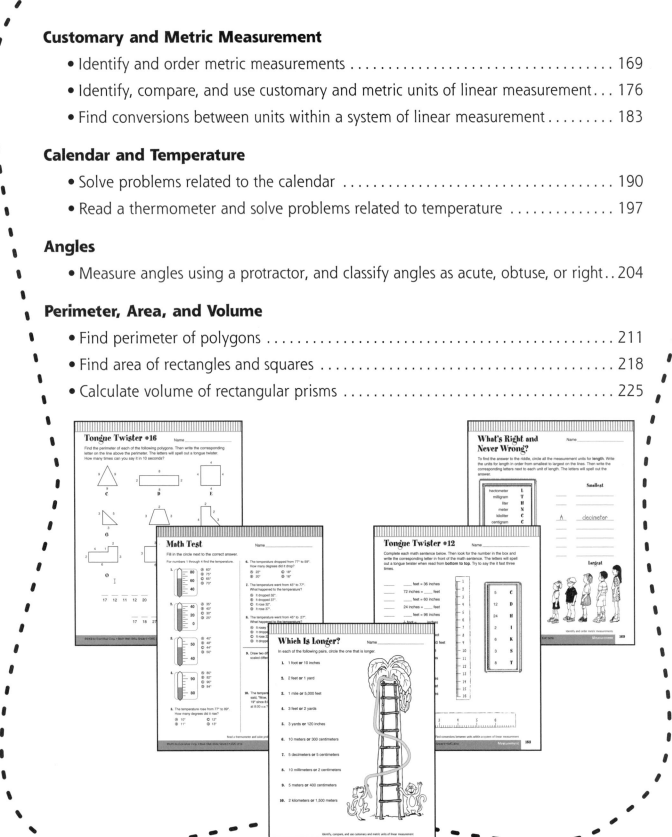

What's Right and Never Wrong?

To find the answer to the riddle, circle all the measurement units for **length**. Write the units for length in order from smallest to largest on the lines. Then write the corresponding letters next to each unit of length. The letters will spell out the answer.

hectometer	L
milligram	T
liter	H
meter	N
kiloliter	C
centigram	C
millimeter	A
hectogram	S
decigram	D
decimeter	A
gram	L
dekagram	F
centimeter	N
kilogram	S
dekaliter	D
deciliter	E
kilometer	E
centiliter	B
hectoliter	R
dekameter	G
milliliter	S

Smallest

____ _____

____ _____

_A_   _decimeter_

____ _____

____ _____

____ _____

Largest

Identify and order metric measurements

What's Furry, Meows, and Chases Mice Underwater?

Name_____

To find the answer to the riddle, circle all the measurement units for **weight**. Write the units for weight in order from smallest to largest on the lines. Then write the corresponding letters next to each unit of length. The letters will spell out the answer.

hectometer	A
milligram	C
liter	E
meter	D
kiloliter	M
centigram	A
millimeter	E
hectogram	S
decigram	T
decimeter	O
gram	F
dekagram	I
centimeter	A
kilogram	H
dekaliter	E
deciliter	I
kilometer	A
centiliter	C
hectoliter	S
dekameter	K
milliliter	H

Smallest

A   centigram

_____   _____

_____   _____

_____   _____

_____   _____

_____   _____

Largest

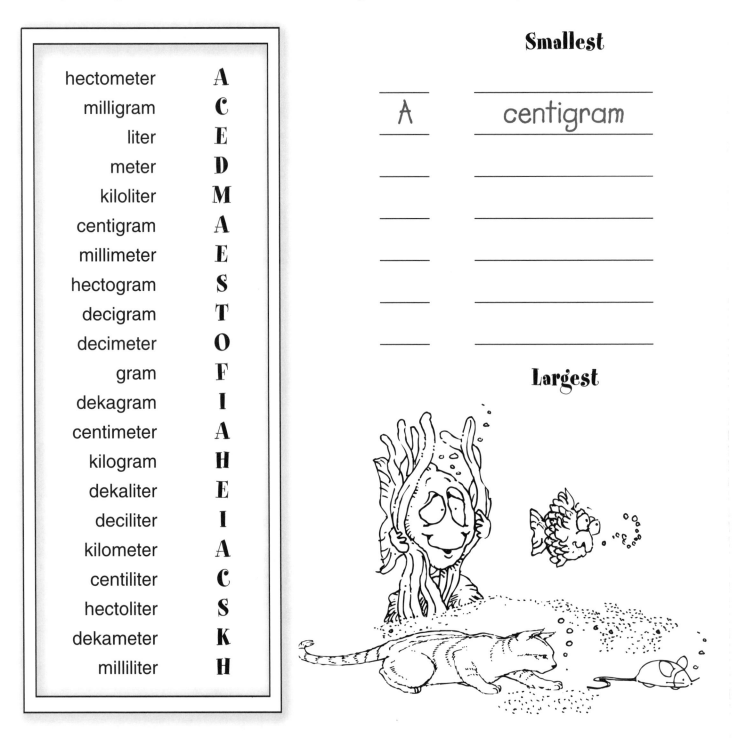

Identify and order metric measurements

EMC 3018 • Basic Math Skills, Grade 5 • ©2003 by Evan-Moor Corp.

Metrics

Three types of metric units are all mixed up in the box below. First, group them by linear measurement units, then by capacity measurement units, and then finally by mass measurement units. Then, within each of these groups, list them in order from smallest (lightest) to largest (heaviest).

Linear	Capacity	Mass
_____	_____	_____
_____	_____	_____
_____	_____	_____
_____	_____	_____
_____	_____	_____
_____	_____	_____
_____	_____	_____

centigram	dekagram	milliliter
kilometer	gram	centimeter
dekameter	decigram	liter
meter	decimeter	millimeter
dekaliter	centiliter	hectoliter
milligram	hectometer	hectogram
kiloliter	kilogram	deciliter

Identify and order metric measurements

Measurement   171

Which Is Which?

Name _____

Next to each of the following units of measurement, write an *M* if the unit is part of the metric system, and write a *C* if the unit is part of the customary measurement system.

1. gram _____

2. meter _____

3. ounce _____

4. pound _____

5. yard _____

6. liter _____

7. kilometer _____

8. decigram _____

9. foot _____

10. cup _____

11. dekameter _____

12. hectogram _____

13. ton _____

14. quart _____

15. milliliter _____

16. mile _____

17. pint _____

18. kiloliter _____

19. inch _____

20. centimeter _____

Identify and order metric measurements

Measurement   EMC 3018 • Basic Math Skills, Grade 5 • ©2003 by Evan-Moor Corp.

Metric Help

Solve each problem.

1. Jerry can't keep track of which units are used for measuring distance and which are used for measuring mass. He has this list in front of him:

dekagram	meter
decigram	decimeter
centigram	kilometer
dekameter	gram
milligram	hectometer

   Write a note to Jerry to help him sort out which units are used for distance and which are used for mass. Include in this note a hint or two that will help him keep this straight in the future.

   _____

2. Mr. Antuna needs your help. He has several metric measuring instruments, but the labels came off. He has one that measures length, and it is a little longer than a yardstick. Another one measures mass and is similar to a few pennies. A third one measures capacity and is slightly larger than a half-gallon pitcher. Help him label each with an appropriate unit of measure.

   _____

3. Mrs. Vierow gave Harold a pile of tools that are used to measure length, including meters, inches, centimeters, kilometers, miles, and yards. Help Harold sort the units into two groups and label each group accordingly.

   _____

Identify and order metric measurements

More Metric Help

Name_____

Solve each problem.

1. Jeanie can't keep track of which units are used for measuring distance and which are used for measuring capacity. She has this list in front of her:

    centiliter   kilometer
    dekameter   liter
    deciliter   decimeter
    milliliter   hectometer
    dekaliter   meter

    Write a note to Jeanie and help her sort the units used for distance and for capacity. Include in this note a hint or two that will help her keep this straight in the future.

    _____

2. Tami has five pieces of wire that are rolled up and labeled as follows:

    1 hectometer, 1 decimeter, 1 meter, 1 centimeter, and 1 kilometer

    Please help her list them in order from the smallest to the largest.

    _____

3. Sean is looking for a piece of string that is longer than 2 meters, but is shorter than 1 hectometer. Can you list three possible lengths of string that would satisfy Sean's need?

    _____

Identify and order metric measurements

EMC 3018 • Basic Math Skills, Grade 5 • ©2003 by Evan-Moor Corp.

Math Test

Name _____

Fill in the circle next to the correct answer.

1. Which unit is used to measure length?
   - Ⓐ kilogram
   - Ⓑ hectogram
   - Ⓒ deciliter
   - Ⓓ millimeter

2. Which unit is used to measure capacity?
   - Ⓐ hectogram
   - Ⓑ deciliter
   - Ⓒ millimeter
   - Ⓓ centigram

3. Which unit is used to measure mass?
   - Ⓐ liter
   - Ⓑ centimeter
   - Ⓒ decigram
   - Ⓓ milliliter

4. Which is shorter than a meter?
   - Ⓐ decimeter
   - Ⓑ hectometer
   - Ⓒ kilometer
   - Ⓓ dekameter

5. Which is heavier than a gram?
   - Ⓐ decigram
   - Ⓑ milligram
   - Ⓒ hectogram
   - Ⓓ centigram

6. Which is less than a liter?
   - Ⓐ dekaliter
   - Ⓑ hectoliter
   - Ⓒ kiloliter
   - Ⓓ centiliter

7. Which list is in order from smallest to largest?
   - Ⓐ millimeter, centimeter, meter, hectometer, decimeter
   - Ⓑ millimeter, decimeter, meter, hectometer, kilometer
   - Ⓒ millimeter, centimeter, meter, hectometer, dekameter
   - Ⓓ millimeter, centimeter, kilometer, meter, dekameter

8. Which list is in order from lightest to heaviest?
   - Ⓐ centigram, decigram, hectogram, kilogram, gram
   - Ⓑ centigram, decigram, gram, dekagram, kilogram
   - Ⓒ centigram, decigram, dekagram, gram, kilogram
   - Ⓓ centigram, decigram, hectogram, gram, kilogram

9. Which of the following does NOT fit and why?

   meter, centiliter, inch, milligram, hectometer, gram

   _____

   _____

10. List the following linear measurements in order from smallest to largest:

    hectometer, decimeter, dekameter, kilometer, centimeter, meter, millimeter

    _____

    _____

Identify and order metric measurements

Tongue Twister #11

Use a ruler that has both metric and customary units of measurement to help you answer the following questions. Complete each statement, writing a number rounded to the nearest whole unit. Then look for the number at the bottom of the page and write the corresponding letter on the line above the answer. The letters will spell out a tongue twister. How many times can you say it in 15 seconds?

2 inches ≈ _____ centimeters **A**   6 inches ≈ _____ centimeters **N**

7 centimeters ≈ _____ inches **C**   10 centimeters ≈ _____ inches **O**

20 centimeters ≈ _____ inches **D**   2.5 centimeters ≈ _____ inch **P**

4 inches ≈ _____ centimeters **E**   10 inches ≈ _____ centimeters **R**

17 centimeters ≈ _____ inches **I**   15 centimeters ≈ _____ inches **S**

30 centimeters ≈ _____ inches **L**   5 centimeters ≈ _____ inches **U**

≈ means "approximately equal to."

$$\frac{P}{1} \quad \frac{}{4} \quad \frac{}{4} \quad \frac{}{1} \quad \frac{}{10} \quad \frac{}{8}$$

$$\frac{}{1} \quad \frac{}{2} \quad \frac{}{25} \quad \frac{}{1} \quad \frac{}{12} \quad \frac{}{10}$$

$$\frac{}{1} \quad \frac{}{10} \quad \frac{}{12} \quad \frac{}{7} \quad \frac{}{3} \quad \frac{}{5} \quad \frac{}{15} \quad \frac{}{6}$$

Identify, compare, and use customary and metric units of linear measurement

What Kind of House Is Always Hot?

Name _____

To solve the riddle, measure each pencil with a metric ruler to the nearest centimeter. Then write the corresponding letter above each length. The letters will spell out the solution to the riddle.

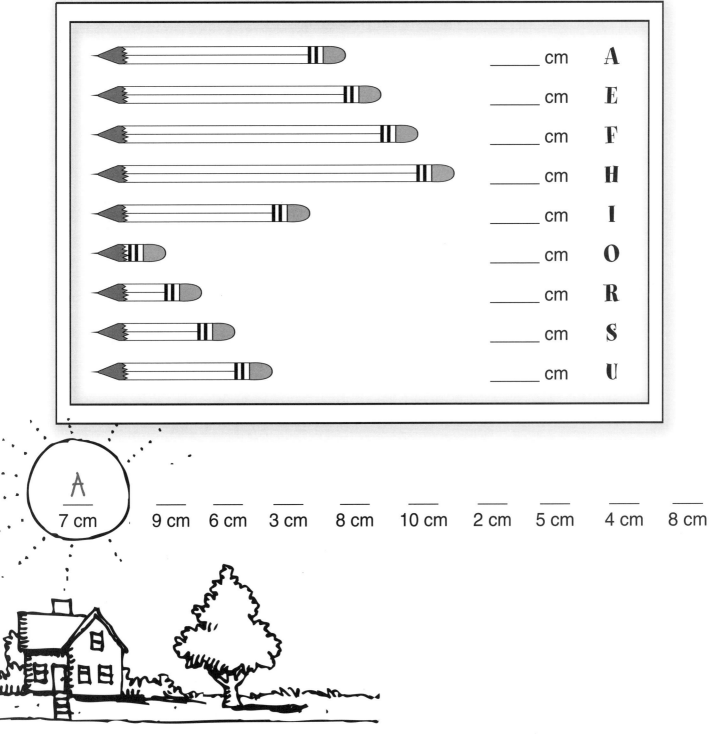

_____ cm   **A**

_____ cm   **E**

_____ cm   **F**

_____ cm   **H**

_____ cm   **I**

_____ cm   **O**

_____ cm   **R**

_____ cm   **S**

_____ cm   **U**

A
___
7 cm   ___   ___   ___   ___   ___   ___   ___   ___   ___
9 cm   6 cm   3 cm   8 cm   10 cm   2 cm   5 cm   4 cm   8 cm

Identify, compare, and use customary and metric units of linear measurement

How Long?

Name _____

Circle the measurement that is longer.

1. 1 millimeter **or** 1 centimeter

2. 1 millimeter **or** 1 decimeter

3. 1 centimeter **or** 1 hectometer

4. 1 dekameter **or** 1 millimeter

5. 1 kilometer **or** 1 centimeter

6. 1 hectometer **or** 1 meter

7. 1 decimeter **or** 1 centimeter

8. 1 dekameter **or** 1 hectometer

9. 1 centimeter **or** 1 meter

10. 1 hectometer **or** 1 millimeter

Identify, compare, and use customary and metric units of linear measurement

EMC 3018 • Basic Math Skills, Grade 5 • ©2003 by Evan-Moor Corp.

Which Is Longer?

In each of the following pairs, circle the one that is longer.

1. 1 foot **or** 10 inches

2. 2 feet **or** 1 yard

3. 1 mile **or** 5,000 feet

4. 3 feet **or** 2 yards

5. 3 yards **or** 120 inches

6. 10 meters **or** 300 centimeters

7. 5 decimeters **or** 5 centimeters

8. 10 millimeters **or** 2 centimeters

9. 5 meters **or** 400 centimeters

10. 2 kilometers **or** 1,500 meters

Identify, compare, and use customary and metric units of linear measurement

What in the World of Metrics?

Look around you at the world you live in. For each of the following lengths, find at least one object that is approximately that length. Write the name of the object next to the length. Then measure the actual length and see how close you were.

Length	Object you think is that length	Actual length
1. 3 centimeters	_____	_____
2. 1 meter	_____	_____
3. 15 centimeters	_____	_____
4. 5 millimeters	_____	_____
5. 2 meters	_____	_____
6. 30 centimeters	_____	_____
7. 10 meters	_____	_____
8. 1 centimeter	_____	_____
9. 1 millimeter	_____	_____
10. 10 centimeters	_____	_____

Identify, compare, and use customary and metric units of linear measurement

The World of Customary

Look around you at the world you live in. For each of the following lengths, find at least one object that is approximately that length. Write the name of the object next to the length. Then measure the actual length and see how close you were.

Length	Object you think is that length	Actual length
1. 10 inches	_____	_____
2. 2 feet	_____	_____
3. 3 inches	_____	_____
4. 1 yard	_____	_____
5. 6 inches	_____	_____
6. 1 foot	_____	_____
7. 2 yards	_____	_____
8. 4 feet	_____	_____
9. 1 inch	_____	_____
10. 5 yards	_____	_____

Identify, compare, and use customary and metric units of linear measurement

Math Test

Name _____

Fill in the circle next to the correct answer.

1. How long is this pencil to the nearest inch?

Ⓐ 5 inches   Ⓑ 6 inches   Ⓒ 7 inches   Ⓓ 12 inches

2. How long is this pencil to the nearest half-inch?

Ⓐ $3\frac{1}{2}$ inches   Ⓑ $4\frac{1}{2}$ inches   Ⓒ 7 inches   Ⓓ $8\frac{1}{2}$ inches

3. How long is this pencil to the nearest centimeter?

Ⓐ 5 centimeters   Ⓑ 6 centimeters   Ⓒ 12 centimeters   Ⓓ 15 centimeters

4. How long is this pencil to the nearest millimeter?

Ⓐ 12 millimeters   Ⓑ 13 millimeters   Ⓒ 110 millimeters   Ⓓ 124 millimeters

5. Which of the following is slightly longer than a yard?

Ⓐ 1 meter   Ⓑ 1 millimeter   Ⓒ 1 kilometer   Ⓓ 1 centimeter

6. Which of the following is a little less than one-half inch?

Ⓐ 1 millimeter   Ⓑ 1 hectometer   Ⓒ 1 centimeter   Ⓓ 1 meter

7. Which of the following is NOT equal to one yard?

Ⓐ 3 feet   Ⓑ 36 inches   Ⓒ 15 miles   Ⓓ All are equal to one yard

8. Which of the following is NOT equal to one meter?

Ⓐ 100 centimeters   Ⓑ 10 decimeters   Ⓒ 1,000 millimeters   Ⓓ All are equal to one meter

---

9. Draw a line that is 12 centimeters long.

10. Which is longer, 2 yards or 7 feet? Explain why.

_____

Identify, compare, and use customary and metric units of linear measurement

Tongue Twister #12

Name _____

Complete each math sentence below. Then look for the number in the box and write the corresponding letter in front of the math sentence. The letters will spell out a tongue twister when read from **bottom to top**. Try to say it fast three times.

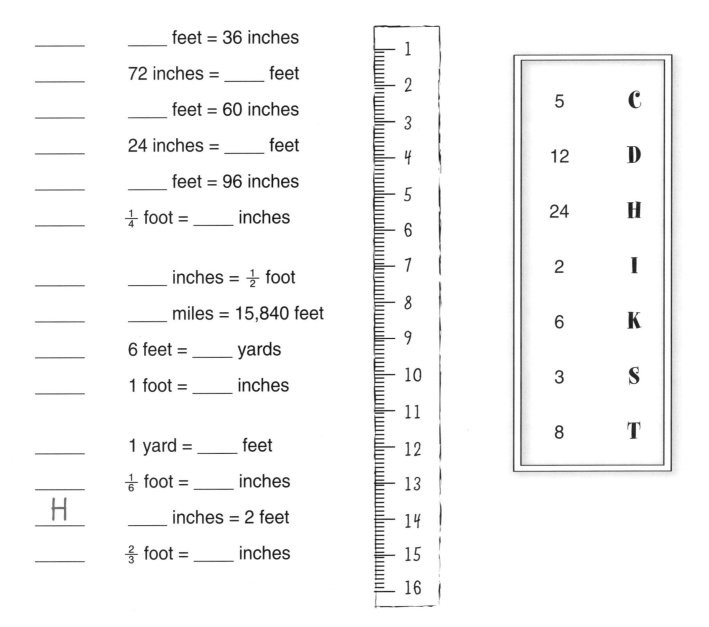

_____   _____ feet = 36 inches

_____   72 inches = _____ feet

_____   _____ feet = 60 inches

_____   24 inches = _____ feet

_____   _____ feet = 96 inches

_____ $\frac{1}{4}$ foot = _____ inches

_____   _____ inches = $\frac{1}{2}$ foot

_____   _____ miles = 15,840 feet

_____   6 feet = _____ yards

_____   1 foot = _____ inches

_____   1 yard = _____ feet

_____ $\frac{1}{6}$ foot = _____ inches

H   _____ inches = 2 feet

_____ $\frac{2}{3}$ foot = _____ inches

5	C
12	D
24	H
2	I
6	K
3	S
8	T

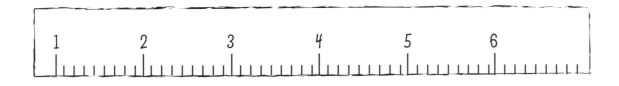

Find conversions between units within a system of linear measurement

Why Was Cinderella Thrown off the Baseball Team?

Name _____

Complete each number sentence with a number. Then write the corresponding letter above that number. The letters will spell out the solution to the riddle.

2,000 millimeters = ___ meters **A**

500 centimeters = ___meters **B**

1 dekameter = ___ meters **C**

300 centimeters = ___ meters **E**

___ kilometers = 4,000 meters **F**

70 decimeters = ___ meters **H**

___ dekameters = 90 meters **L**

___ hectometers = 600 meters **M**

____ meters = 8,000 millimeters **N**

10 decimeters = ___ meter **O**

_____ centimeters = 1 meter **R**

2 meters = _____ centimeters **S**

3 meters = ___ decimeters **T**

_____ meters = 3 hectometers **U**

___ decimeters = 2 meters **W**

___ decimeters = 4 meters **Y**

A
__ __ __ __ __ __ __
5 3 10 2 300 200 3

__ __ __   __ __ __
200 7 3   100 2 8

__ __ __ __
2 20 2 40

__ __ __ __   __ __ __
4 100 1 6   30 7 3

__ __ __ __
5 2 9 9

Find conversions between units within a system of linear measurement

EMC 3018 • Basic Math Skills, Grade 5 • ©2003 by Evan-Moor Corp.

Convert Customary Measurements

Name _____

Complete each of the following to make a true math sentence.

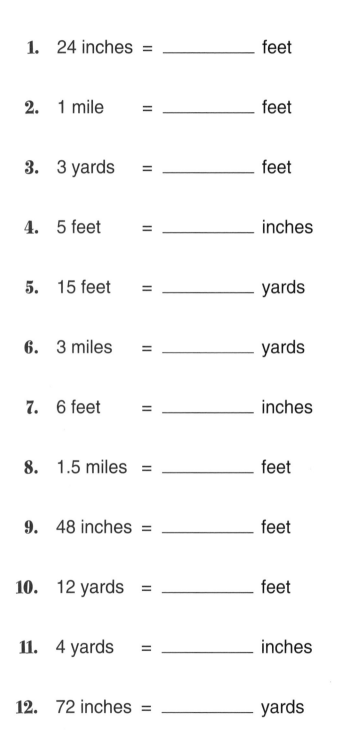

1. 24 inches = _____ feet

2. 1 mile = _____ feet

3. 3 yards = _____ feet

4. 5 feet = _____ inches

5. 15 feet = _____ yards

6. 3 miles = _____ yards

7. 6 feet = _____ inches

8. 1.5 miles = _____ feet

9. 48 inches = _____ feet

10. 12 yards = _____ feet

11. 4 yards = _____ inches

12. 72 inches = _____ yards

Find conversions between units within a system of linear measurement

Convert My Metrics

Name _____

Complete each of the following to make a true math sentence.

1. 1 meter   = _____ centimeters

2. 1 kilometer   = _____ meters

3. $\frac{1}{2}$ meter = _____ centimeters

4. 500 meters   = _____ kilometers

5. 4 hectometers = _____ meters

6. 3 dekameters   = _____ meters

7. 3 meters   = _____ millimeters

8. 0.5 dekameter = _____ meters

9. 3 meters   = _____ millimeters

10. 8,000 meters = _____ kilometers

11. 500 millimeters = _____ meters

12. 500 centimeters = _____ meters

Find conversions between units within a system of linear measurement

EMC 3018 • Basic Math Skills, Grade 5 • ©2003 by Evan-Moor Corp.

Wesley's Problems

Name _____

Wesley was working on the following problems and got most of them wrong. Write positive comments about any of the problems that he got correct. Then show why the other problems are wrong.

For each pair of lengths, circle the one that is longer.

○   1.   4 centimeters **or** (14 millimeters)

2.   5 millimeters **or** (8 meters)

3.   (12 decimeters) **or** 5 meters

4.   (140 centimeters) **or** 10 decimeters

○   5.   7 meters **or** (80 decimeters)

6.   3 hectometers **or** (15 dekameters)

7.   2 kilometers **or** (200 meters)

○   8.   (35 millimeters) **or** 4 centimeters

Find conversions between units within a system of linear measurement

Wayne's Problems

Wayne was working on the following problems and got some of them wrong. Write positive comments about any of the problems that he got correct. Then show why the other problems are wrong.

For each pair of lengths, circle the one that is shorter.

○ **1.** 3 inches **or** (1 foot)

2. (2 feet) **or** 3 yards

3. (1 yard) **or** 40 inches

4. (2 feet) **or** 20 inches

○ **5.** (1 mile) **or** 6000 feet

6. (2 yards) **or** 7 feet

7. 70 inches **or** (5 feet)

○ **8.** (3 miles) **or** 15,000 feet

Find conversions between units within a system of linear measurement

Math Test

Fill in the circle next to the correct answer.

1. 1 yard equals _____.

   Ⓐ 12 inches

   Ⓑ 5,280 feet

   Ⓒ 3 feet

   Ⓓ 24 inches

2. 1 mile equals _____.

   Ⓐ 3 yards

   Ⓑ 50 feet

   Ⓒ 100 yards

   Ⓓ 5,280 feet

3. 5 feet equals _____.

   Ⓐ 2 yards

   Ⓑ 60 inches

   Ⓒ 50 inches

   Ⓓ 3 yards

4. 48 inches equals _____.

   Ⓐ 1 yard

   Ⓑ $\frac{1}{2}$ mile

   Ⓒ 2 yards

   Ⓓ 4 feet

5. 100 meters equals _____.

   Ⓐ 10 centimeters

   Ⓑ 10,000 millimeters

   Ⓒ 1 hectometer

   Ⓓ 1,000 centimeters

6. 1 hectometer equals _____.

   Ⓐ 10 meters

   Ⓑ 100 centimeters

   Ⓒ 1,000 meters

   Ⓓ 100 meters

7. 100 centimeters equals _____.

   Ⓐ 1 meter

   Ⓑ 1 millimeter

   Ⓒ 1 decimeter

   Ⓓ 1 hectometer

8. 1,000 meters equals _____.

   Ⓐ 1 kilometer

   Ⓑ 1 hectometer

   Ⓒ 1 decimeter

   Ⓓ 1 millimeter

9. What are two measurements that are equivalent to 2 meters?

_____

_____

10. What are two measurements that are equivalent to 2 yards?

_____

_____

Find conversions between units within a system of linear measurement

What Do You Call a Frightened Scuba Diver?

Name _____

To solve the riddle, look at the questions below the calendar. Answer each question and write the letter from that date on the line in front of the question. The letters will spell out the answer to the riddle if read from top to bottom.

Sunday		Monday		Tuesday		Wednesday		Thursday		Friday		Saturday	
						1	W	2	Q	3	C	4	S
5	M	6	U	7	F	8	P	9	A	10	R	11	J
12	D	13	N	14	H	15	B	16	E	17	I	18	N
19	X	20	E	21	K	22	T	23	G	24	H	25	Y
26	V	27	L	28	C	29	O	30	Z	31	A		

__C__ The first Friday of the month

_____ Two weeks before the 28th

_____ One week after the 10th

_____ The day before the 4th

_____ Eight days before the 29th

_____ Two weeks after the 6th

_____ Two days after the second Saturday of the month

_____ The fifth Wednesday of the month

_____ The first Tuesday of the month

_____ Three weeks after the 1st

_____ One week before the last day of the month

_____ The middle of the month on a Thursday

_____ The first Saturday of the month

_____ Six days before the last Sunday of the month

_____ The second Thursday of the month

Solve problems related to the calendar

Measurement   EMC 3018 • Basic Math Skills, Grade 5 • ©2003 by Evan-Moor Corp.

Tongue Twister #13

Name _____

Answer each of the questions below the calendar and write the letter from that date on the line in front of the question. The letters will spell out a tongue twister from top to bottom, starting on the left. Try to say it fast three times.

Sunday	Monday	Tuesday	Wednesday	Thursday	Friday	Saturday
	1 L	2 Q	3 E	4 T	5 P	6 Z
7 I	8 W	9 N	10 N	11 M	12 B	13 G
14 X	15 P	16 D	17 A	18 E	19 P	20 U
21 O	22 H	23 S	24 J	25 C	26 F	27 K
28 R	29 Y	30 V				

_____ The first Sunday

_____ Two weeks after the ninth

_T_ The first Thursday

_____ The fourth Monday

_____ The third Thursday

_____ The last Sunday

_____ One week before the twenty-fifth

_____ Two weeks after the third

_____ The first Friday

_____ The first day

_____ One week after the eleventh

_____ Third Wednesday

_____ One week before the thirtieth

_____ Two days after the fifteenth

_____ Second Wednesday

_____ Ten days before the fourteenth

_____ Middle Monday

_____ One day before the nineteenth

_____ Two days after the fifteenth

_____ One week after the sixteenth

_____ Three days after the fourteenth

_____ One week after the third

_____ Three weeks before the twenty-fifth

_____ First Friday

_____ Last Sunday

_____ Two days after the first

_____ One week before the last day

_____ Three days before the sixth

_____ Second Tuesday

? _____ Three weeks before the last Thursday

Solve problems related to the calendar

Calendar This

Answer the following questions using this calendar.

Sunday	Monday	Tuesday	Wednesday	Thursday	Friday	Saturday
					1	2
3	4	5	6	7	8	9
10	11	12	13	14	15	16
17	18	19	20	21	22	23
24	25	26	27	28	29	30

1. How many days are in this month? _____

2. What are the possible months that this calendar could represent? _____

3. What day of the week does the twenty-first fall on? _____

4. What day of the week is seven days after the thirteenth? _____

5. What is the date two days before the twenty-first? _____

6. What is the date of the last Monday of the month? _____

7. What is the date of the day three days after the sixteenth? _____

8. What is the date of the Wednesday before the sixth? _____

9. What is the date two weeks after the eighth? _____

10. In the next month's calendar, what day of the week does the twentieth fall on? _____

Solve problems related to the calendar

EMC 3018 • Basic Math Skills, Grade 5 • ©2003 by Evan-Moor Corp.

Calendar This II

Name _____

Answer the following questions.

1. How many days are there in a week? _____

2. How many months in a year? _____

3. How many days are in the month of March? _____

4. How many days are in a regular year? _____

5. How many days are in a leap year? _____

6. What happens during a leap year that is different from every other year? _____

7. If the first day of the month of May falls on Monday, what day does the last day of May fall on? _____

Use the calendar below to complete questions 8 through 10. Number the days of the month like your current month.

Sunday	Monday	Tuesday	Wednesday	Thursday	Friday	Saturday

8. What day of the week does the twentieth fall on? _____

9. What is the date of the first Wednesday of the month? _____

10. What is the date of the day two weeks after the first Friday of the month? _____

Solve problems related to the calendar

What Month Is This?

Name _____

Answer the following questions using this calendar.

Sunday	Monday	Tuesday	Wednesday	Thursday	Friday	Saturday
					1	2
3	4	5	6	7	8	9
10	11	12	13	14	15	16
17	18	19	20	21	22	23
24	25	26	27	28	29	30
31						

1. What are all the possible months that this calendar could represent?

   _____

2. The date of the Tuesday, one week before the fifth, is the twenty-sixth.
   What month is this calendar? Explain how you got your answer.

   _____

3. Juan and his mother just returned from a vacation on Monday, the fourth.
   They had been gone for ten days. What date did they leave on?

   _____

4. Julie and her family leave on the twenty-seventh for a two-week trip. What
   is the date when they plan to return?

   _____

5. Roberto had an orthodontist appointment on the twenty-seventh of this
   month. The orthodontist would like him to return in six weeks. What is the
   date when he needs to return?

   _____

What Month Is This II?   Name_____

Answer the following questions using this calendar.

Sunday	Monday	Tuesday	Wednesday	Thursday	Friday	Saturday
1	2	3	4	5	6	7
8	9	10	11	12	13	14
15	16	17	18	19	20	21
22	23	24	25	26	27	28
29						

1. What are the possible months that this calendar could represent?
   Explain your reasoning.

   _____

2. Ben went back to the dentist on the 3rd of this month, eight days after his
   last appointment. What was the date of his last appointment?

   _____

3. Julia and her dad are leaving on a trip on March 5th. On what day will they
   be leaving?

   _____

4. Ben wants to know what year this calendar page came from. He knows
   that it is either 2004 or 2005. Can you help him out? What year is this
   calendar from and how do you know?

   _____

5. Tim's birthday is on the 29th of this month. He is in the sixth grade, but he
   says he has had only three birthdays. How is that possible?

   _____

Solve problems related to the calendar

Math Test

Name _____

Fill in the circle next to the correct answer.

1. How many months are in a year?
   - Ⓐ 34
   - Ⓒ 30
   - Ⓑ 12
   - Ⓓ 31

2. How many days are in a regular year?
   - Ⓐ 30
   - Ⓒ 365
   - Ⓑ 31
   - Ⓓ 366

3. How many days are in a leap year?
   - Ⓐ 30
   - Ⓒ 365
   - Ⓑ 31
   - Ⓓ 366

4. Which month has the fewest number of days?
   - Ⓐ March
   - Ⓒ December
   - Ⓑ January
   - Ⓓ February

For Numbers 5 through 8, use the calendar below.

Sunday	Monday	Tuesday	Wednesday	Thursday	Friday	Saturday
	1	2	3	4	5	6
7	8	9	10	11	12	13
14	15	16	17	18	19	20
21	22	23	24	25	26	27
28	29	30				

5. This month could be which of the following?
   - Ⓐ January
   - Ⓒ May
   - Ⓑ March
   - Ⓓ November

6. What is the date of the third Wednesday of the month?
   - Ⓐ 3
   - Ⓒ 17
   - Ⓑ 10
   - Ⓓ 24

7. On what day of the week does the twelfth fall?
   - Ⓐ Monday
   - Ⓑ Wednesday
   - Ⓒ Friday
   - Ⓓ Saturday

8. What day is eight days before the 25th?
   - Ⓐ Wednesday
   - Ⓑ Thursday
   - Ⓒ Friday
   - Ⓓ Saturday

9. What happens during a leap year that is different from every other year?

   _____

   _____

10. If the first day of June falls on a Monday, on what day of the week does the last day of May fall?

    _____

Solve problems related to the calendar

EMC 3018 • Basic Math Skills, Grade 5 • ©2003 by Evan-Moor Corp.

Tongue Twister #14

Name _____

Read each of the thermometers below. Then write the corresponding letter on the line above the temperature. The letters will spell out a tongue twister. Try to say it fast three times.

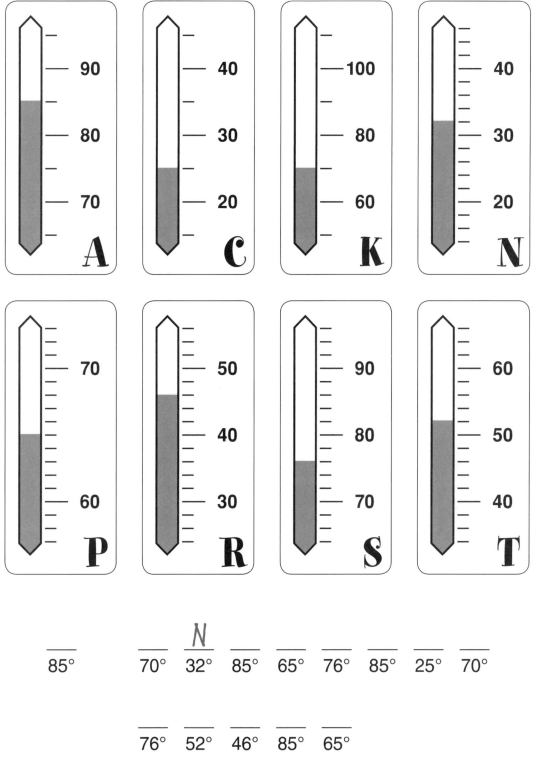

___ $\overset{N}{\underline{}}$ ___ ___ ___ ___ ___ ___ ___
85°   70° 32° 85° 65° 76° 85° 25° 70°

___ ___ ___ ___ ___
76° 52° 46° 85° 65°

Riddle

What do you get when you cross a centipede and a parrot?

Read each of the thermometers below. Then write the corresponding letter on the line above the temperature. The letters will spell out the answer to the riddle.

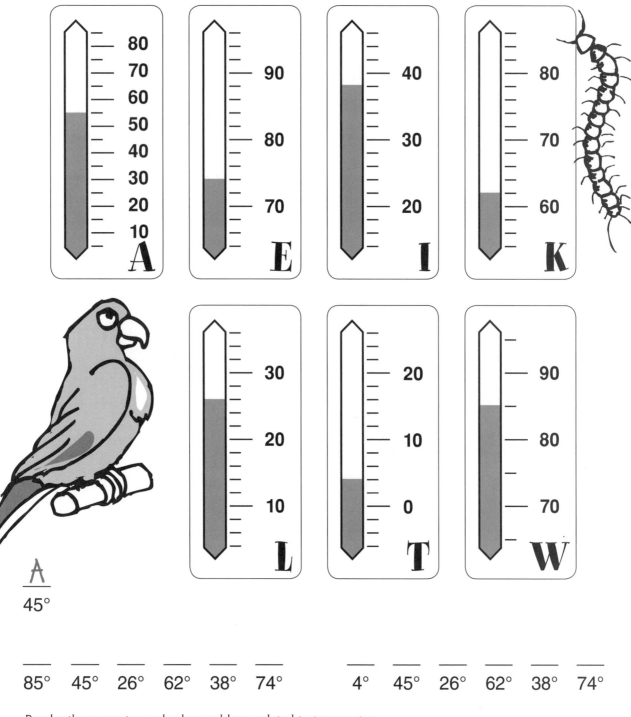

A
—
45°

____ ____ ____ ____ ____ ____   ____ ____ ____ ____ ____ ____
85°   45°   26°   62°   38°   74°   4°   45°   26°   62°   38°   74°

Read a thermometer and solve problems related to temperature

Changing Temperatures

Name _____

Use the thermometer to help you complete this table.

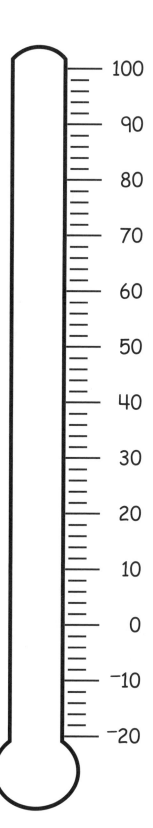

	Starting Temperature	Change in Temperature	Final Temperature
1.	45°	up 15°	
2.	32°	up 10°	
3.	72°	down 8°	
4.	21°		9°
5.	67°		86°
6.		down 11°	80°
7.		down 15°	44°
8.		up 6°	89°
9.	0°	down 10°	
10.	−20°	up 10°	

Read a thermometer and solve problems related to temperature

Daily Temperatures

Name _____

The thermometers show the temperature reading for each day at noon.

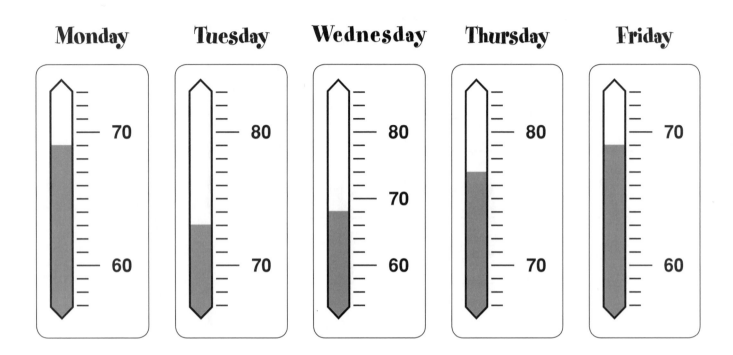

Use the thermometers to answer these questions.

1. Which day had the highest temperature reading at noon? _____

2. Which day had the lowest temperature reading at noon? _____

3. Which two days had the same high temperature at noon? _____

4. How much did the temperature change from Monday to Tuesday? _____

5. How much did the temperature change from Thursday to Friday? _____

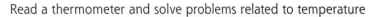

Read a thermometer and solve problems related to temperature

EMC 3018 • Basic Math Skills, Grade 5 • ©2003 by Evan-Moor Corp.

The Bitter Winter

Name _____

The following graph represents the lowest temperatures each day over an eleven-day period. Use this graph to answer the questions below.

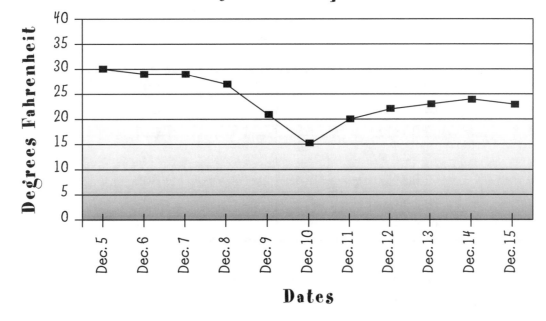

1. During those eleven days, what date had the coolest temperature?

   _____

2. What is the difference between the daily low temperature on December 15th and on December 5th?

   _____

3. What do you think the daily low might have been on December 4th? Why?

   _____

4. What was the hottest temperature during these eleven days?

   _____

5. Compare the daily low on the 9th to the 10th.

   _____

Read a thermometer and solve problems related to temperature

Cold Springs

Name _____

The following table shows the temperatures in Cold Springs during one day in the month of November. Use the table to answer the questions below.

Time of Day	Temperature in Fahrenheit
6:00 A.M.	28°
8:00 A.M.	30°
10:00 A.M.	46°
12:00 noon	54°
2:00 P.M.	62°
4:00 P.M.	??
6:00 P.M.	60°
8:00 P.M.	52°
10:00 P.M.	48°

1. You will notice that they forgot to take the temperature at 4:00 P.M. What temperature do you think it might have been if they had taken the temperature? Why do you think that?

   _____

2. At what time do you think the temperature rose to freezing?

   _____

3. What do you think was the highest temperature of the day? Justify your answer.

   _____

4. How much did the temperature go up from 6:00 A.M. to 12:00 noon?

   _____

5. What temperature do you think it was at 11:00 A.M.?

   _____

Read a thermometer and solve problems related to temperature

EMC 3018 • Basic Math Skills, Grade 5 • ©2003 by Evan-Moor Corp.

Math Test

Name _____

Fill in the circle next to the correct answer.

For Numbers 1 through 4 find the temperature.

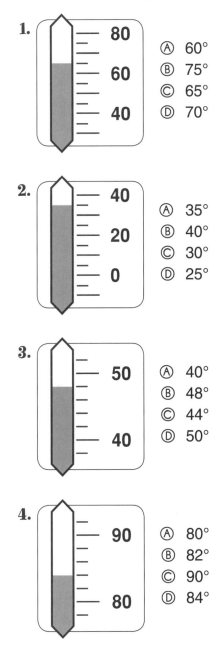

1.
- Ⓐ 60°
- Ⓑ 75°
- Ⓒ 65°
- Ⓓ 70°

2.
- Ⓐ 35°
- Ⓑ 40°
- Ⓒ 30°
- Ⓓ 25°

3.
- Ⓐ 40°
- Ⓑ 48°
- Ⓒ 44°
- Ⓓ 50°

4.
- Ⓐ 80°
- Ⓑ 82°
- Ⓒ 90°
- Ⓓ 84°

5. The temperature rose from 77° to 89°. How many degrees did it rise?
- Ⓐ 10°
- Ⓒ 12°
- Ⓑ 11°
- Ⓓ 13°

6. The temperature dropped from 77° to 59°. How many degrees did it drop?
- Ⓐ 22°
- Ⓒ 18°
- Ⓑ 20°
- Ⓓ 16°

7. The temperature went from 45° to 77°. What happened to the temperature?
- Ⓐ It dropped 32°.
- Ⓑ It dropped 37°.
- Ⓒ It rose 32°.
- Ⓓ It rose 37°.

8. The temperature went from 45° to 27°. What happened to the temperature?
- Ⓐ It rose 18°.
- Ⓑ It dropped 18°.
- Ⓒ It rose 22°.
- Ⓓ It dropped 22°.

9. Draw two different thermometers, each scaled differently, that both show 45°.

10. The temperature at noon was 60°. Jimmy said, "Wow, the temperature has gone up 19° since 8:00." What was the temperature at 8:00 A.M.?

Read a thermometer and solve problems related to temperature

Tongue Twister #15

Name_____

You will need a protractor for this page. Measure each angle to the nearest 10 degrees. Then write the corresponding letter on the line above the angle measure. The letters will spell out a tongue twister. How many times can you say it in 10 seconds?

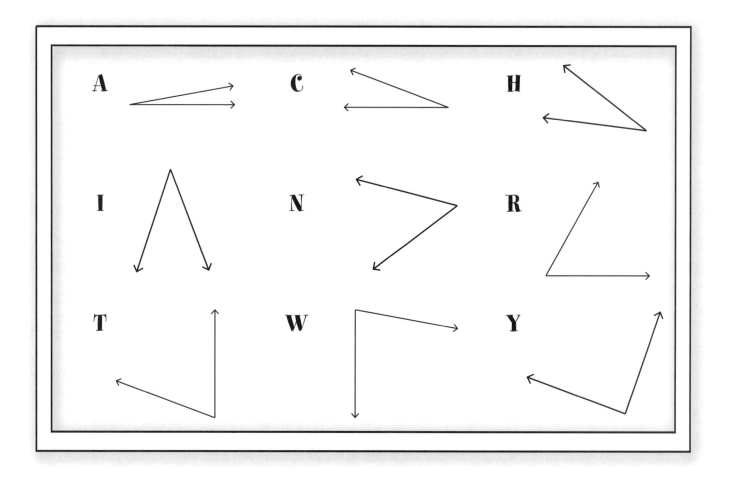

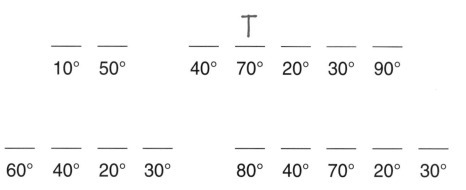

____ ____   ____ T̅ ____ ____ ____
10°   50°   40°   70°   20°   30°   90°

____ ____ ____ ____   ____ ____ ____ ____ ____
60°   40°   20°   30°   80°   40°   70°   20°   30°

Measure angles using a protractor, and classify angles as acute, obtuse, or right

On What Nuts Can Pictures Hang?

Name _____

You will need a protractor for this page. Use a protractor to measure each angle to the nearest 10 degrees. Then write the corresponding letter on the line above the angle measure. The letters will spell out the solution to the riddle.

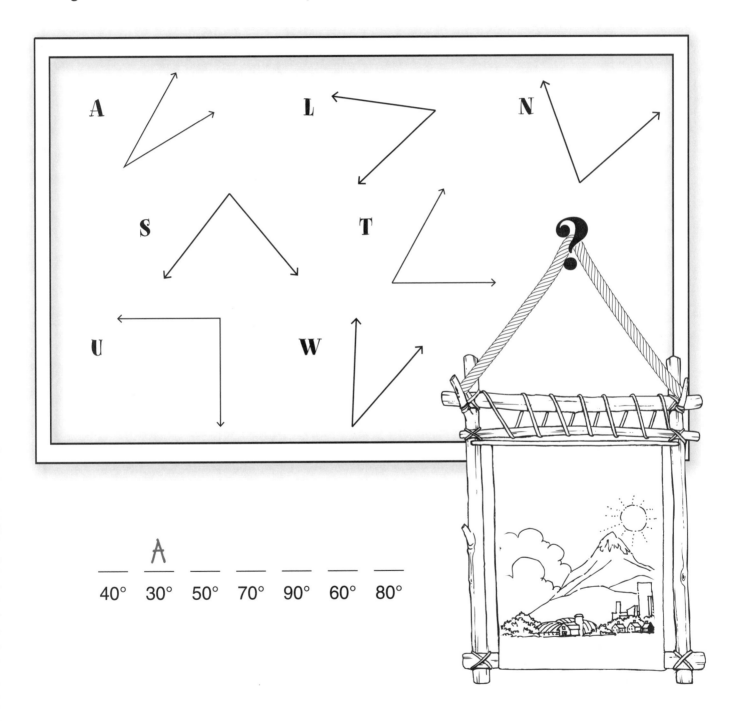

$\underset{40°}{\rule{1.2cm}{0.4pt}}$ $\underset{30°}{\overset{A}{\rule{1.2cm}{0.4pt}}}$ $\underset{50°}{\rule{1.2cm}{0.4pt}}$ $\underset{70°}{\rule{1.2cm}{0.4pt}}$ $\underset{90°}{\rule{1.2cm}{0.4pt}}$ $\underset{60°}{\rule{1.2cm}{0.4pt}}$ $\underset{80°}{\rule{1.2cm}{0.4pt}}$

Measure angles using a protractor, and classify angles as acute, obtuse, or right

What's My Angle?

Name _____

Using a protractor, measure each of the following angles to the
nearest 10 degrees.

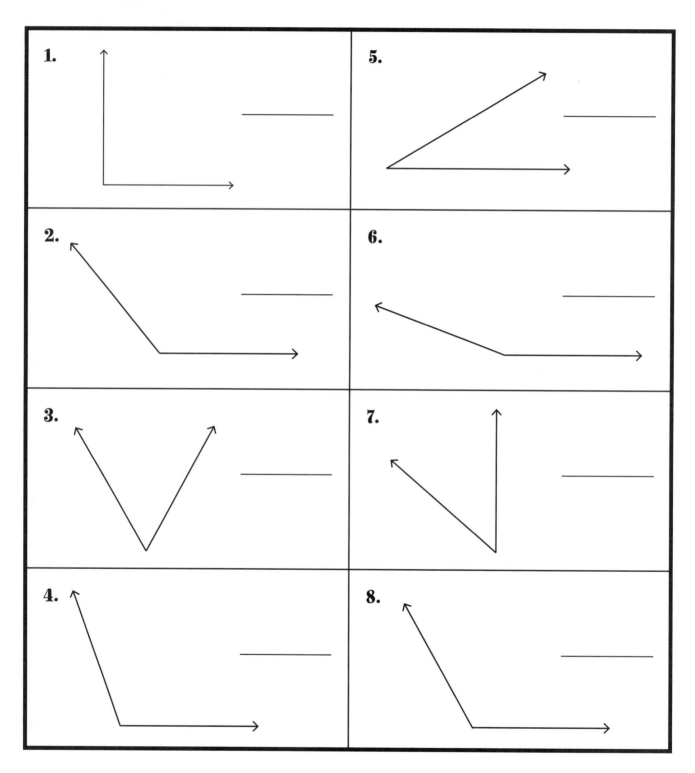

1. _____

2. _____

3. _____

4. _____

5. _____

6. _____

7. _____

8. _____

Measure angles using a protractor, and classify angles as acute, obtuse, or right

EMC 3018 • Basic Math Skills, Grade 5 • ©2003 by Evan-Moor Corp.

What's My Type?

Name _____

Classify each of the following angles as *acute, obtuse,* or *right.*

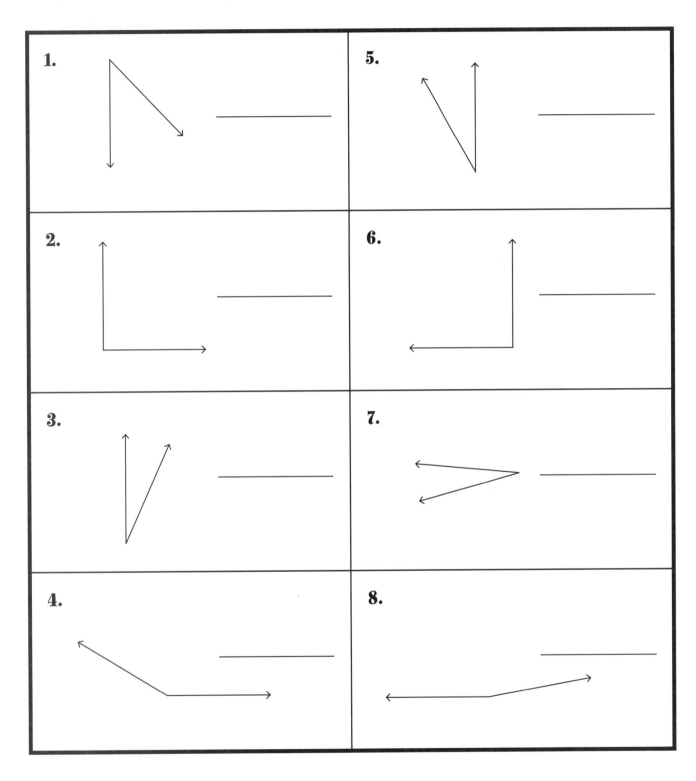

1. _____

2. _____

3. _____

4. _____

5. _____

6. _____

7. _____

8. _____

Measure angles using a protractor, and classify angles as acute, obtuse, or right

The Angles Around Us

Name_____

Look around you to find two examples of each type of angle listed in the chart. Think about the angle where two walls meet, or the edges of your desk, or the angle between the wall and the floor, etc. Write the name of each object and then draw a quick sketch in the chart.

Type of Angle	Real-Life Example (Sketch the object as well as name it)
acute	
acute	
right	
right	
obtuse	
obtuse	

Measure angles using a protractor, and classify angles as acute, obtuse, or right

EMC 3018 • Basic Math Skills, Grade 5 • ©2003 by Evan-Moor Corp.

Large Angles in the World of Skateboards

Name_____

Tim has heard of angles being used with skateboarding, and he has some questions for you to answer.

1. He has heard of people doing "a 180." What does that mean in relation to a skateboard? What does that mean in terms of angle measurement?

   _____

2. Another thing he heard someone do was "a 360." What does that mean in relation to a skateboard? What does that mean in terms of angle measurement?

   _____

3. Keeping those in mind, what do you think 270 degrees would look like? Draw a sketch of someone on a skateboard, looking down on him or her from above. Draw what direction they would be facing initially and then what direction they would be facing after turning 270 degrees. Does it matter if they turn to the right or the left?

   _____

4. Keeping those in mind, what do you think 540 degrees would look like? Draw a sketch of someone on a skateboard, looking down on him or her from above. Draw what direction they would be facing initially and then what direction they would be facing after turning 540 degrees. Does it matter if they turn to the right or the left?

   _____

Measure angles using a protractor, and classify angles as acute, obtuse, or right

Math Test

Fill in the circle next to the correct answer.

For Numbers 1 through 8, use these angles.

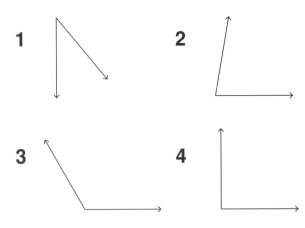

1   2

3   4

1. What is the measure of angle 1?

Ⓐ 30°   Ⓒ 50°
Ⓑ 40°   Ⓓ 60°

2. What is the measure of angle 2?

Ⓐ 80°   Ⓒ 100°
Ⓑ 90°   Ⓓ 110°

3. What is the measure of angle 3?

Ⓐ 60°   Ⓒ 80°
Ⓑ 70°   Ⓓ 120°

4. What is the measure of angle 4?

Ⓐ 45°   Ⓒ 90°
Ⓑ 80°   Ⓓ 100°

5. What type of angle is angle 1?

Ⓐ acute
Ⓑ obtuse
Ⓒ right
Ⓓ straight

6. What type of angle is angle 2?

Ⓐ acute
Ⓑ obtuse
Ⓒ right
Ⓓ straight

7. What type of angle is angle 3?

Ⓐ acute
Ⓑ obtuse
Ⓒ right
Ⓓ straight

8. What type of angle is angle 4?

Ⓐ acute
Ⓑ obtuse
Ⓒ right
Ⓓ straight

9. Draw two different acute angles.

10. Draw two different obtuse angles.

Measure angles using a protractor, and classify angles as acute, obtuse, or right

Tongue Twister #16

Name_____

Find the perimeter of each of the following polygons. Then write the corresponding letter on the line above the perimeter. The letters will spell out a tongue twister. How many times can you say it in 10 seconds?

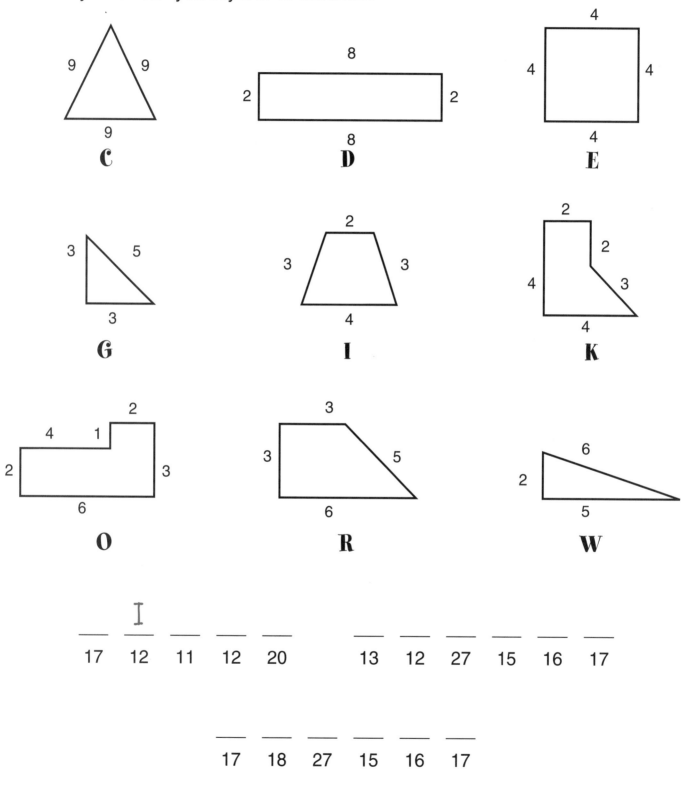

___ I ___ ___ ___ ___   ___ ___ ___ ___ ___ ___
17 12 11 12 20   13 12 27 15 16 17

___ ___ ___ ___ ___ ___
17 18 27 15 16 17

Find perimeter of polygons

What Is the Most Valuable Fish?

Name _____

Find the perimeter of each of the following polygons. Then write the corresponding letter on the line above the perimeter. The letters will spell out the solution to the riddle.

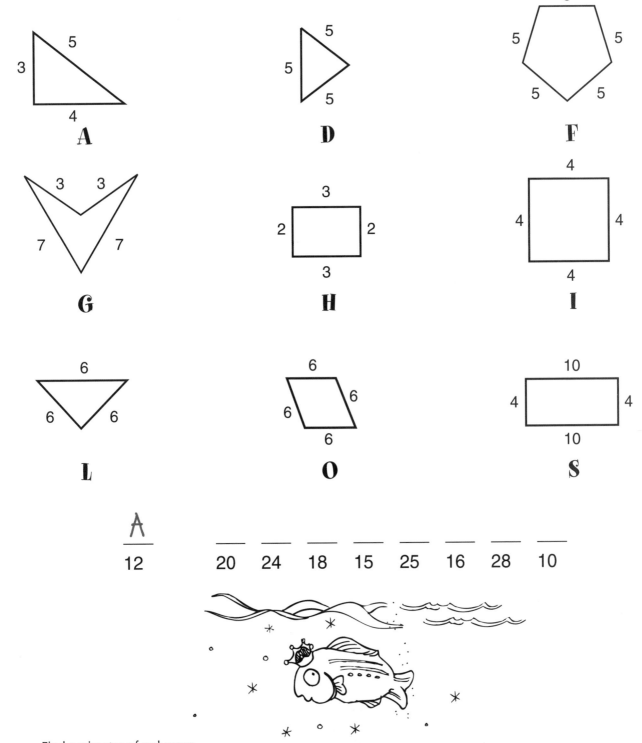

A

D

F

G

H

I

L

O

S

$\overset{A}{\underline{}}$ $\underline{}$ $\underline{}$ $\underline{}$ $\underline{}$ $\underline{}$ $\underline{}$ $\underline{}$ $\underline{}$

12   20   24   18   15   25   16   28   10

Find perimeter of polygons

Perimeters Please

Name _____

Determine the perimeter of each of the following figures.

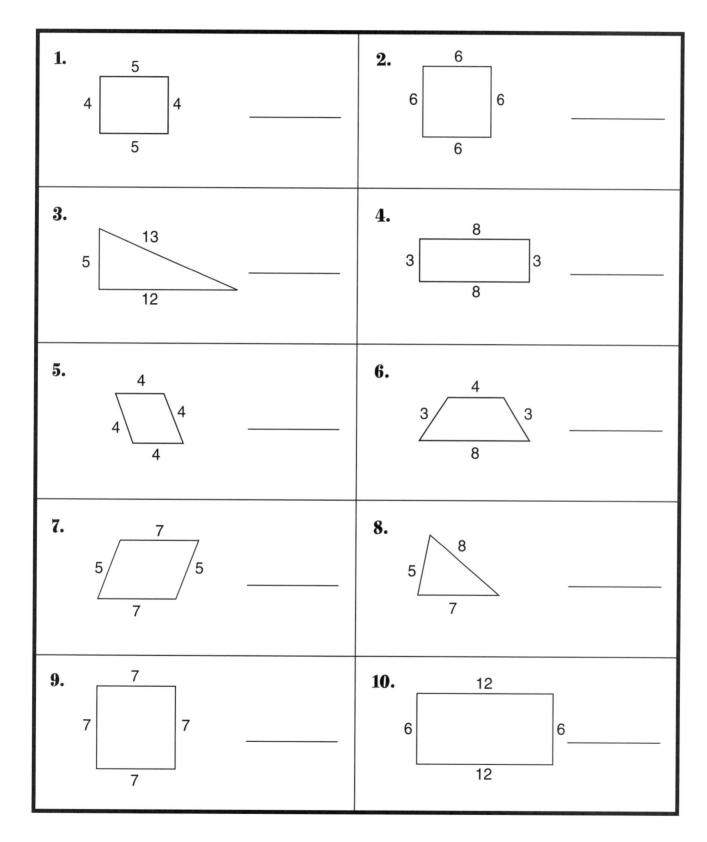

Find perimeter of polygons

What a Strange Perimeter

Name _____

Determine the perimeter of the following figures.

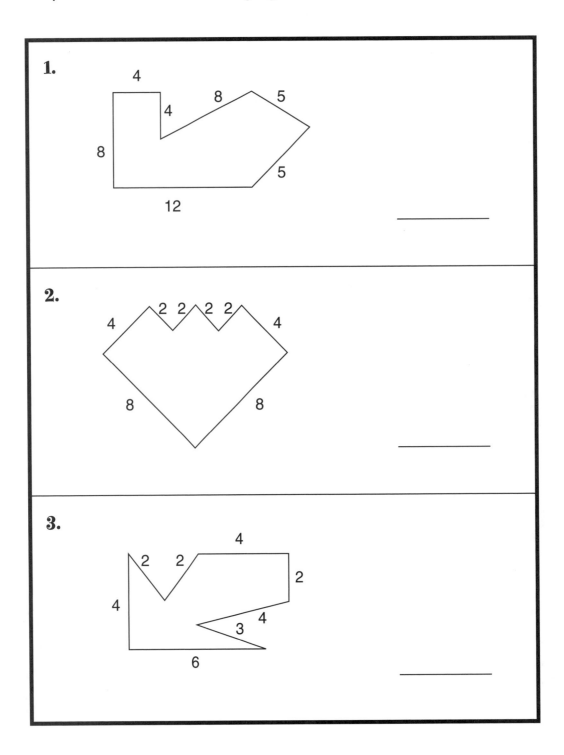

1.

4

8   5

4

8

5

12

_____

2.

2 2 2 2

4   4

8   8

_____

3.

4

2   2

2

4

4

3

6

_____

Perimeters Around You

Look around you and find an example of each of the following polygons in your classroom, at home, on the playground, or somewhere in the world around you. You may only use a certain object once on the chart, but remember that a square is a good example of a rectangle, parallelogram, quadrilateral, etc. Complete the chart by sketching the object, measuring each side of the polygon, and computing the perimeter of each object.

Polygon	Sketch and Measurements	Perimeter
triangle		
square		
rectangle		
trapezoid		
parallelogram		
quadrilateral		
pentagon		
hexagon		
octagon		

Find perimeter of polygons

Perimeter Puzzles

Name _____

Draw a sketch of each of the following polygons using the given clues. Label the length of each side on your drawing.

1. The first polygon has the following characteristics:
   - It has a perimeter of 12 inches.
   - It has four equal sides.
   - It has four right angles.

2. The second polygon has the following characteristics:
   - It has a perimeter of 18 centimeters.
   - It has four sides.
   - It has four right angles.
   - It has two sides that are each 5 centimeters longer than each of the other two sides.

3. The third polygon has the following characteristics:
   - It has a perimeter of 16 inches.
   - It has no right angles.
   - It has four sides.
   - The lengths of all the sides are prime numbers.
   - The lengths of the sides are odd numbers.
   - There are two pairs of congruent, parallel sides.

4. The fourth polygon has the following characteristics:
   - It has a perimeter of 18 centimeters.
   - It has four sides.
   - It has equal sides.
   - It has four right angles.

5. The fifth polygon has the following characteristics:
   - It has a perimeter of 7.5 centimeters.
   - It has three acute angles.
   - It has three sides.
   - The three sides are equal in length.

Find perimeter of polygons

EMC 3018 • Basic Math Skills, Grade 5 • ©2003 by Evan-Moor Corp.

Math Test

Name _____

Fill in the circle next to the correct answer.

1. What is the perimeter of a square with 3 inches on each side?

   Ⓐ 3 inches
   Ⓑ 6 inches
   Ⓒ 9 inches
   Ⓓ 12 inches

2. What is the perimeter of a rectangle that is 3 feet by 2 feet?

   Ⓐ 6 feet
   Ⓑ 10 feet
   Ⓒ 12 feet
   Ⓓ 14 feet

3. What is the perimeter of a right triangle with sides of 7 cm, 24 cm, and 25 cm?

   Ⓐ 56 centimeters
   Ⓑ 25 centimeters
   Ⓒ 24 centimeters
   Ⓓ 49 centimeters

4. What is the perimeter of a rhombus with 5 inches on each side?

   Ⓐ 5 inches
   Ⓑ 4 inches
   Ⓒ 20 inches
   Ⓓ 25 inches

5. What is the perimeter this figure?

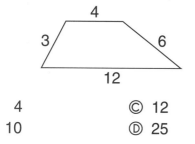

   Ⓐ 4   Ⓒ 12
   Ⓑ 10   Ⓓ 25

6. What is the perimeter of this figure?

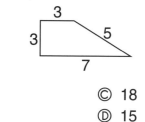

   Ⓐ 10   Ⓒ 18
   Ⓑ 9   Ⓓ 15

7. What is the perimeter of this figure?

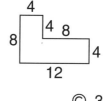

   Ⓐ 96   Ⓒ 36
   Ⓑ 40   Ⓓ 28

8. What is the perimeter of this figure?

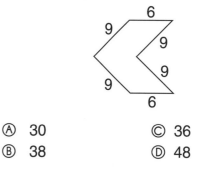

   Ⓐ 30   Ⓒ 36
   Ⓑ 38   Ⓓ 48

9. Draw a figure that has a perimeter of 24 centimeters.

10. Draw a figure that has a perimeter of 15 inches.

Find perimeter of polygons

Tongue Twister #17

Name _____

Find the area of each of the rectangles. Then write the corresponding letter on the line above the area. The letters will spell out a tongue twister. How many times can you say it in 15 seconds?

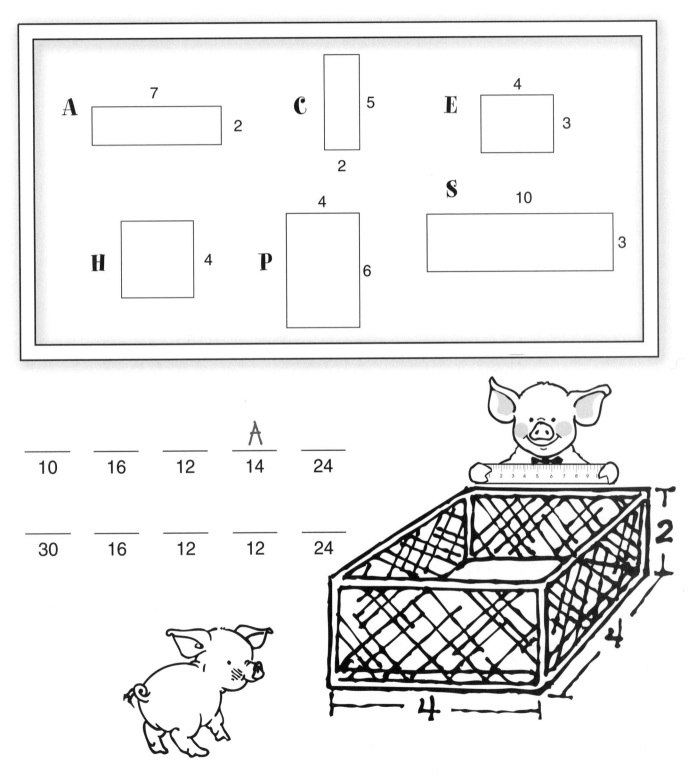

A 7 2

C 5 2

E 4 3

S 10 3

H 4

P 4 6

___ ___ ___ A̶ ___
10   16   12   14   24

___ ___ ___ ___ ___
30   16   12   12   24

T 2 4 4

What Sounds Better the More You Beat It?

Name_____

Find the area of each of the following rectangles. Then write the corresponding letter on the line next to each figure. The letters will spell out the answer to the riddle.

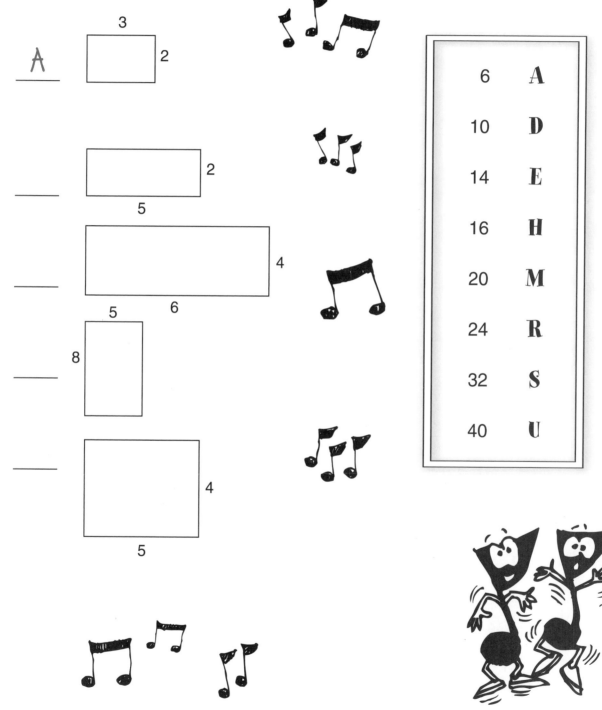

6	**A**
10	**D**
14	**E**
16	**H**
20	**M**
24	**R**
32	**S**
40	**U**

Find area of rectangles and squares

Give Me Your Area

Name _____

Determine the area of each of the following figures.

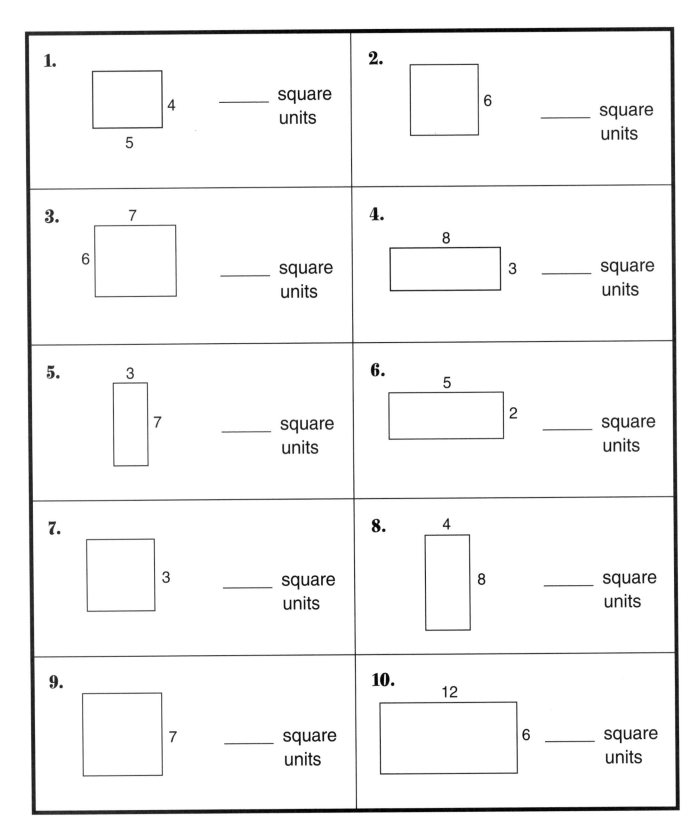

1. 4
   5
   _____ square units

2. 6
   _____ square units

3. 7
   6
   _____ square units

4. 8
   3
   _____ square units

5. 3
   7
   _____ square units

6. 5
   2
   _____ square units

7. 3
   _____ square units

8. 4
   8
   _____ square units

9. 7
   _____ square units

10. 12
    6
    _____ square units

Find area of rectangles and squares

EMC 3018 • Basic Math Skills, Grade 5 • ©2003 by Evan-Moor Corp.

What a Strange Area

Name _____

Determine the shaded area of the following figures.

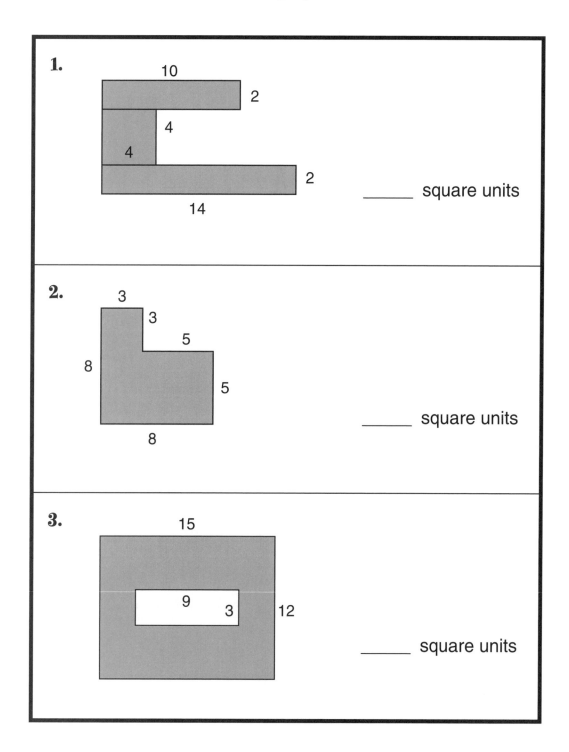

1. 10 2 4 4 2 14 _____ square units

2. 3 3 5 8 5 8 _____ square units

3. 15 9 3 12 _____ square units

Find area of rectangles and squares

Tile My Room

Name _____

A diagram of a room at Tim's house is shown below. His parents are helping him lay tile on the floor so he can use it as a game room with his brother. They need your help to answer the questions below.

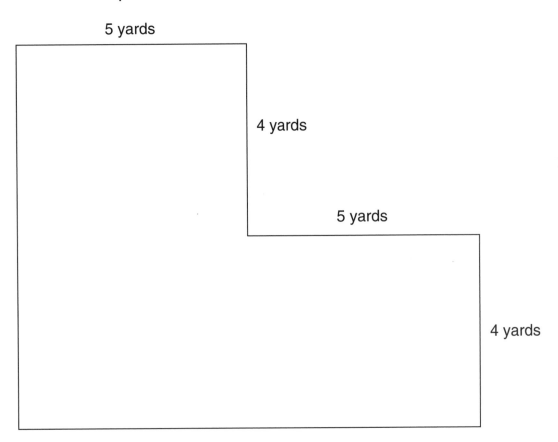

5 yards

4 yards

5 yards

4 yards

1. What is the area of the figure?

_____

2. They want to buy one-foot square tiles. How many tiles do they need? (Be careful as you solve this one.)

_____

3. A box of 12 tiles costs $40. How many boxes of tiles do they need, and how much will they cost?

_____

Find area of rectangles and squares

Painting Project

Karen and her dad are painting her bedroom. Below is a diagram of her bedroom. The room is 5 yards by 3 yards. The door is floor to ceiling and is 4 feet wide. The windows are half the distance from the floor to the ceiling, and there are two of them noted in the diagram. The ceiling in the bedroom is 8 feet high. Use this diagram and information to answer the questions below.

```
┌──────┤ 4-foot wide door ├──────────────────────────┐
│                                                     │
│                                                     │
│                                                     │
│                                                     │
│                                                     │
│                                                     │
│                                                     │
│                                                     │
│                                                     │
└──┤ 3-foot window ├──────────┤ 3-foot window ├───────┘
```

1. What is the area of the ceiling in square feet?

_____

2. If Karen wishes to paint the ceiling in one color and each can of paint covers 400 square feet, how many cans of ceiling paint does she need?

_____

3. What is the area of the walls in her bedroom, accounting for the windows and door?

_____

4. For the walls, Karen is using a different paint. Each can still covers 400 square feet. How many cans of paint will she need to paint the walls?

_____

Find area of rectangles and squares

Math Test

Name _____

Fill in the circle next to the correct answer.

1. What is the area of a rectangle that is 4 feet by 5 feet?

Ⓐ 20 feet
Ⓑ 20 cubic feet
Ⓒ 20 square feet
Ⓓ none of the above

2. What is the area of a square that is 5 feet on a side?

Ⓐ 20 feet
Ⓑ 20 square feet
Ⓒ 25 feet
Ⓓ 25 square feet

3. What is the area of a rectangle that is 7 by 10?

Ⓐ 7 square units
Ⓑ 10 square units
Ⓒ 70 square units
Ⓓ 35 square units

4. What is the area of a rectangle that is 9 cm by 3 cm?

Ⓐ 3 square cm
Ⓑ 9 square cm
Ⓒ 24 square cm
Ⓓ 27 square cm

5. What is the area of a square that is 9 feet on a side?

Ⓐ 9 square yards
Ⓑ 9 square feet
Ⓒ 81 square yards
Ⓓ 18 square feet

6. What is the area of a rectangle that is 3 feet by 6 feet?

Ⓐ 2 square feet
Ⓑ 18 square yards
Ⓒ 18 square feet
Ⓓ 2 cubic yards

7. What is the area of this figure?

Ⓐ 8 square units
Ⓑ 16 square units
Ⓒ 32 square units
Ⓓ 24 square units

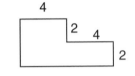

8. What is the area of this figure?

Ⓐ 12 square units
Ⓑ 18 square units
Ⓒ 24 square units
Ⓓ 36 square units

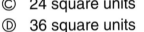

9. Draw a rectangle that has an area of 24 square units.

10. Draw a square that has an area of 36 square units.

Find area of rectangles and squares

EMC 3018 • Basic Math Skills, Grade 5 • ©2003 by Evan-Moor Corp.

What Sea Creature Can Add?

Name _____

Determine the volume of each rectangular prism. Then write the corresponding letter on the line above the volume. The letters will spell out the answer to the riddle.

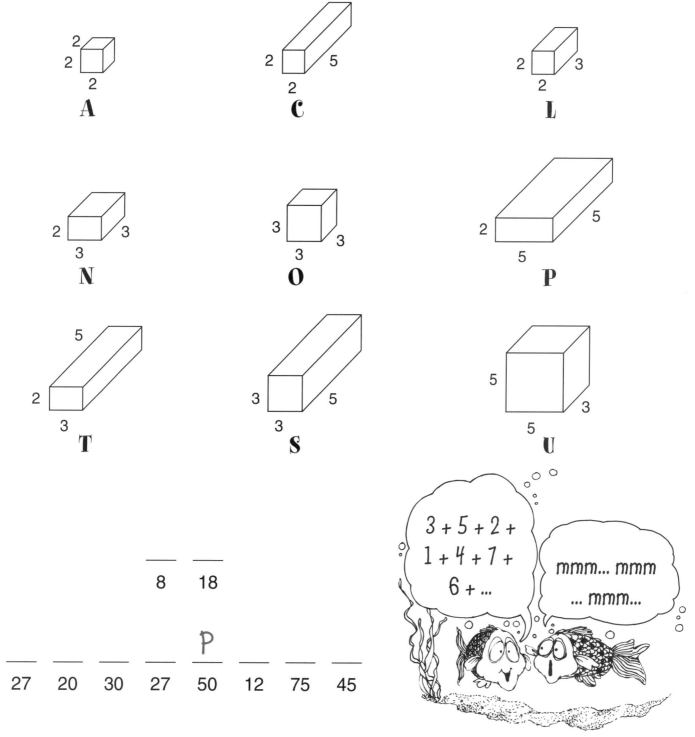

Calculate volume of rectangular prism

Why Did the Baby Wave at His Seat?

Determine the volume of each rectangular prism. Then look at the chart at the bottom of the page and write the corresponding letter on the line below the figure. The letters will spell out the answer to the riddle.

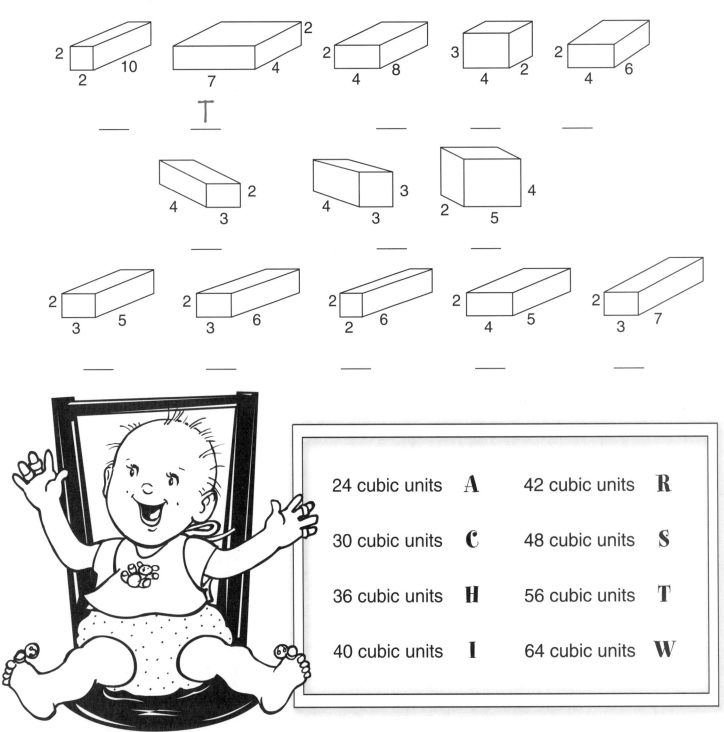

Turn Up the Volume

Name_____

Determine the volume of each of the following rectangular prisms.

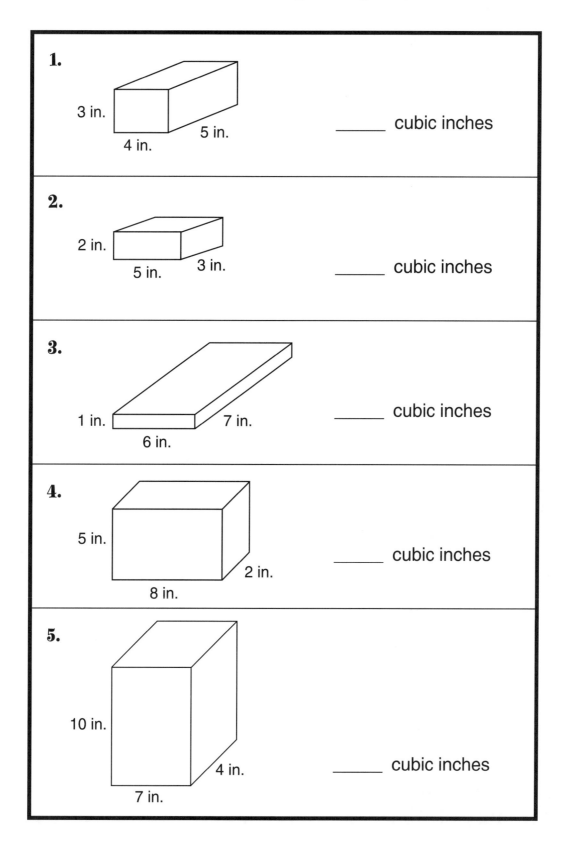

1. 3 in. 4 in. 5 in.   _____ cubic inches

2. 2 in. 5 in. 3 in.   _____ cubic inches

3. 1 in. 6 in. 7 in.   _____ cubic inches

4. 5 in. 8 in. 2 in.   _____ cubic inches

5. 10 in. 7 in. 4 in.   _____ cubic inches

Calculate volume of rectangular prisms

Turn Up the Metric Volume

Name _____

Determine the volume of each of the following rectangular prisms.

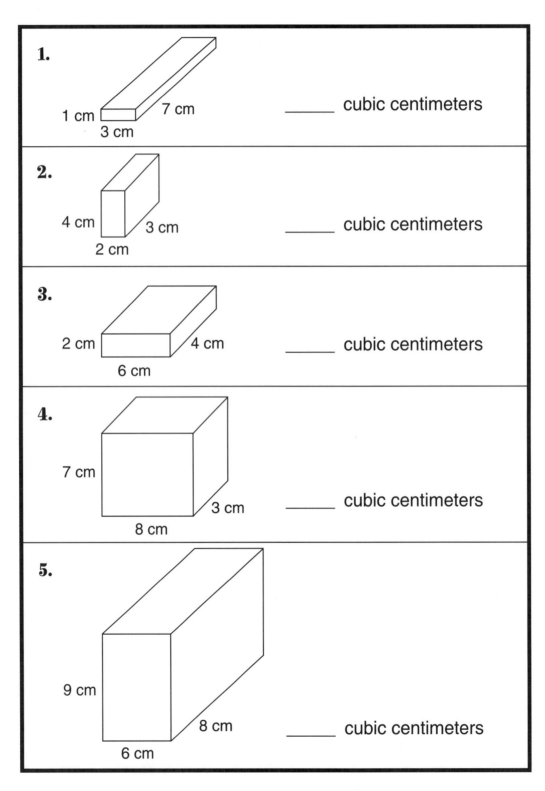

1. 1 cm 7 cm 3 cm   _____ cubic centimeters

2. 4 cm 3 cm 2 cm   _____ cubic centimeters

3. 2 cm 4 cm 6 cm   _____ cubic centimeters

4. 7 cm 3 cm 8 cm   _____ cubic centimeters

5. 9 cm 8 cm 6 cm   _____ cubic centimeters

Calculate volume of rectangular prisms

EMC 3018 • Basic Math Skills, Grade 5 • ©2003 by Evan-Moor Corp.

Helen's Box

Name _____

Helen needs your help with the following task. She has measured a Kleenex box and found that its length is 9 inches, the width is 4 inches, and the height is about 10 centimeters. She started to calculate the volume, and then realized that she has made a drastic mistake.

1. Why can't she multiply the length, width, and height to get the volume?

_____

2. Use a ruler to fix her problem.

_____

3. Now, what is the volume of the Kleenex box?

_____

4. What are the units for your answer?

_____

Calculate volume of rectangular prisms

Here's the Volume, Give Me the Dimensions

Name _____

Use the following clues to find the dimensions of each rectangular prism.

1. The first rectangular prism has the following characteristics:
   - It has a volume of 40 cubic inches.
   - The length is double the width.
   - The length is one less than the height.
   What are the dimensions of the rectangular prism? _____

2. The second rectangular prism has the following characteristics:
   - It has a volume of 72 cubic inches.
   - The sum of the three lengths is 13.
   - The width is half of the height.
   - The length is one more than the width.
   What are the dimensions of the rectangular prism? _____

3. The third rectangular prism has the following characteristics:
   - It has a volume of 70 cubic inches.
   - The lengths of the edges are all prime numbers.
   - The difference between two of the dimensions is 3, and the difference between a different pair of dimensions is 5.
   What are the dimensions of the rectangular prism? _____

4. The fourth rectangular prism has the following characteristics:
   - It has a volume of 360 cubic inches.
   - Two of the dimensions are consecutive numbers.
   - All the dimensions are less than 10, but also greater than 4.
   - All the dimensions are different.
   - The sum of the three dimensions is 22.
   - One of the dimensions is 8 inches.
   What are the dimensions of the rectangular prism? _____

Calculate volume of rectangular prisms

EMC 3018 • Basic Math Skills, Grade 5 • ©2003 by Evan-Moor Corp.

Math Test

Name _____

Fill in the circle next to the correct answer.

1. What units are used when measuring volume?

   Ⓐ square units
   Ⓑ cubic units
   Ⓒ units
   Ⓓ any of the above

2. What is the volume of a rectangular prism that is 4 x 3 x 3?

   Ⓐ 12   Ⓒ 24
   Ⓑ 10   Ⓓ 36

3. What is the volume of a rectangular prism that is 3 x 4 x 4?

   Ⓐ 11   Ⓒ 48
   Ⓑ 16   Ⓓ 12

4. What is the volume of a rectangular prism that is 2 x 5 x 9?

   Ⓐ 16   Ⓒ 10
   Ⓑ 90   Ⓓ 45

5. What is the volume of this rectangular prism?

   Ⓐ 2
   Ⓑ 5
   Ⓒ 8
   Ⓓ 10

   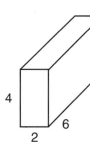

6. What is the volume of this rectangular prism?

   Ⓐ 8
   Ⓑ 48
   Ⓒ 40
   Ⓓ 36

7. What is the volume of this rectangular prism?

   Ⓐ 288
   Ⓑ 48
   Ⓒ 24
   Ⓓ 72

   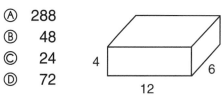

8. What is the volume of this rectangular prism?

   Ⓐ 120
   Ⓑ 70
   Ⓒ 640
   Ⓓ 840

   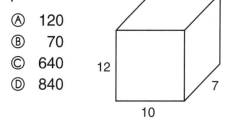

9. Sally is trying to figure out the volume of a box. She has figured out that the area of the bottom is 28 square inches. She measures the height and finds it to be 5 inches. What is the volume?

   _____

10. Tim found the volume of a rectangular prism to be 32 cubic feet. What could be the dimensions of the box?

    _____

    _____

Calculate volume of rectangular prisms

Data Analysis and Probability

Data and Graphs

Probability

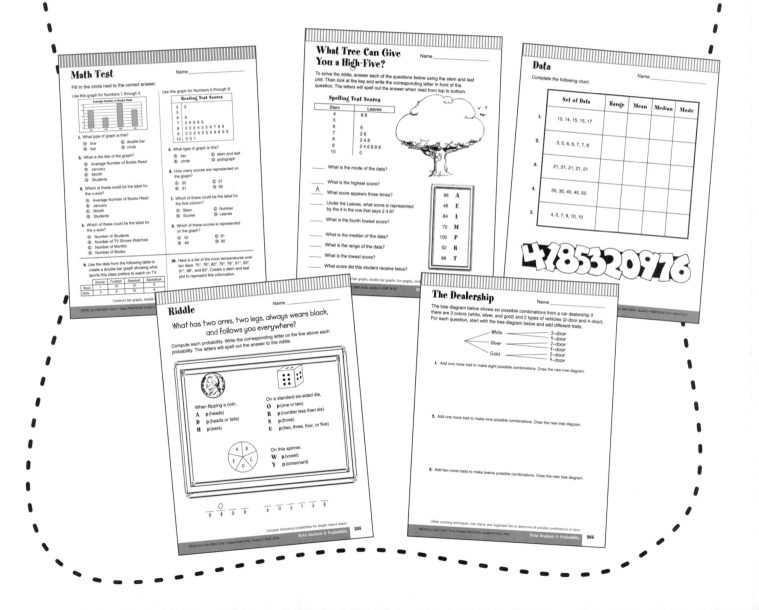

Tongue Twister #18

Name _____

This table represents the sports students like to watch on TV. Use the table to draw a double bar graph on the empty graph below that represents the information.

Gender	Football	Basketball	Soccer	Baseball	Golf
Boys	8	12	5	10	2
Girls	6	9	11	7	5

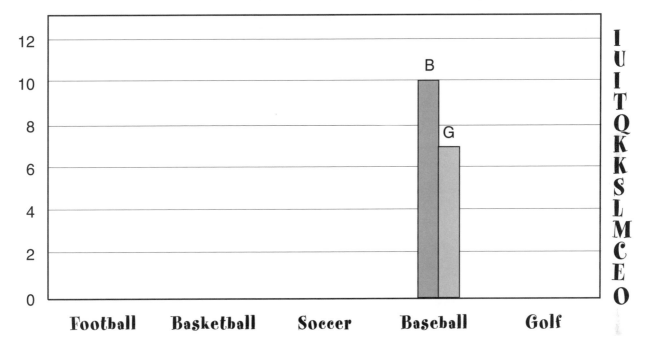

Each line below has a sport and a gender listed under it. This corresponds to one of the bars that you drew on the graph. Go to the top of each bar and look horizontally to the right, and you will see a letter. Write this letter on the line and it will spell out the tongue twister. How many times can you say it in 15 seconds?

I				
___	___	___	___	___
football boys	soccer girls	baseball boys	golf boys	baseball girls

___	___	___	___
football girls	basketball boys	golf girls	soccer boys

Construct bar graphs, double bar graphs, line graphs, circle graphs, and stem and leaf plots

Data Analysis & Probability

What Kind of Pants Do Ghosts Wear?

Name_____

This table represents the favorite flavors of soda for fifth-grade students. Use the table to draw a double bar graph on the empty graph below that represents the information.

Gender	Grape	Lemon-Lime	Orange	Root Beer	Cola
Boys	5	10	3	8	7
Girls	1	0	11	4	9

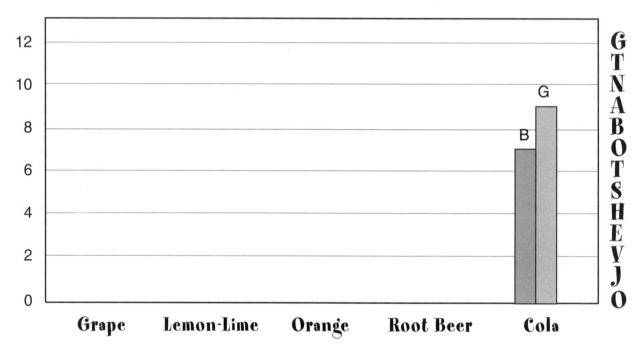

G T N A B O T S H E V J O

Grape   Lemon-Lime   Orange   Root Beer   Cola

Each line below has a flavor and a gender listed under it. This corresponds to one of the bars that you drew on the graph. Go to the top of each bar and look horizontally to the right, and you will see a letter. Write this letter on the line and it will spell out the answer to the riddle.

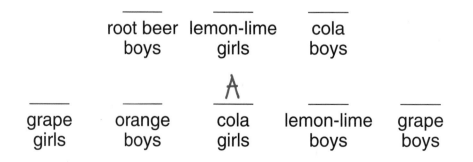

_____   _____   _____
root beer   lemon-lime   cola
boys   girls   boys

_____   _____   A   _____   _____
grape   orange   cola   lemon-lime   grape
girls   boys   girls   boys   boys

Construct bar graphs, double bar graphs, line graphs, circle graphs, and stem and leaf plots

Circle Graph

Name _____

Mr. Smith surveyed thirty students in the fifth grade about their favorite meal of the day. Here are the results:

Breakfast:	5 students
Lunch:	10 students
Dinner:	15 students

Use the information to construct a circle graph. Make a key and color each section a different color. Be sure the colors on your key match the data and your graph.

Favorite Meal

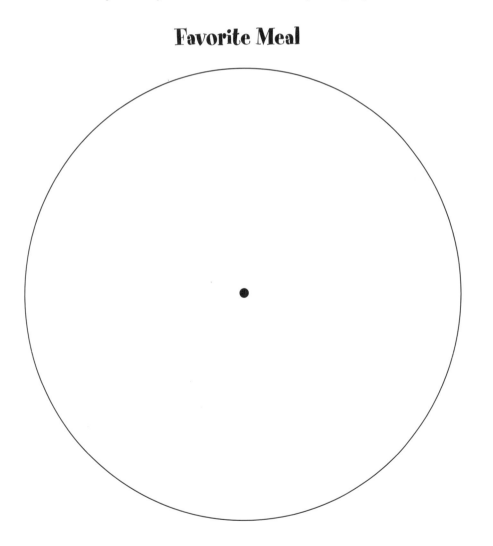

Construct bar graphs, double bar graphs, line graphs, circle graphs, and stem and leaf plots

Stem and Leaf

Name _____

Jordan collected the following data about students' scores on their last spelling test:

100, 95, 94, 89, 82, 70, 88, 92, 94, 95, 93, 88, 95, 72, 97

Construct a stem and leaf plot to represent this data. Remember, the stem is the digit that is in the tens place and the leaves are the digits in the ones place.

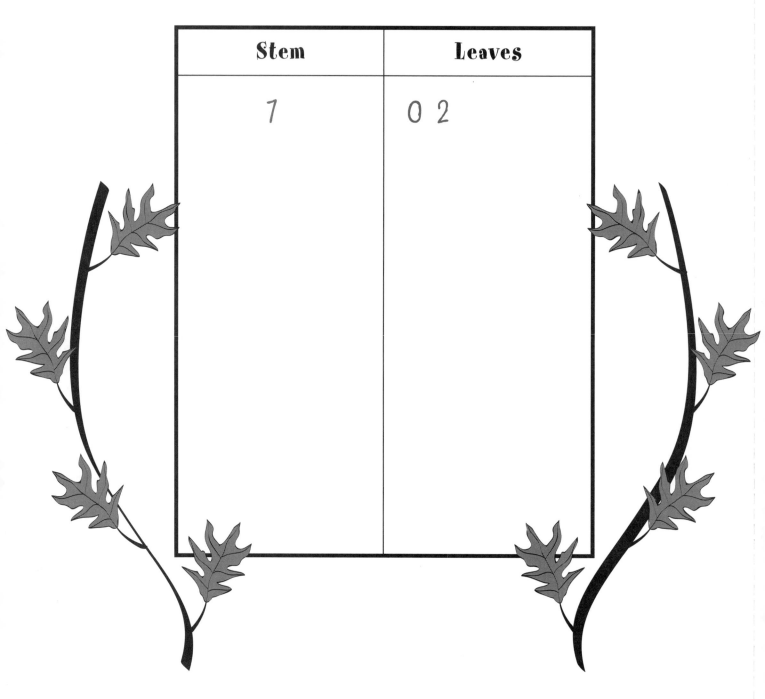

Stem	Leaves
7	0 2

Construct bar graphs, double bar graphs, line graphs, circle graphs, and stem and leaf plots

Data Analysis & Probability   EMC 3018 • Basic Math Skills, Grade 5 • ©2003 by Evan-Moor Corp.

The Unknown Circle

Name_____

Use the following clues to create an appropriate circle graph.

1. The graph represents what month students chose as their favorite month of the year.

2. June and July each had the same number of responses.

3. The largest section of the graph represents one-third of the students.

4. March was the smallest section of the graph.

5. When June and July are put together, they equal one-half of the graph.

6. There are only four months listed on the graph.

7. December is the largest section.

8. The following months are NOT listed on the graph: January, February, April, May, August, September, October, and November.

Favorite Month

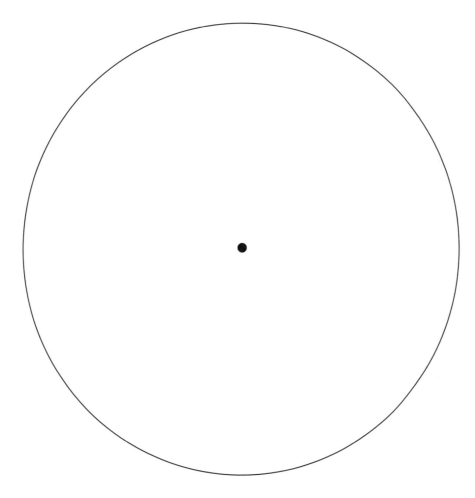

Interpret bar graphs, double bar graphs, line graphs, circle graphs, and stem and leaf plots

Data Analysis & Probability

Line Graph

Name _____

1. During the next day, take the outside temperature every hour. Start when you first get up in the morning until you go to bed at night. Try to take the temperature at the same time each hour, for example, on the hour. Use this chart to record your findings.

Time of Day										
Outside Temperature										

2. After you have collected one day's worth of data, draw a line graph to represent the information. Use the graph below to do your work. Be sure to label each axis and title the graph.

0

3. Use your graph to answer the following questions:

- What was the highest temperature during your recording? _____

- During the time you were recording temperatures, what was the lowest temperature? _____

- Even though you didn't take the temperature, what do you think the temperature might have been one hour before your first reading? _____

Construct bar graphs, double bar graphs, line graphs, circle graphs, and stem and leaf plots

Data Analysis & Probability   EMC 3018 • Basic Math Skills, Grade 5 • ©2003 by Evan-Moor Corp.

Math Test

Name_____

Fill in the circle next to the correct answer.

Use this graph for Numbers 1 through 4.

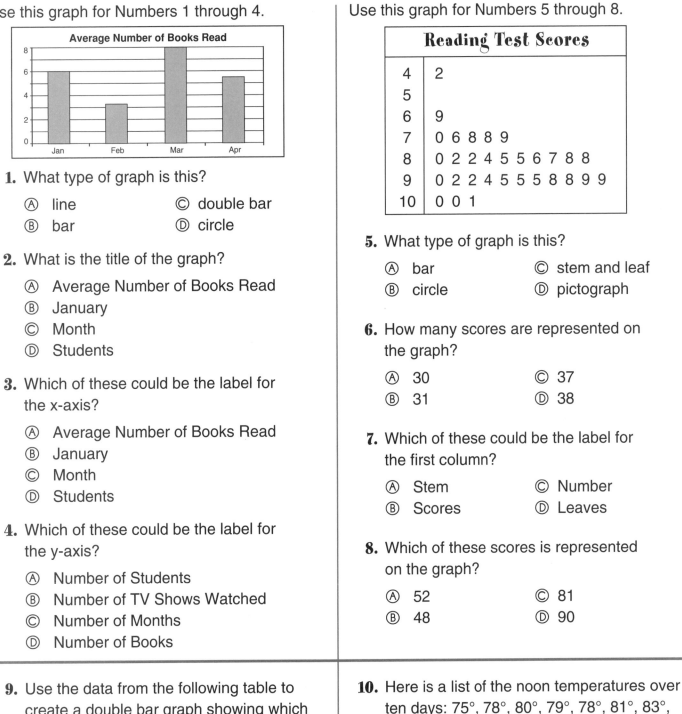

Average Number of Books Read

1. What type of graph is this?

   Ⓐ line   Ⓒ double bar
   Ⓑ bar   Ⓓ circle

2. What is the title of the graph?

   Ⓐ Average Number of Books Read
   Ⓑ January
   Ⓒ Month
   Ⓓ Students

3. Which of these could be the label for the x-axis?

   Ⓐ Average Number of Books Read
   Ⓑ January
   Ⓒ Month
   Ⓓ Students

4. Which of these could be the label for the y-axis?

   Ⓐ Number of Students
   Ⓑ Number of TV Shows Watched
   Ⓒ Number of Months
   Ⓓ Number of Books

Use this graph for Numbers 5 through 8.

Reading Test Scores

4	2
5	
6	9
7	0 6 8 8 9
8	0 2 2 4 5 5 6 7 8 8
9	0 2 2 4 5 5 5 8 8 9 9
10	0 0 1

5. What type of graph is this?

   Ⓐ bar   Ⓒ stem and leaf
   Ⓑ circle   Ⓓ pictograph

6. How many scores are represented on the graph?

   Ⓐ 30   Ⓒ 37
   Ⓑ 31   Ⓓ 38

7. Which of these could be the label for the first column?

   Ⓐ Stem   Ⓒ Number
   Ⓑ Scores   Ⓓ Leaves

8. Which of these scores is represented on the graph?

   Ⓐ 52   Ⓒ 81
   Ⓑ 48   Ⓓ 90

9. Use the data from the following table to create a double bar graph showing which sports this class prefers to watch on TV.

	Soccer	Football	Baseball	Basketball
Boys	1	10	12	8
Girls	3	9	15	5

10. Here is a list of the noon temperatures over ten days: 75°, 78°, 80°, 79°, 78°, 81°, 83°, 91°, 88°, and 83°. Create a stem and leaf plot to represent this information.

Construct bar graphs, double bar graphs, line graphs, circle graphs, and stem and leaf plots

Trivia #3

Name _____

Use the circle graph below and answer the questions. After you answer each question, write the corresponding letter on the line in front of the question. The letters will spell out the name of a worm that can grow to forty feet in length.

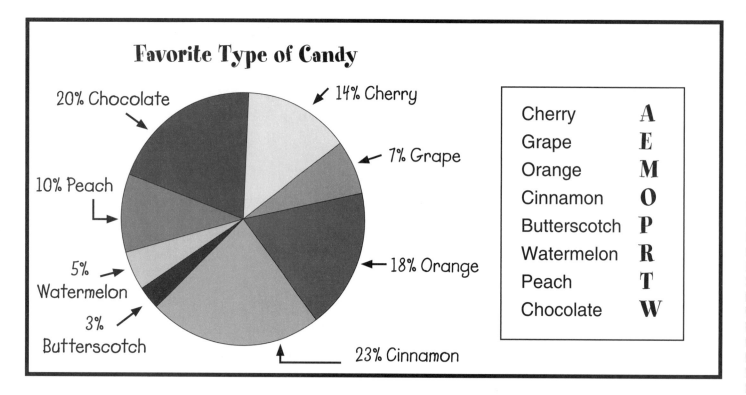

Favorite Type of Candy

20% Chocolate
14% Cherry
7% Grape
10% Peach
18% Orange
5% Watermelon
3% Butterscotch
23% Cinnamon

Cherry	**A**
Grape	**E**
Orange	**M**
Cinnamon	**O**
Butterscotch	**P**
Watermelon	**R**
Peach	**T**
Chocolate	**W**

_____ What flavor did only 10% of students list as their favorite?

_____ What flavor did 14% of students list as their favorite?

_____ What flavor was the least favorite?

__E__ What flavor did half as many students list as their favorite compared to Cherry?

_____ What flavor is listed as the second most popular flavor?

_____ What flavor was the most popular?

_____ What flavor did half as many students list as their favorite compared to Peach?

_____ What flavor did 18% of students list as their favorite?

Interpret bar graphs, double bar graphs, line graphs, circle graphs, and stem and leaf plots

Data Analysis & Probability
EMC 3018 • Basic Math Skills, Grade 5 • ©2003 by Evan-Moor Corp.

What Tree Can Give You a High-Five?

Name_____

To solve the riddle, answer each of the questions below using the stem and leaf plot. Then look at the key and write the corresponding letter in front of the question. The letters will spell out the answer when read from top to bottom.

Spelling Test Scores

Stem	Leaves
4	8 8
5	
6	6
7	2 6
8	2 4 8
9	2 4 6 8 8 8
10	0

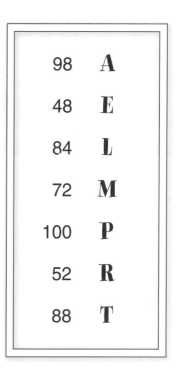

_____ What is the mode of the data?

_____ What is the highest score?

__A__ What score appears three times?

_____ Under the Leaves, what score is represented by the 4 in the row that says 2 4 8?

_____ What is the fourth lowest score?

_____ What is the median of the data?

_____ What is the range of the data?

_____ What is the lowest score?

_____ What score did this student receive twice?

98	**A**
48	**E**
84	**L**
72	**M**
100	**P**
52	**R**
88	**T**

Interpret bar graphs, double bar graphs, line graphs, circle graphs, and stem and leaf plots

The Clark Family

Name_____

Use the information below to label each bar with the correct name.

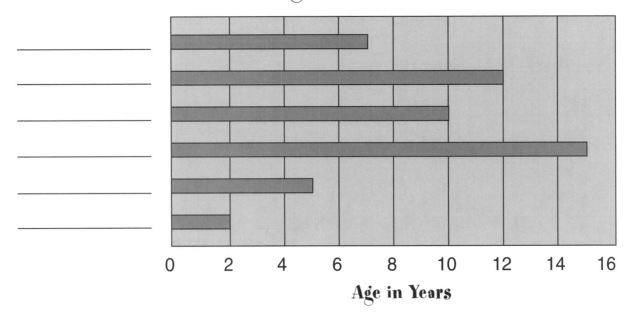

Ages of the Clark Children

Age in Years

1. The six children are named Sarah, Mitch, Michael, Sally, Kenny, and Kathy.

2. One of the girls is the youngest.

3. The boy who is 12 years old has a name that starts with the letter K.

4. Kathy is five years younger than Sarah.

5. Mitch is seven.

6. Michael is five years older than Sarah.

Interpret bar graphs, double bar graphs, line graphs, circle graphs, and stem and leaf plots

Data Analysis & Probability   EMC 3018 • Basic Math Skills, Grade 5 • ©2003 by Evan-Moor Corp.

High Temperatures

Name _____

Use the graph about high temperatures to answer the questions below.

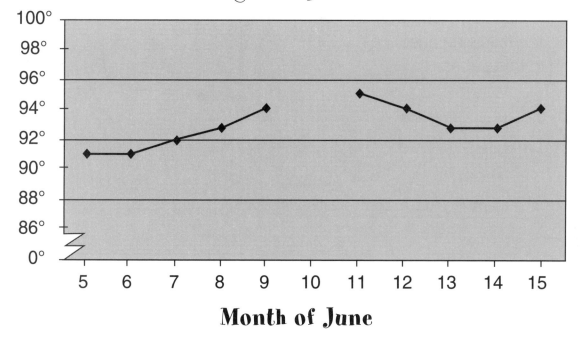

1. What was the highest temperature on June 9th? _____

2. What was the highest temperature on June 11th? _____

3. The high temperature for June 10th didn't get recorded. What do you think the high temperature on that day might have been? _____

4. What was the lowest temperature on June 13th? _____

5. How much hotter was June 11th than June 13th? _____

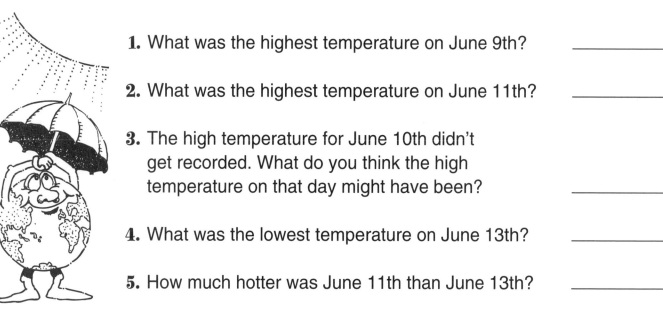

Interpret bar graphs, double bar graphs, line graphs, circle graphs, and stem and leaf plots

Data Analysis & Probability

Graphs in the Newspaper

Name _____

Find a graph in a newspaper or magazine and cut it out. Answer the following questions in relation to your graph. After completing the following questions, attach your graph to this paper.

1. What is the title of your graph?

   _____

2. What type of graph is yours a representation of?

   _____

3. What are the labels in the graph other than the title (axis, slices of the pie, stem and leaves, etc.)?

   _____

4. Is there a clear winner or a majority in your graph? If so, which one?

   _____

5. What is the purpose or message of the graph?

   _____

6. Do you think the graph is persuasive? Why or why not?

   _____

Interpret bar graphs, double bar graphs, line graphs, circle graphs, and stem and leaf plots

Data Analysis & Probability   EMC 3018 • Basic Math Skills, Grade 5 • ©2003 by Evan–Moor Corp.

Jerel's Graph

Name_____

Jerel created this graph to represent the number of books that he read from January through April.

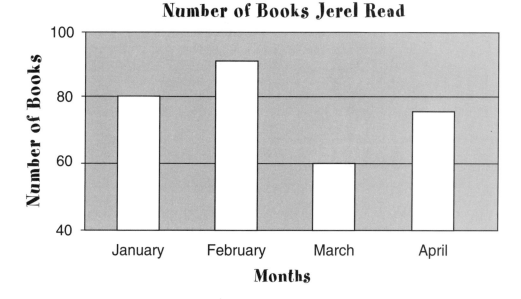

Number of Books Jerel Read

1. After looking over the graph, Juanita commented that Jerel read twice as many books in the month of January as he did in the month of March. Jerel disagreed with Juanita's observation and pointed something out to Juanita. What do you think Jerel pointed out to Juanita to help clear up her misunderstanding?

_____

2. What are some other things that people can do when they create graphs that might give misleading information?

_____

3. Use the same data from Jerel's graph to create another bar graph that is NOT misleading.

Interpret bar graphs, double bar graphs, line graphs, circle graphs, and stem and leaf plots

Data Analysis & Probability

Math Test

Name _____

Fill in the circle next to the correct answer.

For Numbers 1 through 3, use this circle graph.

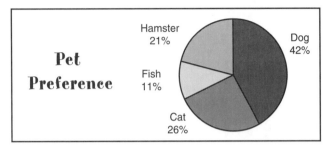

1. Which pet did the students most prefer?

   Ⓐ hamster   Ⓒ cat

   Ⓑ fish   Ⓓ dog

2. Which was the least favorite pet?

   Ⓐ hamster   Ⓒ cat

   Ⓑ fish   Ⓓ dog

3. How many students were surveyed?

   Ⓐ 100   Ⓒ 26

   Ⓑ 11   Ⓓ can't tell from the graph

For Numbers 4 and 5, use this bar graph.

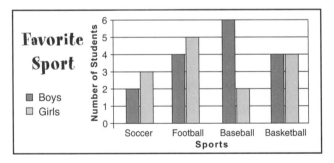

4. How many students were surveyed?

   Ⓐ 14   Ⓒ 30

   Ⓑ 7   Ⓓ can't tell from the graph

5. Which sport was the most favorite?

   Ⓐ soccer   Ⓒ baseball

   Ⓑ football   Ⓓ basketball

For Numbers 6 through 10, use this stem and leaf plot.

Number of Pages Read During Spring Break

Stem	Leaves
4	0
5	5 6 8
6	0 9 9
7	0 5 5 5 6
8	0 8 9
9	0 2 2 4
10	0 9

6. How many students kept track of their reading?

   Ⓐ 40   Ⓒ 21

   Ⓑ 20   Ⓓ 100

7. What is the mode of the data?

   Ⓐ 0   Ⓒ 75

   Ⓑ 5   Ⓓ 109

8. What was the highest number of pages read during the spring break?

   Ⓐ 40   Ⓒ 100

   Ⓑ 200   Ⓓ 109

9. How do you find the median value on the stem and leaf plot? What is the median value on this chart?

_____

_____

10. If one of the students had read 124 pages during spring break, how would you enter that on the chart?

_____

Interpret bar graphs, double bar graphs, line graphs, circle graphs, and stem and leaf plots

   EMC 3018 • Basic Math Skills, Grade 5 • ©2003 by Evan–Moor Corp.

What's a Ghost's Favorite Dinner?

Name _____

To solve the riddle, answer each of the questions about the given data.
Then write the corresponding letter on the line in front of the question.
The letters will spell out the answer to the riddle when read from
top to bottom.

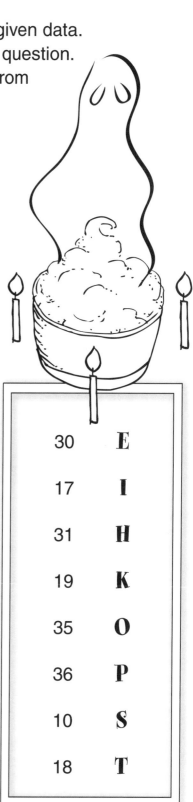

Data Set 1:	30, 35, 35, 35, 38, 39, 40
Data Set 2:	20, 21, 24, 30, 31, 31, 39
Data Set 3:	11, 15, 16, 17, 17, 21, 29

__*S*__ What is the range of the first data set?

_____ What is the mean of the first data set?

_____ What is the median of the first data set?

_____ What is the mode of the first data set?

_____ What is the range of the second data set?

_____ What is the mode of the second data set?

_____ What is the median of the second data set?

_____ What is the mean of the third data set?

_____ What is the range of the third data set?

_____ What is the mode of the third data set?

30	**E**
17	**I**
31	**H**
19	**K**
35	**O**
36	**P**
10	**S**
18	**T**

Analyze data utilizing range, mean, median, and mode

Data Analysis & Probability

What Did the Baseball Glove Say to the Baseball?

Name _____

To solve the riddle, answer each of the questions below the stem and leaf plot. Then write the corresponding letter in front of the question. The letters will spell out the answer when read from top to bottom.

Mother's Ages

Stem	Leaves
2	8 8
3	1 2 4 4 4 5 6 7 9
4	2 6
5	8
6	0
7	
8	2

_____ What is the mode of the data?

__A__ How many ages are represented in this table?

_____ What is the lowest age?

_____ Which age appears three times?

_____ What is the sum of all the ages?

_____ What is the median of the data?

_____ What is the range of the data?

_____ How old is the third youngest mother?

_____ What is the mean of all the ages?

_____ These ages represent how many mothers?

_____ How old is the second youngest mother?

_____ Under the Leaves, what score is represented by the 6 in the row that says 2 6?

_____ What is the age of the oldest mother?

16	**A**
34	**C**
46	**E**
656	**H**
41	**L**
54	**O**
82	**R**
28	**T**
31	**U**
35.5	**Y**

Analyze data utilizing range, mean, median, and mode

EMC 3018 • Basic Math Skills, Grade 5 • ©2003 by Evan–Moor Corp.

What's Your Range?

Name_____

Find the **range** of each set of data.

1. 2, 5, 7, 12, 15 _____
2. 26, 44, 47, 53, 57, 69 _____
3. 36, 42, 56, 35, 74, 26, 61 _____
4. 80, 49, 30, 72, 84, 14, 42 _____

Find the **mean** of each set of data.

5. 1, 4, 6, 3, 6 _____
6. 5, 15, 45, 33, 47 _____
7. 44, 26, 31, 41 _____
8. 53, 82, 94, 38, 43 _____

Find the **median** of each set of data.

9. 5, 7, 9, 11, 14 _____
10. 2, 4, 6, 9 _____
11. 15, 12, 16, 18, 11, 17 _____
12. 23, 26, 27, 21, 24, 23, 26 _____

Find the **mode** of each set of data.

13. 4, 7, 9, 9, 11, 13 _____
14. 5, 6, 6, 7, 8, 8, 9, 10 _____
15. 25, 25, 25, 25 _____
16. 5, 8, 3, 7, 4, 3, 6, 4, 5, 3, 7 _____

Analyze data utilizing range, mean, median, and mode

Data Analysis & Probability

Data

Name _____

Complete the following chart.

	Set of Data	Range	Mean	Median	Mode
1.	10, 14, 15, 15, 17				
2.	3, 5, 6, 6, 7, 7, 8				
3.	21, 21, 21, 21, 21				
4.	30, 35, 40, 45, 50				
5.	4, 5, 7, 9, 10, 10				

Analyze data utilizing range, mean, median, and mode

EMC 3018 • Basic Math Skills, Grade 5 • ©2003 by Evan–Moor Corp.

Adding Data

Name _____

Solve each of the following problems.

1. Sharon was given the following set of data: 45, 40, 38, 37, 37, 35, and 33.
   She was asked to add one number to the data set to change the value of
   the median. What value could Sharon add?

   _____

2. Jeff was given the following data: 20, 22, 24, 25, 25, 27, 27, and 30.
   Jeff was asked to add one number to the data set to get only one mode.
   What value could Jeff add to accomplish this?

   _____

3. Marlis was given the following data set: 7, 8, 9, 10, 11, 12, and 13.
   She was asked to add one number to the data set without changing the
   median value or the range of the set of data. What value could she add?

   _____

4. Austin was given the following data set: 35, 39, 40, 42, and 44. He was
   asked to add one value to the data set that would change the mean to 42.
   What value should he add?

   _____

Analyze data utilizing range, mean, median, and mode

Adding Data II

Solve each of the following problems.

1. Carlos was given the following set of data: 29, 30, 31, 35, and 37. He was asked to add one value to the data set to make the range of the data 20. What are two different values Carlos could add that would accomplish this?

   _____

2. Amy was given the following set of data: 40, 41, 42, 42, 43, 43, 44, 45, 45, 45, and 47. She was asked to add two values to the set of data to create two modes. What are two numbers that she could add so the data would have two modes? What is another pair of numbers that she could have added to accomplish the same task?

   _____

3. Tate was given the following set of data: 4, 6, 6, 8, 9, and 11. He was asked to add one value to the data set that would change the mean to 12. What value should Tate add?

   _____

4. Ben was given the following set of data: 13, 15, 15, 16, 17, 17, 18, and 25. He was asked to add two values to the data set, but keep the same mean. What two values could he add?

   _____

5. Arlene was given the following set of data: 1, 5, 6, 6, 7, 9, and 10. She was asked to add two values to create a different single mode for the set of data. What values could she add?

   _____

Analyze data utilizing range, mean, median, and mode

Math Test

Name _____

Fill in the circle next to the correct answer.

Use the following data set for Numbers 1 through 4.

30, 31, 33, 33, 35, 36, 36, 38

1. What is the mode of the data?

Ⓐ 33
Ⓒ both 33 and 36
Ⓑ 36
Ⓓ 38

2. What is the median of the data?

Ⓐ 33
Ⓒ 35
Ⓑ 34
Ⓓ 36

3. What is the range of the data?

Ⓐ 8
Ⓒ 38
Ⓑ 30
Ⓓ 10

4. What is the mean of the data?

Ⓐ 272
Ⓒ 35
Ⓑ 33
Ⓓ 34

Use the following data set for Numbers 5 and 6.

1, 3, 5, 7, 9

5. What is the mode of the data?

Ⓐ There is no mode.
Ⓑ 1
Ⓒ 7
Ⓓ 9

6. What is the median of the data?

Ⓐ 3
Ⓑ 5
Ⓒ 7
Ⓓ 9

Use this stem and leaf plot to answer Numbers 7 and 8.

Number of Fish in Aquariums

Stem	Leaves
0	2 9 9
1	0 2 4 4 6 7 7 7 8 9
2	1 6 7 7 9
3	9
4	5
5	
6	2

7. What is the range of the data?

Ⓐ 2
Ⓒ 62
Ⓑ 60
Ⓓ 50

8. What is the mode of the data?

Ⓐ 27
Ⓒ 17
Ⓑ 14
Ⓓ 9

9. Jim was given the following set of data: 3, 6, 8, 9, and 10. He was asked to add one number that would change the median of the data. What number could he add? What is the new median?

_____

10. Suzy was given the following set of data: 5, 5, 5, 5, and 5. She was asked to add one number that wouldn't change the median or the mode, but would change the mean and the range of the data. If the new mean should be 6, what number should Suzy add?

_____

Analyze data utilizing range, mean, median, and mode

Tongue Twister #19

Name _____

Compute each probability. Write the corresponding letter on the line above each probability. The letters will spell out a tongue twister. Try to say it fast three times.

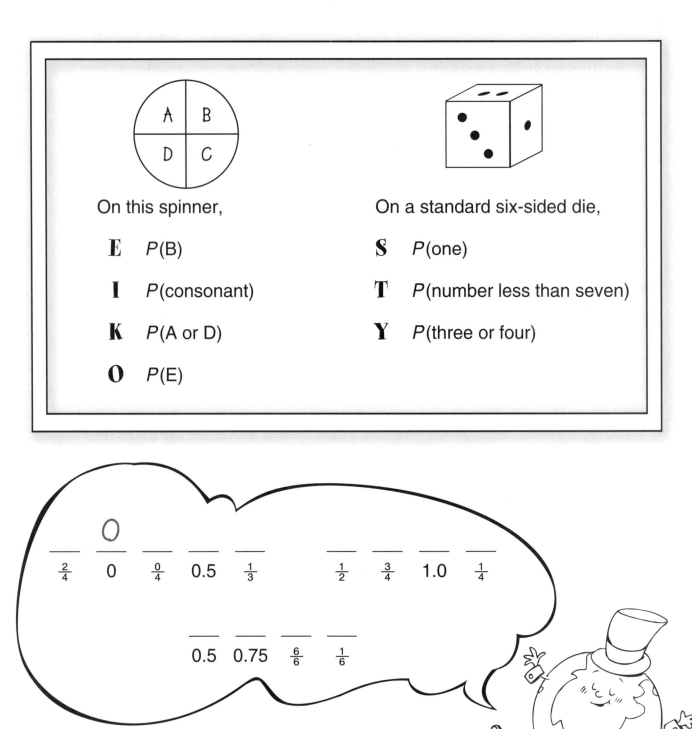

On this spinner,

E $P(\text{B})$

I $P(\text{consonant})$

K $P(\text{A or D})$

O $P(\text{E})$

On a standard six-sided die,

S $P(\text{one})$

T $P(\text{number less than seven})$

Y $P(\text{three or four})$

$\dfrac{O}{\frac{2}{4}}$ $\overline{}$ $\overline{}$ $\overline{}$ $\overline{}$ $\overline{}$ $\overline{}$ $\overline{}$ $\overline{}$
$\frac{2}{4}$ 0 $\frac{0}{4}$ 0.5 $\frac{1}{3}$ $\frac{1}{2}$ $\frac{3}{4}$ 1.0 $\frac{1}{4}$

$\overline{}$ $\overline{}$ $\overline{}$ $\overline{}$
0.5   0.75 $\frac{6}{6}$ $\frac{1}{6}$

Compute theoretical probabilities for simple chance events

Data Analysis & Probability   EMC 3018 • Basic Math Skills, Grade 5 • ©2003 by Evan–Moor Corp.

Riddle

Name_____

What has two arms, two legs, always wears black, and follows you everywhere?

Compute each probability. Write the corresponding letter on the line above each probability. The letters will spell out the answer to the riddle.

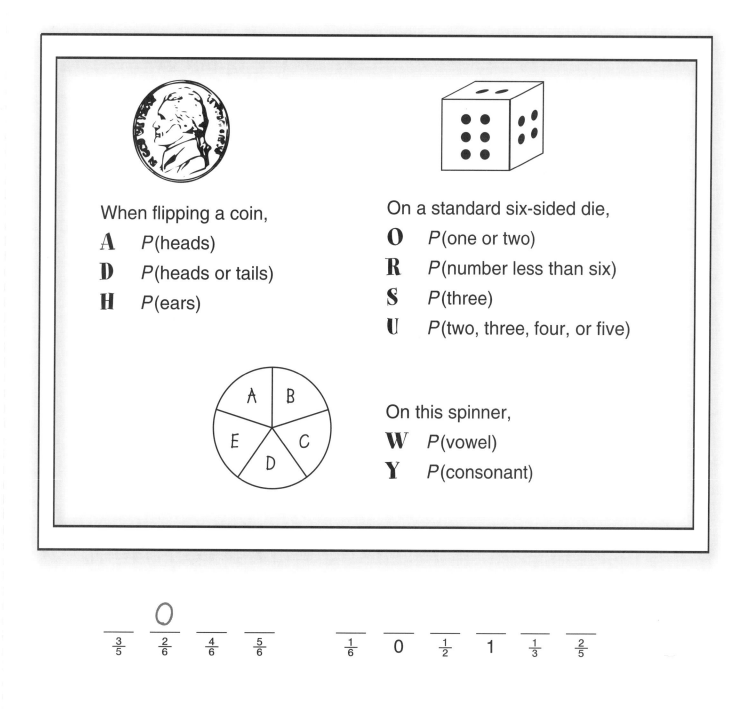

When flipping a coin,

A P(heads)

D P(heads or tails)

H P(ears)

On a standard six-sided die,

O P(one or two)

R P(number less than six)

S P(three)

U P(two, three, four, or five)

On this spinner,

W P(vowel)

Y P(consonant)

_____ O _____ _____   _____ _____ _____ _____ _____ _____
$\frac{3}{5}$ $\frac{2}{6}$ $\frac{4}{6}$ $\frac{5}{6}$ $\frac{1}{6}$ 0 $\frac{1}{2}$ 1 $\frac{1}{3}$ $\frac{2}{5}$

Compute theoretical probabilities for simple chance events

Data Analysis & Probability   **255**

Probability

Determine the probability of each of the following events.

When rolling a standard six-sided die, what is the probability of getting…?

1. a 2 _____

2. a 5 _____

3. a 1 or a 2 _____

4. an odd number _____

5. an even number _____

6. a 9 _____

When flipping a coin, what is the probability of getting…?

7. heads _____

8. tails _____

When spinning this spinner, what is the probability of getting...?

9. white _____

10. red _____

11. brown _____

12. red or white _____

Compute theoretical probabilities for simple chance events

More Probability

Determine the probability of each of the following events.

When rolling a standard six-sided die, what is the probability of getting…?

1. a 6 _____

2. a 2 _____

3. a 5 or a 6 _____

4. an odd number _____

5. an even number _____

6. a 0 _____

If you had a bag with four black marbles and eight gray marbles inside, what is the probability of randomly selecting a marble that is…?

7. black _____

8. gray _____

9. white _____

When you are spinning this spinner, what is the probability of getting…?

10. red _____

11. white _____

12. purple _____

red	white
blue	blue
white	red
blue	white

Compute theoretical probabilities for simple chance events

Spinners

Name _____

Use the following clues to determine what spinner is being described. Draw the spinner for each set of clues.

1.

Spinner #1
$P(1) = \frac{1}{2}$
$P(2) = \frac{1}{4}$
$P(3) = \frac{1}{4}$

2.

Spinner #2
$P(\text{red}) = \frac{1}{3}$
$P(\text{red, blue, or green}) = 1$
$P(\text{red or blue}) = \frac{2}{3}$

3.

Spinner #3
$P(A, B, C, D, \text{or } E) = 1$
$P(A) = P(B) = P(C) = P(D) = \frac{1}{5}$

4.

Spinner #4
$P(\text{white}) = \frac{2}{3}$
$P(\text{red}) = 0$
$P(\text{red, white, or blue}) = 1$

5.

Spinner #5
$P(1, 2, 3, \text{or } 4) = 1$
$P(1) = P(2) + P(3)$
$P(4) = \frac{1}{2}$
$P(2) = P(3)$

Compute theoretical probabilities for simple chance events

Number Cube

Name _____

Each of the following scenarios describes a six-sided number cube. Your task is to tell what is on each of the six sides.

1. $P(\text{even number}) = \frac{1}{2}$

$P(\text{odd number}) = \frac{1}{2}$

$P(7) = \frac{1}{6}$

$P(5) = \frac{2}{6}$

$P(2) = \frac{1}{2}$

____ ____ ____

____ ____ ____

3. $P(\text{even number}) = 0$

$P(3, 5, 7, 9, \text{ or } 11) = 1$

$P(3) = \frac{2}{6}$

The sum of six sides is 38.

____ ____ ____

____ ____ ____

2. $P(\text{odd number}) = \frac{2}{6}$

$P(6) = \frac{1}{6}$

Four of the numbers are
  consecutive numbers.

The sum of all six sides is 54.

The largest number is 13.

____ ____ ____

____ ____ ____

4. $P(\text{odd number}) = 0$

$P(\text{number larger than 4}) = 0$

$P(\text{number smaller than 4}) = 0$

The sum of all six sides is 24.

____ ____ ____

____ ____ ____

Compute theoretical probabilities for simple chance events

Math Test

Name _____

Fill in the circle next to the correct answer.

1. On a standard six-sided die, the $P(1)$ is _____.

   Ⓐ $\frac{1}{6}$ Ⓒ $\frac{3}{6} = \frac{1}{2}$

   Ⓑ $\frac{2}{6} = \frac{1}{3}$ Ⓓ $\frac{6}{6} = 1$

2. On a standard six-sided die, the $P(\text{even number})$ is _____.

   Ⓐ $\frac{1}{6}$ Ⓒ $\frac{1}{2}$

   Ⓑ $\frac{1}{3}$ Ⓓ 1

3. On a standard six-sided die, the $P(9)$ is _____.

   Ⓐ $\frac{1}{6}$ Ⓑ $\frac{1}{2}$ Ⓒ 0 Ⓓ 1

4. On a standard coin, the $P(\text{heads})$ is _____.

   Ⓐ $\frac{1}{4}$ Ⓑ $\frac{1}{6}$ Ⓒ 1 Ⓓ $\frac{1}{2}$

5. A bag contains 5 red beads and 7 gold beads, and 1 bead is selected at random. What is the probability of drawing a red bead?

   Ⓐ $\frac{5}{7}$ Ⓑ $\frac{5}{14}$ Ⓒ $\frac{5}{12}$ Ⓓ $\frac{7}{12}$

6. A bag contains 3 green marbles, 6 yellow marbles, and 8 blue marbles, and 1 marble is selected at random. What is the probability of drawing a yellow marble?

   Ⓐ 6 Ⓒ $\frac{3}{8}$

   Ⓑ $\frac{6}{11}$ Ⓓ $\frac{6}{17}$

Use this spinner for Numbers 7 and 8.

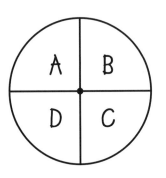

7. What is the probability of spinning an A?

   Ⓐ $\frac{1}{4}$ Ⓒ 0

   Ⓑ $\frac{3}{4}$ Ⓓ 1

8. What is the probability of spinning an F?

   Ⓐ 1 Ⓒ $\frac{1}{2}$

   Ⓑ $\frac{1}{4}$ Ⓓ 0

9. Draw a spinner that would have a probability of $\frac{1}{2}$ for spinning a red section.

10. What is the probability of getting a 7 on a six-sided number cube? Why?

   _____

   _____

Compute theoretical probabilities for simple chance events

What Do Insects Learn in School?

Name _____

On the line in front of each list, write the number of combinations that can be made with the items listed. Then write the corresponding letter on the line. The letters will spell out the answer to the riddle when read from **the bottom up**.

_____ 9 types of plates in 2 different colors

_____ 2 different cups with 2 different saucers with 2 different plates

_____ 3 different colored pants and 4 different shirts

_____ 5 types of cars in 4 different colors

__A__ 3 different colors of sheets in 2 different patterns

_____ 5 different colors of paper with 3 different colors of glitter

_____ 3 colors of thread with 3 different patches

_____ 5 different colors of carpet with 2 different colors of paint

_____ 4 types of ice-cream cones and 5 ice-cream flavors

_____ 8 different types of sandwiches and 2 different drinks

_____ 5 different computers and 3 different sizes of monitors

6	**A**	10	**H**	16	**O**
8	**C**	12	**I**	18	**S**
9	**E**	15	**M**	20	**T**

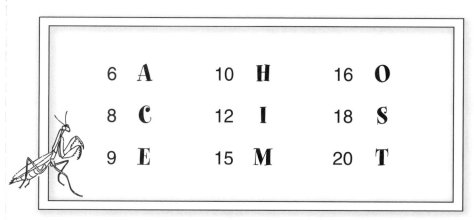

Utilize counting techniques, tree charts, and organized lists to determine all possible combinations of items

Data Analysis & Probability

Tongue Twister #20

Name _____

On the line in front of each list, write the number of combinations that can be made with the items listed. Then write the corresponding letter on the line in front of the question. The letters will spell out a tongue twister when read from top to bottom. Try to say it fast three times.

_____ 3 types of ice-cream cones and 2 flavors of ice cream

__O__ 7 colors of socks and 2 types of shoes

_____ 3 colors of shirts and 4 colors of buttons

_____ 4 types of vans in 2 different colors

_____ 2 colors of paper and 5 colors of glue

_____ 9 different dishes that are all blue

_____ 2 types of cars in 3 different colors

_____ 5 colors of glitter and 2 colors of construction paper

_____ 5 colors of shirts and 3 colors of scarves

_____ 3 colors of jeans and 3 different name brands

_____ 6 different shades and 3 different colors

6	C
8	E
9	I
10	K
12	M
14	O
15	S
16	T
18	X

_____ 3 types of computers and 5 different sizes of monitors

_____ 8 types of vegetables and 2 different ways of cooking them

_____ 3 types of dogs and 3 different colors of collars

_____ 3 colors of shirts and 2 colors of pants

_____ 2 types of shoes and 5 different name brands

_____ 3 different colors of light bulbs and 5 different styles of lamps

Utilize counting techniques, tree charts, and organized lists to determine all possible combinations of items

Data Analysis & Probability   EMC 3018 • Basic Math Skills, Grade 5 • ©2003 by Evan–Moor Corp.

Trees

Name _____

This tree diagram shows the number of outfits that can be created from 2 pairs of pants (red and green) and 2 shirts (white and black). Each "branch" lists one possible outfit. There are a total of 4 different outfits on this tree diagram.

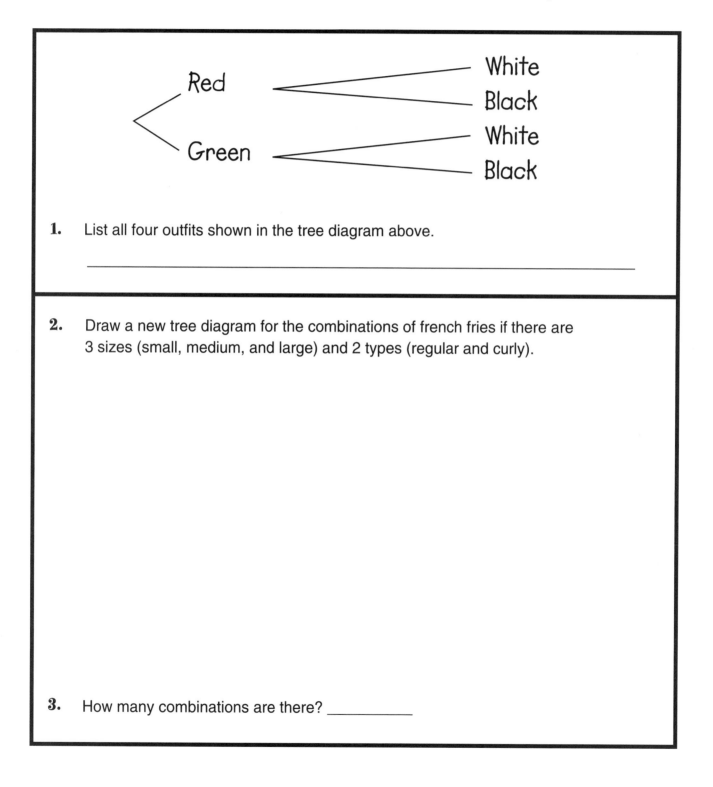

1. List all four outfits shown in the tree diagram above.

    _____

2. Draw a new tree diagram for the combinations of french fries if there are 3 sizes (small, medium, and large) and 2 types (regular and curly).

3. How many combinations are there? _____

Utilize counting techniques, tree charts, and organized lists to determine all possible combinations of items

Organized Lists

This organized list shows the number of outfits that could be created from 2 pairs of pants (red and green) and 2 shirts (white and black). Each row lists one possible outfit. There are a total of 4 different outfits in this organized list.

Pants	Shirts
Red	White
Red	Black
Green	White
Green	Black

Make an organized list for each of the following:

1. 3 sizes of soda (small, medium, and large) and 2 flavors (orange and cola)

2. 3 types of ice-cream cones (sugar, waffle, and plain) and 3 flavors of ice cream (chocolate, strawberry, and vanilla)

Utilize counting techniques, tree charts, and organized lists to determine all possible combinations of items

The Dealership

Name _____

The tree diagram below shows six possible combinations from a car dealership if there are 3 colors (white, silver, and gold) and 2 types of vehicles (2-door and 4-door). For each question, start with the tree diagram below and add different traits.

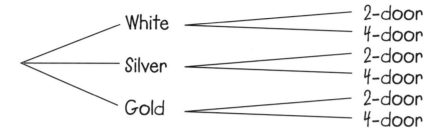

1. Add one more trait to make eight possible combinations. Draw the new tree diagram.

2. Add one more trait to make nine possible combinations. Draw the new tree diagram.

3. Add two more traits to make twelve possible combinations. Draw the new tree diagram.

Utilize counting techniques, tree charts, and organized lists to determine all possible combinations of items

Organized Problems

Name _____

Julie created organized lists for the problems below and needs your help. Read each problem and then help Julie correct her mistakes.

1. There are 3 colors of cars (red, blue, and silver) and there are 2 styles (2-door and 4-door). Julie listed all the possible combinations. Has she left any out? What hint can you give that might help her organize her list better?

Color of Car	Style of Car
red	2-door
blue	4-door
silver	2-door
blue	2-door
red	4-door
silver	2-door

_____

_____

2. There are 3 spelling lists (blue, green, and red) and each list has a set of words (20 words **or** 25 words). Julie made this list of all the combinations. Write a note to Julie telling her if she has completed the list accurately.

Spelling List	# of Words
blue	20
blue	25
green	20
green	25
red	20
red	25

_____

_____

3. There are 2 types of ice-cream cones and 2 flavors of ice cream for cones with two scoops. Julie made this list to show how many combinations are possible. She's not sure if she has listed them all. Check her list and write a note to her about what you observe.

Type of Cone	Flavor of 1st Scoop	Flavor of 2nd Scoop	
sugar	chocolate	chocolate	_____
sugar	chocolate	vanilla	_____
sugar	vanilla	chocolate	_____
sugar	vanilla	vanilla	_____
waffle	chocolate	chocolate	_____
waffle	chocolate	vanilla	_____

Utilize counting techniques, tree charts, and organized lists to determine all possible combinations of items

Data Analysis & Probability　　　　EMC 3018 • Basic Math Skills, Grade 5 • ©2003 by Evan-Moor Corp.

Math Test

Name _____

Fill in the circle next to the correct answer.

1. If there are 4 shirts and 3 pairs of pants, how many different outfits can be created?

Ⓐ 3 Ⓒ 7
Ⓑ 4 Ⓓ 12

2. If there are 3 types of ice-cream cones and 3 different flavors of ice cream, how many different single scoop ice-cream cones can be made?

Ⓐ 3 Ⓒ 12
Ⓑ 9 Ⓓ 27

Use the tree diagram below for Numbers 3 and 4.

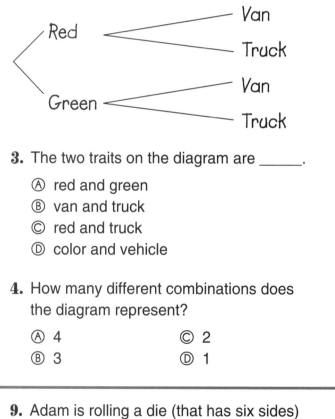

3. The two traits on the diagram are _____.

Ⓐ red and green
Ⓑ van and truck
Ⓒ red and truck
Ⓓ color and vehicle

4. How many different combinations does the diagram represent?

Ⓐ 4 Ⓒ 2
Ⓑ 3 Ⓓ 1

Use this organized list for Numbers 5 through 8.

Jersey	Mascot
orange	eagle
blue	eagle
red	eagle
orange	bronco
blue	bronco
red	bronco
orange	lions
blue	lions
red	lions

5. What does the list represent?

Ⓐ flavors of ice cream
Ⓑ colors and types of cars
Ⓒ colors of jerseys and mascots
Ⓓ colors of mascots

6. How many different colors are listed?

Ⓐ 2 Ⓒ 6
Ⓑ 3 Ⓓ 9

7. How many different mascots are listed?

Ⓐ 2 Ⓒ 6
Ⓑ 3 Ⓓ 9

8. How many different combinations does the list represent?

Ⓐ 2 Ⓒ 6
Ⓑ 3 Ⓓ 9

9. Adam is rolling a die (that has six sides) and spinning a spinner with two equal sections (red and green). Draw a tree diagram to represent all the possible combinations.

10. Sarah has a coin and a spinner with five sections (1, 2, 3, 4, and 5). Create a list to show all the possible combinations there are if she is flips the coin once and spins the spinner once.

Utilize counting techniques, tree charts, and organized lists to determine all possible combinations of items

Data Analysis & Probability

Resources

Name _____

Time: _____   Number Correct: _____

7 − 7 = _____	6 + 2 = _____	7 + 9 = _____	8 + 2 = _____
8 − 1 = _____	12 − 4 = _____	9 − 6 = _____	9 + 3 = _____
4 + 5 = _____	2 − 2 = _____	2 + 6 = _____	2 + 9 = _____
9 − 9 = _____	11 − 10 = _____	1 + 10 = _____	11 − 5 = _____
2 + 2 = _____	10 − 5 = _____	10 − 3 = _____	18 − 9 = _____
7 − 4 = _____	1 + 5 = _____	19 − 10 = _____	6 − 6 = _____
12 − 3 = _____	8 − 3 = _____	8 + 8 = _____	11 − 3 = _____
15 − 9 = _____	7 + 5 = _____	1 + 2 = _____	7 + 3 = _____
5 + 8 = _____	8 − 0 = _____	5 + 5 = _____	3 + 8 = _____
10 + 0 = _____	14 − 5 = _____	10 + 6 = _____	10 + 1 = _____
2 + 7 = _____	10 + 3 = _____	4 + 9 = _____	9 + 8 = _____
6 − 3 = _____	12 − 7 = _____	5 + 9 = _____	12 − 2 = _____
10 − 9 = _____	4 + 1 = _____	7 − 2 = _____	0 + 7 = _____
13 − 6 = _____	9 + 5 = _____	9 − 8 = _____	13 − 10 = _____
18 − 10 = _____	3 + 9 = _____	18 − 8 = _____	3 + 6 = _____
6 + 6 = _____	7 − 6 = _____	2 − 1 = _____	14 − 10 = _____
4 + 3 = _____	10 − 10 = _____	9 + 0 = _____	3 + 10 = _____
6 − 4 = _____	2 + 3 = _____	8 − 2 = _____	14 − 8 = _____
0 + 0 = _____	5 + 6 = _____	16 − 9 = _____	3 + 1 = _____
10 − 7 = _____	0 + 8 = _____	5 + 7 = _____	10 − 1 = _____
8 + 1 = _____	10 + 10 = _____	5 − 3 = _____	10 + 4 = _____
10 − 6 = _____	4 − 2 = _____	6 + 4 = _____	6 + 5 = _____
1 + 0 = _____	14 − 4 = _____	8 + 3 = _____	17 − 8 = _____
1 − 0 = _____	7 + 8 = _____	9 − 2 = _____	12 − 9 = _____
6 − 1 = _____	16 − 7 = _____	9 − 4 = _____	3 + 2 = _____

Name _____

Time: _____   Number Correct: _____

$6 + 10 =$ _____	$10 - 4 =$ _____	$7 - 3 =$ _____	$16 - 10 =$ _____
$15 - 10 =$ _____	$10 + 5 =$ _____	$14 - 6 =$ _____	$2 + 1 =$ _____
$7 - 5 =$ _____	$7 + 6 =$ _____	$7 + 7 =$ _____	$7 + 10 =$ _____
$0 + 4 =$ _____	$10 - 2 =$ _____	$5 - 2 =$ _____	$6 - 0 =$ _____
$3 - 2 =$ _____	$8 - 5 =$ _____	$8 - 4 =$ _____	$0 - 0 =$ _____
$3 + 7 =$ _____	$9 - 1 =$ _____	$11 - 9 =$ _____	$5 + 3 =$ _____
$7 + 2 =$ _____	$9 + 7 =$ _____	$12 - 5 =$ _____	$15 - 8 =$ _____
$15 - 7 =$ _____	$5 + 2 =$ _____	$4 - 4 =$ _____	$6 + 0 =$ _____
$0 + 1 =$ _____	$7 - 1 =$ _____	$1 + 7 =$ _____	$5 - 1 =$ _____
$8 + 6 =$ _____	$2 + 4 =$ _____	$0 + 10 =$ _____	$3 + 5 =$ _____
$17 - 9 =$ _____	$11 - 7 =$ _____	$9 + 4 =$ _____	$8 + 4 =$ _____
$11 - 11 =$ _____	$9 - 3 =$ _____	$14 - 9 =$ _____	$2 - 2 =$ _____
$3 - 3 =$ _____	$1 + 8 =$ _____	$6 + 8 =$ _____	$10 + 8 =$ _____
$5 - 4 =$ _____	$12 - 8 =$ _____	$13 - 5 =$ _____	$16 - 6 =$ _____
$6 + 7 =$ _____	$3 - 1 =$ _____	$2 + 0 =$ _____	$4 + 6 =$ _____
$3 + 0 =$ _____	$7 + 0 =$ _____	$13 - 9 =$ _____	$1 + 6 =$ _____
$9 - 7 =$ _____	$2 + 10 =$ _____	$0 + 5 =$ _____	$4 - 1 =$ _____
$1 + 9 =$ _____	$6 - 5 =$ _____	$15 - 6 =$ _____	$5 - 0 =$ _____
$9 + 10 =$ _____	$0 + 6 =$ _____	$11 - 4 =$ _____	$4 + 8 =$ _____
$11 - 6 =$ _____	$3 - 0 =$ _____	$5 + 0 =$ _____	$10 - 0 =$ _____
$0 + 9 =$ _____	$13 - 7 =$ _____	$4 + 4 =$ _____	$4 + 10 =$ _____
$4 - 3 =$ _____	$17 - 10 =$ _____	$9 + 2 =$ _____	$19 - 9 =$ _____
$6 - 2 =$ _____	$8 + 10 =$ _____	$15 - 5 =$ _____	$9 - 5 =$ _____
$3 + 4 =$ _____	$2 + 8 =$ _____	$1 + 4 =$ _____	$5 + 10 =$ _____
$6 + 9 =$ _____	$5 + 4 =$ _____	$10 - 8 =$ _____	$9 + 9 =$ _____

Time: _____   Number Correct: _____

5 × 5 = _____	9 × 5 = _____	4 × 10 = _____	2 × 8 = _____
7 × 9 = _____	3 × 8 = _____	1 × 4 = _____	1 × 9 = _____
10 × 4 = _____	6 × 2 = _____	5 × 7 = _____	10 × 6 = _____
6 × 9 = _____	9 × 9 = _____	8 × 9 = _____	3 × 5 = _____
2 × 0 = _____	1 × 3 = _____	6 × 1 = _____	10 × 8 = _____
2 × 9 = _____	2 × 3 = _____	0 × 2 = _____	5 × 2 = _____
6 × 3 = _____	8 × 6 = _____	6 × 0 = _____	2 × 10 = _____
10 × 0 = _____	2 × 7 = _____	3 × 7 = _____	9 × 1 = _____
3 × 10 = _____	5 × 1 = _____	5 × 10 = _____	6 × 10 = _____
3 × 3 = _____	7 × 10 = _____	9 × 3 = _____	8 × 7 = _____
9 × 6 = _____	1 × 0 = _____	4 × 5 = _____	9 × 4 = _____
8 × 1 = _____	4 × 8 = _____	4 × 4 = _____	8 × 8 = _____
4 × 3 = _____	7 × 3 = _____	0 × 10 = _____	0 × 9 = _____
6 × 8 = _____	3 × 2 = _____	7 × 6 = _____	2 × 4 = _____
7 × 2 = _____	2 × 5 = _____	10 × 2 = _____	4 × 1 = _____
3 × 4 = _____	0 × 8 = _____	6 × 4 = _____	5 × 8 = _____
0 × 1 = _____	7 × 5 = _____	3 × 6 = _____	7 × 7 = _____
4 × 0 = _____	4 × 2 = _____	0 × 6 = _____	6 × 5 = _____
10 × 5 = _____	2 × 6 = _____	3 × 0 = _____	8 × 4 = _____
1 × 2 = _____	7 × 8 = _____	4 × 6 = _____	2 × 2 = _____
5 × 6 = _____	10 × 10 = _____	5 × 4 = _____	0 × 4 = _____
9 × 0 = _____	8 × 3 = _____	1 × 6 = _____	7 × 0 = _____
3 × 9 = _____	5 × 9 = _____	7 × 1 = _____	6 × 6 = _____
6 × 7 = _____	2 × 1 = _____	8 × 5 = _____	9 × 7 = _____
7 × 4 = _____	0 × 5 = _____	9 × 8 = _____	8 × 10 = _____

Name _____

Time: _____   Number Correct: _____

1 × 9 = _____	3 × 6 = _____	2 × 3 = _____	4 × 3 = _____
4 × 4 = _____	2 × 9 = _____	1 × 6 = _____	6 × 10 = _____
5 × 7 = _____	1 × 10 = _____	0 × 9 = _____	8 × 7 = _____
7 × 1 = _____	5 × 9 = _____	4 × 5 = _____	9 × 9 = _____
9 × 4 = _____	7 × 10 = _____	9 × 7 = _____	10 × 2 = _____
10 × 8 = _____	9 × 0 = _____	5 × 2 = _____	8 × 6 = _____
0 × 5 = _____	4 × 1 = _____	6 × 5 = _____	9 × 1 = _____
1 × 3 = _____	3 × 8 = _____	6 × 6 = _____	8 × 5 = _____
4 × 0 = _____	10 × 0 = _____	9 × 2 = _____	7 × 7 = _____
5 × 5 = _____	10 × 5 = _____	10 × 1 = _____	4 × 6 = _____
0 × 3 = _____	6 × 9 = _____	4 × 8 = _____	6 × 3 = _____
5 × 3 = _____	7 × 6 = _____	4 × 10 = _____	2 × 8 = _____
8 × 2 = _____	2 × 10 = _____	3 × 3 = _____	1 × 0 = _____
9 × 10 = _____	8 × 4 = _____	10 × 6 = _____	10 × 3 = _____
5 × 8 = _____	7 × 3 = _____	6 × 4 = _____	1 × 4 = _____
3 × 1 = _____	5 × 1 = _____	2 × 1 = _____	5 × 4 = _____
2 × 4 = _____	1 × 5 = _____	1 × 7 = _____	2 × 2 = _____
6 × 0 = _____	2 × 6 = _____	6 × 8 = _____	1 × 1 = _____
2 × 7 = _____	3 × 9 = _____	8 × 3 = _____	2 × 0 = _____
8 × 1 = _____	6 × 7 = _____	4 × 2 = _____	8 × 0 = _____
7 × 2 = _____	7 × 5 = _____	2 × 5 = _____	9 × 5 = _____
8 × 9 = _____	10 × 4 = _____	1 × 8 = _____	9 × 8 = _____
3 × 10 = _____	6 × 2 = _____	0 × 10 = _____	5 × 6 = _____
4 × 7 = _____	7 × 4 = _____	3 × 5 = _____	10 × 10 = _____
9 × 6 = _____	3 × 2 = _____	0 × 7 = _____	0 × 0 = _____

EMC 3018 • Basic Math Skills, Grade 5 • ©2003 by Evan-Moor Corp.

Name _____

Time: _____   Number Correct: _____

$36 \div 6 =$	$63 \div 7 =$	$100 \div 10 =$	$0 \div 3 =$
$49 \div 7 =$	$60 \div 6 =$	$56 \div 8 =$	$20 \div 10 =$
$25 \div 5 =$	$20 \div 5 =$	$50 \div 5 =$	$40 \div 8 =$
$45 \div 9 =$	$0 \div 7 =$	$35 \div 5 =$	$63 \div 9 =$
$80 \div 10 =$	$30 \div 3 =$	$4 \div 2 =$	$81 \div 9 =$
$64 \div 8 =$	$42 \div 6 =$	$24 \div 4 =$	$8 \div 1 =$
$54 \div 6 =$	$18 \div 3 =$	$54 \div 9 =$	$18 \div 2 =$
$0 \div 1 =$	$6 \div 3 =$	$32 \div 4 =$	$21 \div 3 =$
$18 \div 6 =$	$2 \div 2 =$	$28 \div 7 =$	$72 \div 8 =$
$6 \div 2 =$	$0 \div 10 =$	$24 \div 8 =$	$40 \div 4 =$
$12 \div 3 =$	$24 \div 3 =$	$8 \div 2 =$	$60 \div 10 =$
$5 \div 5 =$	$0 \div 9 =$	$15 \div 3 =$	$8 \div 4 =$
$16 \div 8 =$	$9 \div 9 =$	$40 \div 10 =$	$12 \div 4 =$
$0 \div 5 =$	$4 \div 1 =$	$36 \div 9 =$	$18 \div 9 =$
$50 \div 10 =$	$12 \div 2 =$	$70 \div 10 =$	$3 \div 3 =$
$56 \div 7 =$	$9 \div 1 =$	$36 \div 4 =$	$80 \div 8 =$
$42 \div 7 =$	$14 \div 7 =$	$2 \div 1 =$	$27 \div 3 =$
$12 \div 6 =$	$6 \div 6 =$	$30 \div 10 =$	$72 \div 9 =$
$30 \div 6 =$	$48 \div 8 =$	$90 \div 9 =$	$7 \div 1 =$
$16 \div 4 =$	$4 \div 4 =$	$8 \div 8 =$	$10 \div 5 =$
$21 \div 7 =$	$32 \div 8 =$	$30 \div 5 =$	$7 \div 7 =$
$20 \div 4 =$	$28 \div 4 =$	$24 \div 6 =$	$90 \div 10 =$
$14 \div 2 =$	$27 \div 9 =$	$15 \div 5 =$	$45 \div 5 =$
$40 \div 5 =$	$10 \div 2 =$	$6 \div 1 =$	$48 \div 6 =$
$20 \div 2 =$	$9 \div 3 =$	$35 \div 7 =$	$16 \div 2 =$

Name _____

Time: _____   Number Correct: _____

$18 \div 6 =$ _____ $20 \div 4 =$ _____ $12 \div 4 =$ _____ $56 \div 8 =$ _____

$32 \div 8 =$ _____ $36 \div 4 =$ _____ $20 \div 5 =$ _____ $80 \div 10 =$ _____

$8 \div 2 =$ _____ $42 \div 6 =$ _____ $21 \div 7 =$ _____ $28 \div 4 =$ _____

$48 \div 8 =$ _____ $24 \div 4 =$ _____ $9 \div 9 =$ _____ $2 \div 2 =$ _____

$49 \div 7 =$ _____ $70 \div 10 =$ _____ $30 \div 5 =$ _____ $10 \div 5 =$ _____

$6 \div 1 =$ _____ $7 \div 1 =$ _____ $81 \div 9 =$ _____ $10 \div 2 =$ _____

$90 \div 10 =$ _____ $70 \div 7 =$ _____ $6 \div 3 =$ _____ $32 \div 4 =$ _____

$5 \div 5 =$ _____ $30 \div 6 =$ _____ $14 \div 2 =$ _____ $9 \div 1 =$ _____

$63 \div 9 =$ _____ $72 \div 9 =$ _____ $48 \div 6 =$ _____ $30 \div 3 =$ _____

$15 \div 5 =$ _____ $45 \div 5 =$ _____ $21 \div 3 =$ _____ $35 \div 5 =$ _____

$6 \div 6 =$ _____ $50 \div 10 =$ _____ $5 \div 1 =$ _____ $56 \div 7 =$ _____

$40 \div 8 =$ _____ $2 \div 1 =$ _____ $12 \div 3 =$ _____ $100 \div 10 =$ _____

$14 \div 7 =$ _____ $0 \div 3 =$ _____ $9 \div 3 =$ _____ $16 \div 8 =$ _____

$15 \div 3 =$ _____ $18 \div 9 =$ _____ $8 \div 4 =$ _____ $7 \div 7 =$ _____

$64 \div 8 =$ _____ $24 \div 6 =$ _____ $8 \div 8 =$ _____ $40 \div 10 =$ _____

$60 \div 6 =$ _____ $50 \div 5 =$ _____ $0 \div 6 =$ _____ $12 \div 6 =$ _____

$30 \div 10 =$ _____ $0 \div 1 =$ _____ $40 \div 4 =$ _____ $27 \div 9 =$ _____

$0 \div 8 =$ _____ $6 \div 2 =$ _____ $18 \div 2 =$ _____ $20 \div 10 =$ _____

$4 \div 1 =$ _____ $72 \div 8 =$ _____ $35 \div 7 =$ _____ $0 \div 4 =$ _____

$4 \div 2 =$ _____ $40 \div 5 =$ _____ $0 \div 5 =$ _____ $45 \div 9 =$ _____

$16 \div 2 =$ _____ $16 \div 4 =$ _____ $24 \div 8 =$ _____ $18 \div 3 =$ _____

$10 \div 1 =$ _____ $12 \div 2 =$ _____ $36 \div 9 =$ _____ $63 \div 7 =$ _____

$28 \div 7 =$ _____ $20 \div 2 =$ _____ $24 \div 3 =$ _____ $0 \div 10 =$ _____

$25 \div 5 =$ _____ $54 \div 6 =$ _____ $42 \div 7 =$ _____ $4 \div 4 =$ _____

$54 \div 9 =$ _____ $27 \div 3 =$ _____ $36 \div 6 =$ _____ $80 \div 8 =$ _____

Name _____

Time: _____   Number Correct: _____

$3 \times 1 =$ _____	$7 \times 2 =$ _____	$6 \times 11 =$ _____	$8 \times 9 =$ _____
$2 \times 8 =$ _____	$11 \times 7 =$ _____	$7 \times 4 =$ _____	$11 \times 1 =$ _____
$7 \times 10 =$ _____	$10 \times 6 =$ _____	$2 \times 1 =$ _____	$2 \times 5 =$ _____
$10 \times 10 =$ _____	$11 \times 6 =$ _____	$11 \times 2 =$ _____	$1 \times 8 =$ _____
$10 \times 11 =$ _____	$8 \times 11 =$ _____	$3 \times 9 =$ _____	$1 \times 4 =$ _____
$4 \times 10 =$ _____	$1 \times 2 =$ _____	$3 \times 11 =$ _____	$2 \times 3 =$ _____
$11 \times 8 =$ _____	$7 \times 9 =$ _____	$11 \times 5 =$ _____	$7 \times 11 =$ _____
$2 \times 4 =$ _____	$8 \times 3 =$ _____	$9 \times 4 =$ _____	$5 \times 3 =$ _____
$4 \times 9 =$ _____	$9 \times 6 =$ _____	$2 \times 6 =$ _____	$4 \times 8 =$ _____
$7 \times 8 =$ _____	$7 \times 5 =$ _____	$4 \times 3 =$ _____	$1 \times 9 =$ _____
$8 \times 8 =$ _____	$6 \times 9 =$ _____	$9 \times 7 =$ _____	$6 \times 7 =$ _____
$5 \times 1 =$ _____	$7 \times 6 =$ _____	$5 \times 5 =$ _____	$3 \times 4 =$ _____
$4 \times 11 =$ _____	$5 \times 11 =$ _____	$4 \times 7 =$ _____	$6 \times 10 =$ _____
$5 \times 2 =$ _____	$9 \times 8 =$ _____	$1 \times 6 =$ _____	$8 \times 5 =$ _____
$9 \times 1 =$ _____	$9 \times 9 =$ _____	$11 \times 4 =$ _____	$3 \times 6 =$ _____
$6 \times 6 =$ _____	$8 \times 1 =$ _____	$2 \times 10 =$ _____	$5 \times 7 =$ _____
$3 \times 7 =$ _____	$10 \times 4 =$ _____	$1 \times 3 =$ _____	$2 \times 11 =$ _____
$5 \times 4 =$ _____	$3 \times 2 =$ _____	$1 \times 11 =$ _____	$9 \times 11 =$ _____
$3 \times 5 =$ _____	$5 \times 8 =$ _____	$5 \times 10 =$ _____	$7 \times 3 =$ _____
$6 \times 3 =$ _____	$11 \times 9 =$ _____	$6 \times 5 =$ _____	$10 \times 8 =$ _____
$10 \times 3 =$ _____	$4 \times 1 =$ _____	$5 \times 9 =$ _____	$8 \times 10 =$ _____
$1 \times 7 =$ _____	$9 \times 10 =$ _____	$6 \times 4 =$ _____	$1 \times 5 =$ _____
$4 \times 4 =$ _____	$3 \times 10 =$ _____	$11 \times 3 =$ _____	$7 \times 7 =$ _____
$6 \times 2 =$ _____	$6 \times 1 =$ _____	$10 \times 9 =$ _____	$9 \times 2 =$ _____
$3 \times 3 =$ _____	$11 \times 10 =$ _____	$4 \times 6 =$ _____	$11 \times 11 =$ _____

Name _____

Time: _____ Number Correct: _____

6 × 3 = _____	9 × 6 = _____	4 × 10 = _____	8 × 12 = _____
11 × 1 = _____	2 × 9 = _____	6 × 1 = _____	9 × 5 = _____
12 × 7 = _____	8 × 6 = _____	5 × 3 = _____	4 × 11 = _____
8 × 2 = _____	2 × 11 = _____	12 × 11 = _____	2 × 6 = _____
5 × 10 = _____	1 × 11 = _____	11 × 5 = _____	2 × 12 = _____
11 × 12 = _____	9 × 7 = _____	6 × 5 = _____	7 × 10 = _____
10 × 2 = _____	4 × 2 = _____	7 × 4 = _____	11 × 6 = _____
11 × 8 = _____	3 × 7 = _____	9 × 3 = _____	10 × 5 = _____
6 × 10 = _____	2 × 4 = _____	10 × 9 = _____	7 × 11 = _____
2 × 10 = _____	12 × 6 = _____	12 × 10 = _____	2 × 5 = _____
7 × 6 = _____	11 × 2 = _____	8 × 5 = _____	5 × 4 = _____
12 × 12 = _____	1 × 1 = _____	3 × 2 = _____	10 × 10 = _____
4 × 5 = _____	2 × 7 = _____	6 × 8 = _____	11 × 3 = _____
4 × 1 = _____	7 × 12 = _____	7 × 9 = _____	4 × 8 = _____
7 × 3 = _____	11 × 4 = _____	8 × 4 = _____	1 × 3 = _____
3 × 6 = _____	4 × 7 = _____	10 × 7 = _____	3 × 10 = _____
1 × 9 = _____	5 × 6 = _____	1 × 8 = _____	12 × 8 = _____
9 × 11 = _____	7 × 8 = _____	11 × 9 = _____	8 × 3 = _____
4 × 12 = _____	3 × 3 = _____	8 × 7 = _____	9 × 8 = _____
11 × 10 = _____	8 × 10 = _____	3 × 9 = _____	11 × 7 = _____
3 × 4 = _____	12 × 9 = _____	6 × 6 = _____	3 × 5 = _____
2 × 8 = _____	3 × 8 = _____	8 × 9 = _____	2 × 2 = _____
9 × 2 = _____	9 × 9 = _____	12 × 2 = _____	1 × 12 = _____
6 × 2 = _____	1 × 10 = _____	1 × 4 = _____	5 × 8 = _____
3 × 11 = _____	4 × 9 = _____	9 × 1 = _____	11 × 11 = _____

EMC 3018 • Basic Math Skills, Grade 5 • ©2003 by Evan–Moor Corp.

Math Timed Tests–Class Record Sheet

Student Names	Test 1 +/– Facts	Test 2 +/– Facts	Test 3 × Facts Through 10s	Test 4 × Facts Through 10s	Test 5 ÷ Facts	Test 6 ÷ Facts	Test 7 × Facts Through 11s	Test 8 × Facts Through 11s

Name _____

Math Test Page _____

1. Ⓐ Ⓑ Ⓒ Ⓓ   5. Ⓐ Ⓑ Ⓒ Ⓓ
2. Ⓐ Ⓑ Ⓒ Ⓓ   6. Ⓐ Ⓑ Ⓒ Ⓓ
3. Ⓐ Ⓑ Ⓒ Ⓓ   7. Ⓐ Ⓑ Ⓒ Ⓓ
4. Ⓐ Ⓑ Ⓒ Ⓓ   8. Ⓐ Ⓑ Ⓒ Ⓓ

9. | 10.

Name _____

Math Test Page _____

1. Ⓐ Ⓑ Ⓒ Ⓓ   5. Ⓐ Ⓑ Ⓒ Ⓓ
2. Ⓐ Ⓑ Ⓒ Ⓓ   6. Ⓐ Ⓑ Ⓒ Ⓓ
3. Ⓐ Ⓑ Ⓒ Ⓓ   7. Ⓐ Ⓑ Ⓒ Ⓓ
4. Ⓐ Ⓑ Ⓒ Ⓓ   8. Ⓐ Ⓑ Ⓒ Ⓓ

9. | 10.

Name _____

Math Test Page _____

1. Ⓐ Ⓑ Ⓒ Ⓓ   5. Ⓐ Ⓑ Ⓒ Ⓓ
2. Ⓐ Ⓑ Ⓒ Ⓓ   6. Ⓐ Ⓑ Ⓒ Ⓓ
3. Ⓐ Ⓑ Ⓒ Ⓓ   7. Ⓐ Ⓑ Ⓒ Ⓓ
4. Ⓐ Ⓑ Ⓒ Ⓓ   8. Ⓐ Ⓑ Ⓒ Ⓓ

9. | 10.

Name _____

Math Test Page _____

1. Ⓐ Ⓑ Ⓒ Ⓓ   5. Ⓐ Ⓑ Ⓒ Ⓓ
2. Ⓐ Ⓑ Ⓒ Ⓓ   6. Ⓐ Ⓑ Ⓒ Ⓓ
3. Ⓐ Ⓑ Ⓒ Ⓓ   7. Ⓐ Ⓑ Ⓒ Ⓓ
4. Ⓐ Ⓑ Ⓒ Ⓓ   8. Ⓐ Ⓑ Ⓒ Ⓓ

9. | 10.

You're a ST★R

You're doing GREAT!
Keep up the good work!

MATH Genius

#1 in MATH

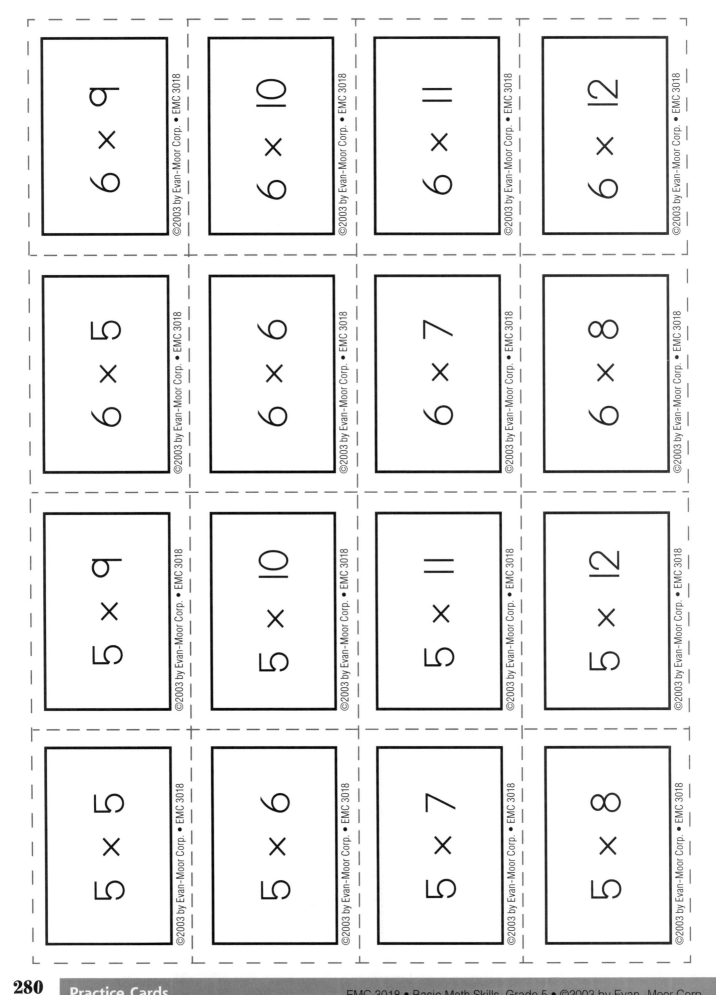

6 × 9	6 × 5	5 × 9	5 × 5
6 × 10	6 × 6	5 × 10	5 × 6
6 × 11	6 × 7	5 × 11	5 × 7
6 × 12	6 × 8	5 × 12	5 × 8

©2003 by Evan-Moor Corp. • EMC 3018

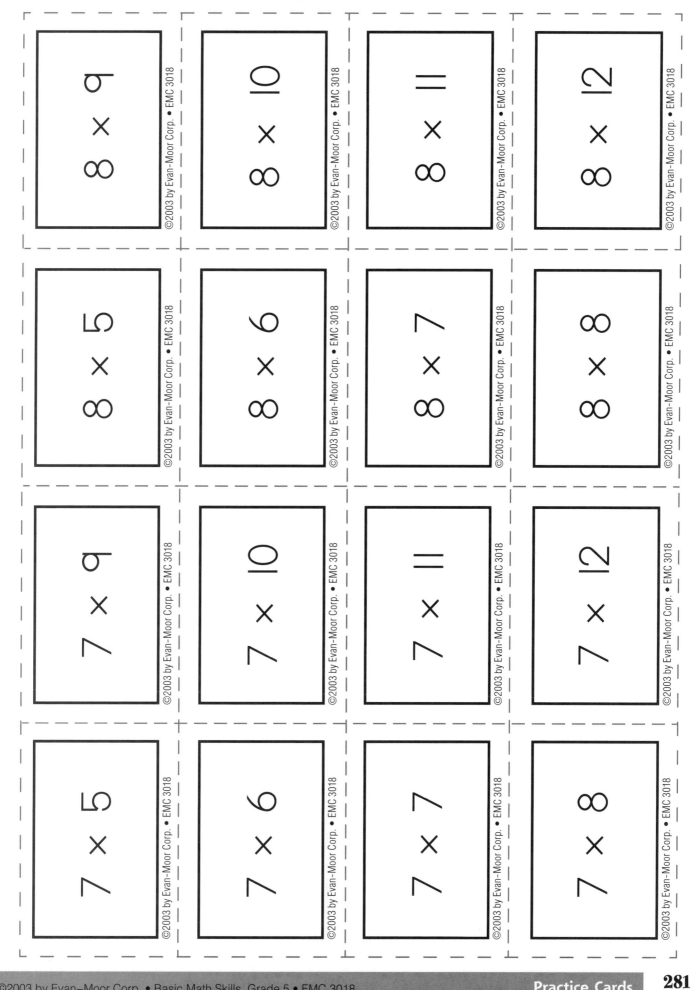

8 × 9

©2003 by Evan-Moor Corp. • EMC 3018

8 × 10

©2003 by Evan-Moor Corp. • EMC 3018

8 × 11

©2003 by Evan-Moor Corp. • EMC 3018

8 × 12

©2003 by Evan-Moor Corp. • EMC 3018

8 × 5

©2003 by Evan-Moor Corp. • EMC 3018

8 × 6

©2003 by Evan-Moor Corp. • EMC 3018

8 × 7

©2003 by Evan-Moor Corp. • EMC 3018

8 × 8

©2003 by Evan-Moor Corp. • EMC 3018

7 × 9

©2003 by Evan-Moor Corp. • EMC 3018

7 × 10

©2003 by Evan-Moor Corp. • EMC 3018

7 × 11

©2003 by Evan-Moor Corp. • EMC 3018

7 × 12

©2003 by Evan-Moor Corp. • EMC 3018

7 × 5

©2003 by Evan-Moor Corp. • EMC 3018

7 × 6

©2003 by Evan-Moor Corp. • EMC 3018

7 × 7

©2003 by Evan-Moor Corp. • EMC 3018

7 × 8

©2003 by Evan-Moor Corp. • EMC 3018

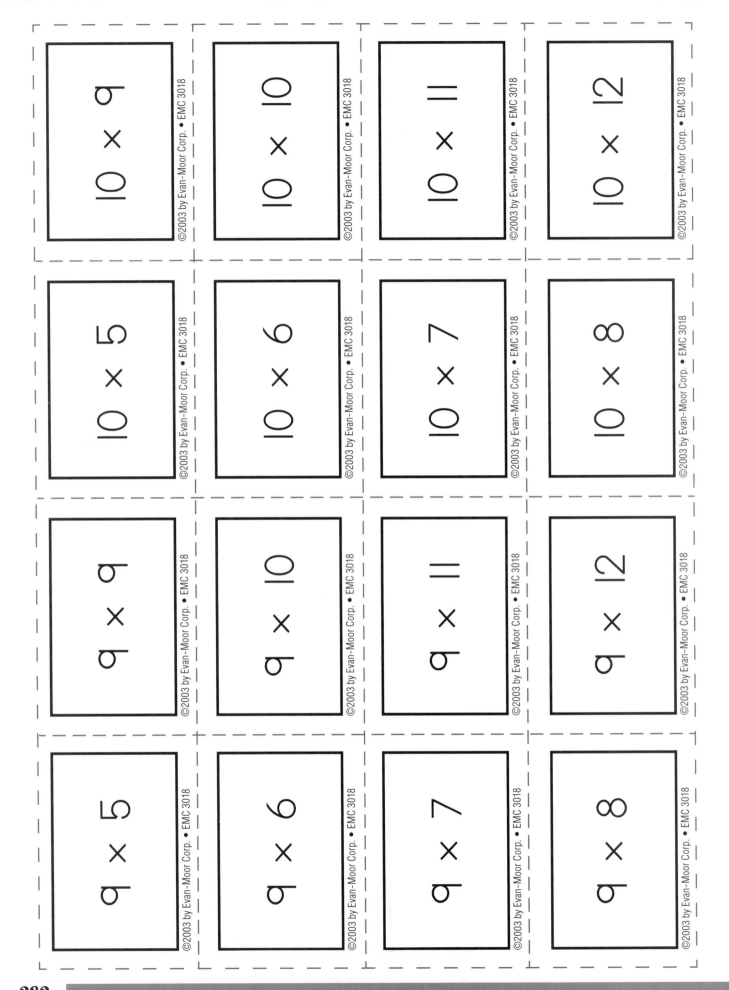

EMC 3018 • Basic Math Skills, Grade 5 • ©2003 by Evan–Moor Corp.

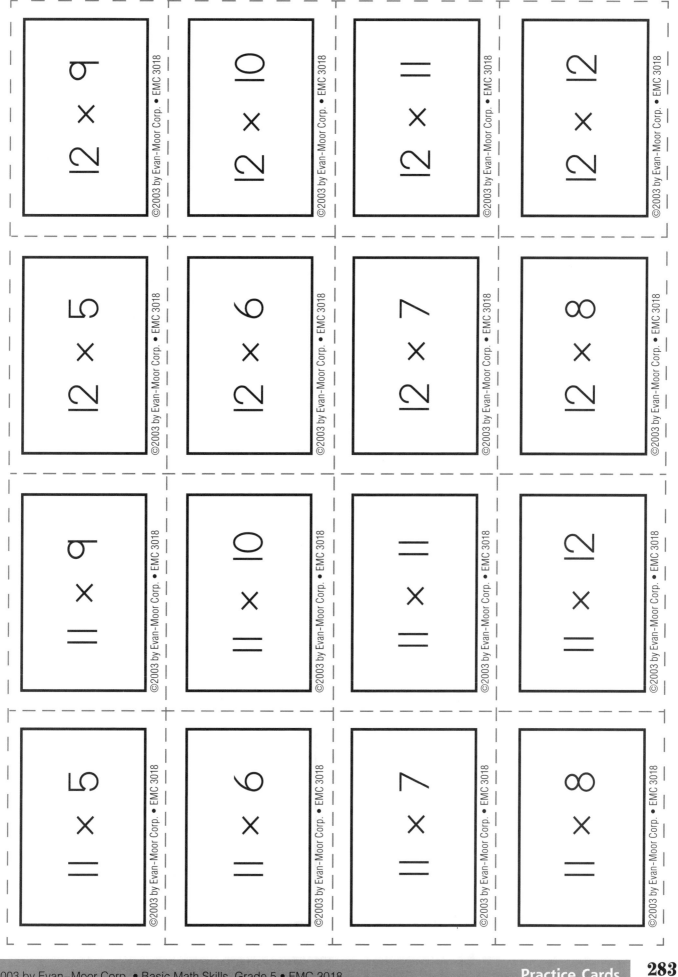

12 × 9	12 × 5	11 × 9	11 × 5
12 × 10	12 × 6	11 × 10	11 × 6
12 × 11	12 × 7	11 × 11	11 × 7
12 × 12	12 × 8	11 × 12	11 × 8

©2003 by Evan-Moor Corp. • EMC 3018

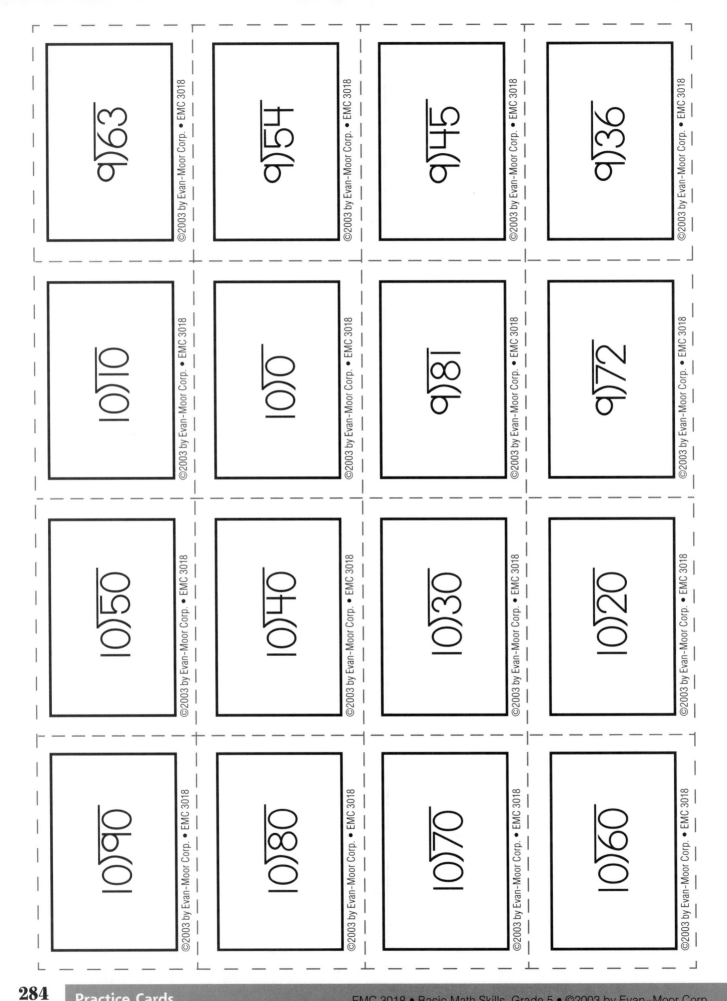

$9\overline{)63}$ $9\overline{)54}$ $9\overline{)45}$ $9\overline{)36}$

$10\overline{)10}$ $10\overline{)0}$ $9\overline{)81}$ $9\overline{)72}$

$10\overline{)50}$ $10\overline{)40}$ $10\overline{)30}$ $10\overline{)20}$

$10\overline{)90}$ $10\overline{)80}$ $10\overline{)70}$ $10\overline{)60}$

EMC 3018 • Basic Math Skills, Grade 5 • ©2003 by Evan–Moor Corp.

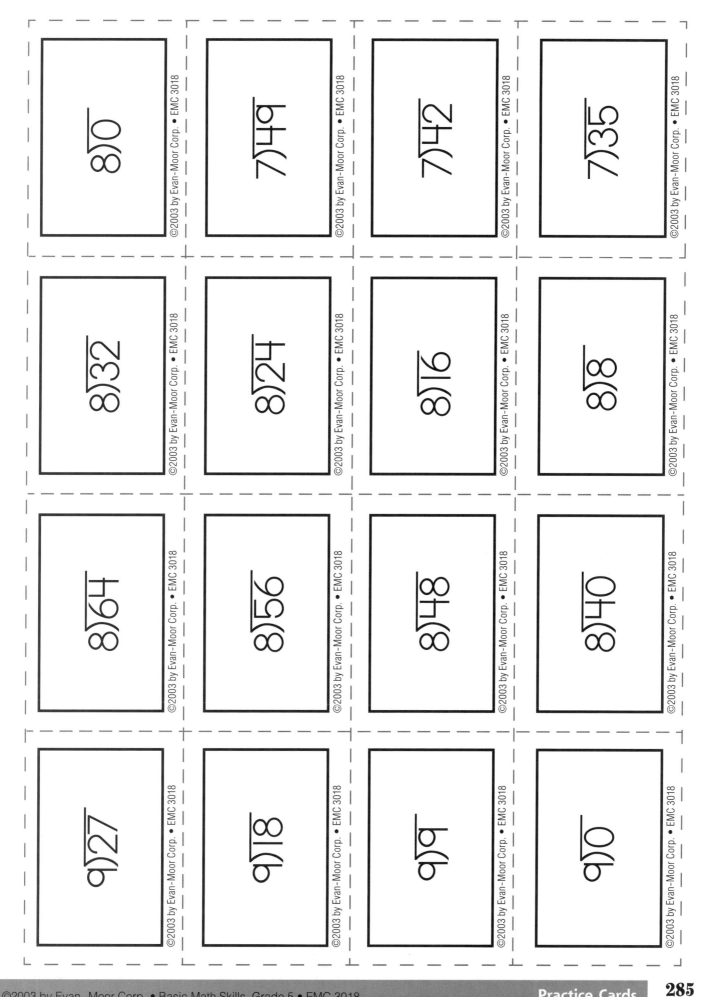

Answer Key

Page 5: Tricky crickets

Page 6: A purple people eater

Page 7

1. 17, 25, 34, 74, 75, 83
2. 37, 170, 175, 208, 382, 491
3. 15.3, 15.7, 15.9, 16.2, 17, 26.4
4. $7\frac{1}{5}$, $7\frac{1}{3}$, $7\frac{1}{2}$, 8, $8\frac{1}{2}$, $8\frac{2}{3}$
5. 6, $6\frac{1}{4}$, $6\frac{1}{3}$, $6\frac{1}{2}$, $6\frac{2}{3}$, $6\frac{3}{4}$
6. 0.0159, 0.159, 1.59, 15.9, 159, 1,590
7. 25.9, 25.99, 26, 26.25, 26.3, 26.34
8. $6\frac{4}{9}$, $6\frac{2}{3}$, $7\frac{1}{10}$, $7\frac{3}{5}$, $7\frac{9}{10}$, $8\frac{3}{10}$
9. 0.0256, 0.256, 2.56, 25.6, 256, 2,560
10. 14, 14.19, 14.2, 14.21, 14.3, 14.8

Page 8

1. 9,524, 843, 264, 249, 190, 125
2. 267, 264, 263, 261, 260, 259
3. 825, 820, 802, 799, 798, 795
4. 6.85, 6.8, 6.24, 6, 5.9, 5.2
5. 14.95, 14.9, 14.53, 14.5, 13.94, 13.85
6. 309.2, 309, 308.95, 308.92, 308.9, 308.75
7. $10\frac{4}{5}$, $10\frac{1}{2}$, $10\frac{1}{10}$, 10, $9\frac{2}{3}$, $9\frac{1}{4}$
8. $8\frac{1}{2}$, $8\frac{1}{3}$, $7\frac{3}{4}$, $7\frac{1}{2}$, $7\frac{1}{3}$, $6\frac{3}{4}$
9. $2\frac{1}{3}$, 2, $1\frac{3}{4}$, $1\frac{1}{2}$, $1\frac{1}{3}$, $\frac{3}{4}$
10. 10.2, 10, 9.5, $9\frac{1}{3}$, 8.9, $8\frac{3}{4}$

Page 9

1. 14, 19, 21, 27, 30, 34
2. yes
3. $2\frac{1}{2}$ feet
4. 84, 75, 29
5. 29.5, 29, $28\frac{3}{4}$, 28.6, 28.5, 25.75, 25

Page 10

1. 2 feet, 22 inches, 18 inches, 1 foot, 8 inches
2. 6 inches because 6″ is slightly more than 15 cm
3. 1.5 feet, 14.2 inches, 8.95 inches
4. no

Page 11

1. D
2. C
3. B
4. A
5. B
6. A
7. C
8. A
9. Mint Chocolate Chip has the most votes.
10. 24, 24.6, 27, 28

Page 12: Six crisp snacks

Page 13: A rainbow

Page 14

1. 300
2. 49,000
3. 27,540
4. 180,000
5. 300,000
6. 1,700,000
7. 6,000,000
8. 7,500,000
9. 3,000,000
10. 15,000,000

Page 15

1. tens
2. hundreds
3. ones
4. thousands
5. hundred thousands
6. tens
7. hundreds
8. millions
9. ten thousands
10. ones
11. 2
12. 3
13. 4
14. 8
15. 9
16. 3
17. 8
18. 1
19. 4
20. 7

Page 16

1. 196
2. 8,403
3. 763
4. 8,912
5. 17,514

Page 17

1. 201
2. 999
3. 245
4. 6,203
5. 4,983

Page 18

1. D
2. B
3. D
4. D
5. C
6. B
7. A
8. D
9. Answers will vary, but should have a 0 in the tens place and 0, 1, 2, 3, or 4 in the ones place.
10. 289

Page 19: A baa-baa shop

EMC 3018 • Basic Math Skills, Grade 5 • ©2003 by Evan-Moor Corp.

Page 20: Stop paying the water bill

Page 21
1. 2,275
2. 493
3. 10,416
4. 42,177
5. 15,960
6. 1,827
7. 480
8. 19,100
9. 8,596
10. 25,311

Page 22
1. 4,032
2. 2,100
3. 14,459
4. 20,130
5. 60,160
6. 2,632
7. 3,360
8. 6,976
9. 32,400
10. 28,618

Page 23
1. 364 sunflower seeds
2. 630 fish
3. dogs
4. 36 inches by 108 inches
5. 1,736 miles; no, it is 1,064 miles short

Page 24
1. $336
2. $4,704
3. $1,060
4. $468
5. yes, $192

Page 25
1. C
2. B
3. A
4. D
5. D
6. A
7. B
8. C
9. 5,880 pages
10. yes, 220 miles

Page 26: He makes a swish

Page 27: Take it on a joy ride

Page 28
1. 3   4   6
2. 6   8   10
3. 3   6   9
4. 7   8   5
5. 7   1   7
6. 7   5   9
7. 3   6   7
8. 3   5   6
9. 4   3   3
10. 5   10   7

Page 29
1. 4   6   4   1
2. 4   6   7   7
3. 6   7   6   2
4. 9   7   7   11
5. 5   6   12   2
6. 9   6   4   5
7. 6   5   7   4
8. 3   2   7   11

Page 30
1. 12 bundles
2. $8
3. 8 fish
4. 9 pieces
5. 4 treats
6. 2 juice boxes

Page 31
1. no, needs 42 pieces
2. 7 fish
3. 8 cards
4. 4 friends
5. 5 people
6. 3 flowers

Page 32
1. B
2. B
3. C
4. D
5. C
6. B
7. B
8. A
9. 4 pieces
10. $10

Page 33: To the hoptician

Page 34: 3 complete stars

Page 35
1. 10 R2   10 R2   11 R6
2. 5 R1   3 R1   14
3. 4   10 R4   8 R8
4. 6   10 R8   2 R4
5. 7 R6   8 R3   13
6. 7 R7   8   13 R5
7. 9   42   3
8. 9 R3   19 R1   9 R4
9. 8   18   6 R3
10. 7 R5   20 R1   7

Page 36
1. 6   7 R6   3 R3   7 R7
2. 7 R1   9 R4   7   1 R7
3. 3 R4   5 R5   3 R5   16 R1
4. 8   5   11 R1   10 R7
5. 16 R4   6 R4   16 R1   14 R1
6. 5   3 R5   9 R2   7 R1
7. 3 R5   6 R1   4 R3   8 R1
8. 6   9   6   8 R2

Page 37
1. 10 cookies with 4 extras; Answers will vary—maybe divide them so each person gets part of another cookie.
2. 12 days
3. 7 pencils with 1 extra; Answers will vary—maybe give the extra to the teacher.
4. 8 fish with 2 extras; Answers will vary, but should indicate that fish can't be divided like cookies, so maybe put one extra in each of two tanks.
5. 10 days

Page 38
1. 24
2. 31
3. 42
4. 29 and 49; Answers will vary.

Page 39
1. D
2. A
3. D
4. C
5. B
6. A
7. C
8. D

9. 7 pieces with 4 extras; Answers will vary, but maybe give them to Mom.

10. 8 cookies with 3 extras; Answers will vary, but maybe break them apart or give them to Dad.

Page 40: Free flag

Page 41: Udder chaos

Page 42
1. 7 R5
2. 8 R13
3. 26 R13
4. 58 R4
5. 49 R1
6. 32 R17
7. 16 R31
8. 54 R5
9. 160 R21
10. 130 R68

Page 43
1. 20 R11   14 R17   257 R4
2. 17 R12   43 R9   52 R26
3. 21 R12   34 R12   81 R3
4. 18 R6   273 R7   64 R28

Page 44
1. 15 books with 24 extras
2. 20 shelves
3. 42 bundles with 8 extras; Answers will vary, but maybe give the extras to an orphanage.
4. 40 cards, no extras
5. 29 hours

Page 45
1. 21 inches
2. 25 snowballs with 17 extras; Answers will vary.
3. almost 14 hours
4. 57 spaces

Page 46
1. C
2. A
3. D
4. B
5. C
6. A
7. A
8. D

9. 10 rolls with 29 extras; Answers will vary, but maybe wait and collect more pennies to make another roll.

10. 32 packages with 2 extras; Answers will vary.

Page 47
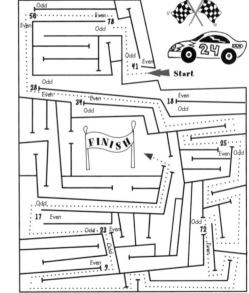

Page 48
Circled numbers: 2, 3, 5, 7, 11, 13, 17, 19, 23, 29, 31, 37, 41, 43, 47, 53, 59, 61, 67, 71, 73, 79, 83, 89, and 97

Page 49

1. even	odd	even
2. odd	odd	even
3. odd	odd	even
4. even	odd	even
5. odd	even	odd
6. even	even	even
7. even	even	even
8. even	odd	odd
9. even	even	odd
10. even	even	even

Page 50

1. composite	composite	composite
2. composite	prime	prime
3. prime	prime	prime
4. composite	composite	composite
5. composite	prime	prime
6. prime	composite	composite
7. composite	composite	prime
8. composite	prime	prime
9. prime	composite	composite
10. prime	prime	prime

Page 51

1. 26 dusty rose and 39 emerald green

2. no

3. no, 19 is prime and the only way to lay them into a rectangle is 1 by 19.

4. yes

Page 52

1. Answers will vary, but should address the fact that 37 is prime and you can't make it into a rectangle other than 1 by 37.

2. yes

3. 6 x 8 or 8 x 6

4. no

Page 53

1. B	5. D
2. A	6. C
3. D	7. D
4. B	8. D

9. 23, 29, 31, 37, 41, 43, 47

10. Answers will vary; maybe divide them evenly between 2 people with each getting 7.

Page 54: A posse cat

Page 55

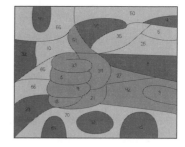

Page 56

1. 1, 2, 3, 4, 6, 8, 12, 24
2. 1, 2, 4, 8, 16, 32, 64
3. 1, 2, 4, 8, 16, 32
4. 1, 5, 25
5. 1, 2, 3, 5, 6, 9, 10, 15, 18, 30, 45, 90
6. 1, 2, 3, 4, 6, 8, 12, 16, 24, 48
7. 1, 2, 3, 6, 9, 18
8. 1, 83
9. 1, 3, 9, 11, 33, 99
10. 1, 5, 25, 125

Page 57

1. 1, 2, 3, 4, 5, 6, 7, 8
2. 2, 4, 6, 8, 10, 12, 14, 16
3. 3, 6, 9, 12, 15, 18, 21, 24
4. 4, 8, 12, 16, 20, 24, 28, 32
5. 5, 10, 15, 20, 25, 30, 35, 40
6. 6, 12, 18, 24, 30, 36, 42, 48
7. 7, 14, 21, 28, 35, 42, 49, 56
8. 8, 16, 24, 32, 40, 48, 56, 64
9. 9, 18, 27, 36, 45, 54, 63, 72
10. 10, 20, 30, 40, 50, 60, 70, 80

Page 58

1. 3, 6, 9, 12, 15, 18, 21, 24, 27, 30
2. 1 × 24, 2 × 12, 3 × 8, 4 × 6
3. 27; Answers will vary.
4. Answers will vary, but should mention that 149 is prime and that Tate needs to eat 1 more to get to another composite number.
5. 60 bottles

Page 59

1. 56
2. 30
3. 105
4. 120
5. 120

Page 60

1. D
2. B
3. A
4. D
5. C
6. A
7. C
8. A

9. 1, 2, 3, 6, 9, 18
10. Answers will vary, but should include five of the following: 44, 48, 52, 56, 60, 64, 68, 72, 76

Page 61: In case they get a hole in one

Page 62: A cardigan

Page 63

1. ☆☆☆ (3)

2. □□□□□ (5)

3. ◇◇◇◇◇◇◇◇ (8)

4. △△△△△△△△ △△△△△△△ (15)

5. ○○○○○○○○○○ (10)

6. ☀ (1)

7. ☾☾☾☾☾☾☾☾☾☾ (10)

8. ☺☺☺☺☺ (5)

9. ⇨⇨⇨ (3)

10. ଚଚଚଚଚଚଚ (7)

Page 64

1. ✿✿✿✿ (4)

2. 🐭🐭🐭🐭 (4)

3. ⊘⊘⊘⊘⊘ (5)

4. ⌂⌂ (2)

5. ⊿⊿⊿⊿ (4)

6. □□□□□□□□ (8)

7. ⋈⋈⋈ (3)

8. ⋈⋈⋈ (3)

9. ☀☀ (2)

10. ▤▤▤ (3)

Page 65

1. 36 baseball cards
2. 40 trolls
3. 48 blank pages
4. 125 pounds
5. 6 decks of cards

Page 66

1. 40 tulip bulbs
2. 3 potato plants
3. 10 hills
4. 5 plants

Page 67

1. C
2. A
3. D
4. B
5. B
6. D
7. D
8. A

9. ☆☆☆☆☆☆☆★★★★

10. Drawing should have 6 unshaded triangles, 9 shaded triangles, and 5 triangles circled.

Page 68: Francis fries fresh fish fillets

Page 69: Envelope

Page 70

1. $\frac{5}{5} = 1$
2. $4\frac{3}{3} = 5$
3. $4\frac{6}{4} = 5\frac{1}{2}$
4. $1\frac{3}{4}$
5. $5\frac{7}{10}$
6. $8\frac{17}{15} = 9\frac{2}{15}$
7. $4\frac{5}{6}$
8. $7\frac{6}{7}$
9. $\frac{23}{40}$
10. $12\frac{9}{6} = 13\frac{1}{2}$

Page 71

1. $\frac{4}{8} = \frac{1}{2}$
2. $3\frac{1}{3}$
3. $3\frac{3}{4}$
4. $2\frac{2}{3}$
5. $3\frac{2}{4} = 3\frac{1}{2}$
6. $2\frac{3}{5}$
7. $7\frac{1}{9}$
8. $3\frac{1}{4}$
9. $4\frac{7}{9}$
10. $1\frac{9}{10}$

EMC 3018 • Basic Math Skills, Grade 5 • ©2003 by Evan-Moor Corp.

Page 72

1. $14\frac{1}{6}$ yards
2. yes, $47\frac{1}{4}$ yards left
3. $16\frac{1}{6}$ yards
4. $2\frac{7}{12}$ yards
5. no, she only has $7\frac{5}{12}$ yards

Page 73

1. $\frac{5}{12}$ of a pizza
2. 18 pizzas
3. $\frac{5}{12}$ of a pizza
4. 5:50 P.M.
5. none

Page 74

1. D
2. A
3. D
4. D
5. C
6. C
7. A
8. D

9. Answers will vary, but should include something about before you add, you need to get common denominators.
10. $1\frac{5}{6}$ yards

Page 75: Two yards

Page 76: A chapped chap chopped chips

Page 77

1. $\frac{3}{8}$
2. $\frac{2}{15}$
3. $\frac{4}{21}$
4. $\frac{8}{25}$
5. $\frac{1}{12}$
6. $\frac{3}{20}$
7. $\frac{25}{42}$
8. $\frac{2}{15}$
9. $\frac{4}{63}$
10. $\frac{20}{63}$

Page 78

1. $\frac{2}{15}$
2. $\frac{21}{40}$
3. $\frac{3}{64}$
4. $\frac{20}{63}$
5. $\frac{5}{18}$
6. $\frac{6}{35}$
7. $\frac{70}{99}$
8. $\frac{10}{39}$
9. $\frac{12}{49}$
10. $\frac{3}{56}$

Page 79

1. Answers will vary, but should address the commutative property in the numerators, where $1 \times 2 = 2 \times 1$.
2. Answers will vary, but should address that when you multiply by a number less than 1, then answer will be smaller.
3. yes

Page 80

1. Answers will vary. (Example is 8 people and $\frac{1}{2}$ of them wear glasses. How many wear glasses?)
2. Answers will vary. (Example is $5 and you give $\frac{1}{4}$ to a charity. How much did you give to the charity?)
3. Answers will vary. (Example is $\frac{1}{4}$ yard of fabric and you use $\frac{1}{2}$ of that to make a scarf. How much fabric did it take to make the scarf?)
4. Answers will vary. (Example is $5\frac{1}{2}$ pizzas and Kenny ate $\frac{1}{5}$ of them. How much pizza did Kenny eat?)

Page 81

1. A
2. C
3. D
4. A
5. B
6. A
7. D
8. C

9. Answers will vary. (Example is $5 and you spent half of that. How much did you spend?)
10. Answers will vary. (Example is you have $\frac{1}{2}$ pizza and Jim ate $\frac{1}{4}$ of that. How much of a whole pizza did Jim eat?)

Page 82: A slug has four noses

Page 83: In the Pussific

Page 84

1. 8.9
2. 7.9
3. 8.6
4. 136.3
5. 106.92
6. 31.42
7. 21.215
8. 15.4
9. 55.6
10. 27.27
11. 99.9
12. 55.7
13. 21.4
14. 10.74
15. 97.63
16. 11.494
17. 851.524
18. 931.495
19. 11.492
20. 8.92

Page 85

1. 1.1
2. 3.6
3. 0.2
4. 3.7
5. 8.1
6. 6.3
7. 9.77
8. 2.59
9. 80.54
10. 2.88
11. 37.1
12. 91.2
13. 33.3
14. 88.5
15. 10.8
16. 2.88
17. 6.46
18. 15.16
19. 17.608
20. 4.389

Page 86

1. $4.05
2. $10.49
3. $7.67
4. $2.85
5. yes; total was $38.90

Page 87

1. $18.93; 1 ten, 1 five, 3 ones, 3 quarters, 1 dime, 1 nickel, and 3 pennies
2. lost 0.003 pounds
3. 0.389 pounds
4. 4.275 pounds
5. 0.03 meters

Page 88

1. D
2. B
3. A
4. C
5. B
6. A
7. B
8. D
9. $80.90
10. Answers will vary.

Page 89: Edgar ate eight eggs a day

Page 90: It goes back for seconds

Page 91

1. 0.2
2. 2.0
3. 2.0
4. 2.5
5. 0.75
6. 0.75
7. 0.08
8. 4.0
9. 3.8
10. 1.74

Page 92

1. 1.08
2. 0.1
3. 4.8
4. 25.6
5. 0.42
6. 0.105
7. 0.0038
8. 31.5
9. 0.899
10. 13.0845

Page 93

1. $540
2. $20.14
3. $20.70
4. $161
5. 76.36 square meters

Page 94

1. $78.75
2. 26.9 tons
3. 227.6 square feet
4. 2.16 ounces; Answers will vary, but maybe a small bird
5. 74 feet

Page 95

1. C
2. B
3. A
4. C
5. B
6. D
7. A
8. C

9. Answers will vary, but should address the need for a "0" place holder to the right of the 30 and that the correct answer should be 39.0.

10. Answers will vary; solution is 1.792.

Page 96: A lobster has ten legs

Page 97: Beacon and eggs

Page 98

Problem Number	Fraction	Decimal	Percent
1	$\frac{1}{4}$	0.25	25%
2	$\frac{1}{2}$	0.5	50%
3	$\frac{1}{3}$	$0.\overline{3}$	$33\frac{1}{3}\%$
4	$\frac{3}{4}$	0.75	75%
5	$\frac{4}{5}$	0.8	80%
6	$\frac{3}{8}$	0.375	37.5%
7	$\frac{1}{8}$	0.125	12.5%
8	$\frac{1}{10}$	0.1	10%
9	$\frac{9}{10}$	0.9	90%
10	$\frac{5}{8}$	0.625	62.5%

Page 99

Problem Number	Fraction	Decimal	Percent
1	$\frac{3}{4}$	0.75	75%
2	$\frac{1}{4}$	0.25	25%
3	$\frac{1}{2}$	0.5	50%
4	$\frac{3}{10}$	0.3	30%
5	$\frac{3}{5}$	0.6	60%
6	$\frac{1}{10}$	0.1	10%
7	$\frac{4}{5}$	0.8	80%
8	$\frac{2}{5}$	0.4	40%
9	$\frac{9}{10}$	0.9	90%
10	1	1.0	100%

Page 100
1. 0.3
2. Answers will vary, but should address that 0.6 would be 60% and 6% should be 0.06.
3. 20%
4. 25%; Answers will vary, for example, the discount was $15 off $60 or 15/60 = 0.25 = 25%.
5. 50%

Page 101
1. 75%
2. 90%
3. 100%
4. 20%
5. 27 correct

Page 102
1. B
2. C
3. D
4. D
5. C
6. B
7. D
8. A

9. $\frac{1}{4}$ and 0.25 or other equivalent values
10. Answers will vary.

Page 103: Voltswagon

Page 104

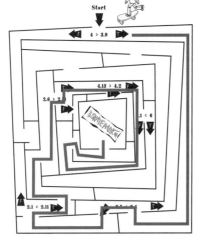

Page 105
1. true
2. true
3. false
4. false
5. true
6. true
7. true
8. true
9. true
10. true

Page 106
1. true
2. true
3. true
4. true
5. false
6. true
7. false
8. true
9. true
10. true

Page 107
1. >; Explanations will vary.
2. Answers will vary, but should include an agreement with Stacy that they could also use the $\leq$, $\geq$, and = symbols.
3. < or $\leq$

Page 108
1. Answers will vary.
2. <; Answers will vary.
3. Answers will vary, but should support the > symbol.

Page 109
1. A
2. C
3. D
4. A
5. D
6. B
7. D
8. B
9. 5.4 > 4.9
10. 2.9 $\leq$ 7.4

Page 111: A loafer

Page 112: A leek

Page 113
1. add 2
2. add 2
3. add 5
4. add 4
5. subtract 8
6. multiply by 2 **or** double the number
7. divide by 3
8. add 19

Page 114

1. 11
2. 36
3. 31
4. 60
5. 25
6. 3
7. −2
8. 486

Page 115

1. 24 tiles
2. 75 gray and 50 white
3. 30 tiles

Page 116

1. 36 railings, 13 poles
2. 280 feet
3. 204 bales of hay

Page 117

1. B
2. C
3. B
4. D
5. A
6. D
7. A
8. D
9. subtract 6
10. 3 times itself

Page 118: Three blind mice

Page 119: Urgent detergent

Page 120

From top to bottom:
1. 4, 7, 13, 7, 8, 12
2. 2, 4, 6, 6, 4, 5
3. 1, 5, 13, 5, 3, 8
4. 3, 5, 10, 4, 7, 13

Page 121

From top to bottom:
1. 5, 7, 17, 5, 8, 17
2. 3, 5, 24, 7, 36, 15
3. 4, 19, 4, 39, 10, −1
4. 12, 19, 43, 8, 88, 85

Page 122

W (width)	L (length)	Number of Decorative Tile
8	10	$(2 \times 8) + (2 \times 10) + 4 =$ $(16) + (20) + 4 =$ $36 + 4 = 40$
10	12	$(2 \times 10) + (2 \times 12) + 4 =$ $(20) + (24) + 4 =$ $44 + 4 = 48$

Page 123

8	6	$(4 \times 8) + (2 \times 6) =$ $(32) + (12) =$ 44
9	8	$(4 \times 9) + (2 \times 8) =$ $(36) + (16) =$ 52

4 cows and 3 ducks

Page 124

1. A
2. C
3. D
4. B
5. C
6. D
7. B
8. C
9. Answers will vary, but should follow the rule.
10. Answers will vary, but should follow the rule.

Page 125: Humburgers

Page 126: Hiccup teacup

Page 127

1. +2
2. −1
3. ×2
4. ×4
5. ÷2
6. +5

Page 128

1. −1
2. +4
3. ÷3
4. × itself (squared)
5. ÷2
6. −8

Page 129

1. Answers will vary, for example, +14 **or** ×4 +2.
2. Answers will vary, for example, +1 **or** +2 −1.
3. Answers will vary, for example, −3 **or** +1 −4.
4. Answers will vary, for example, +20 **or** ×5 −4.

Page 130

1. Answers will vary, for example, +15 **or** ×3 −5.
2. Answers will vary: for example, +11 **or** ×5 +4.
3. Answers will vary, for example, −2 **or** ÷3 +2.
4. Answers will vary, for example, +12 **or** ×3 −6.

Page 131

1. A
2. C
3. A
4. D
5. C
6. A
7. D
8. B
9. Answers will vary, for example, −5 **or** ÷2.
10. Answers will vary, for example, +1 **or** ×2 −1.

EMC 3018 • Basic Math Skills, Grade 5 • ©2003 by Evan-Moor Corp.

Page 132: Morse cod

Page 133: A boo and arrow

Page 134

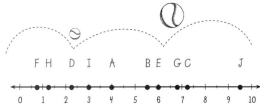

Page 135

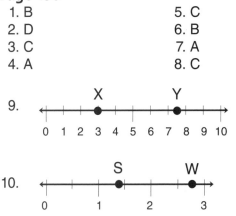

Page 136

1. Good job (all correct)

2. $5\frac{1}{2}$ should be halfway between 5 and 6, not a point at 5 and a point at $\frac{1}{2}$.

3. 3.75 should be between 3 and 4 and 8.5 should be halfway between 8 and 9.

Page 137

1. Board should show cut mark for the requested length, $5\frac{1}{2}$ feet.

2. Board should show two cut marks for the requested lengths: 4 feet and $3\frac{1}{4}$ feet.

3. Board should show three cut marks for the requested lengths: $2\frac{2}{3}$ feet, $3\frac{1}{3}$ feet, and $2\frac{1}{2}$ feet.

Page 138

1. B   5. C
2. D   6. B
3. C   7. A
4. A   8. C

9.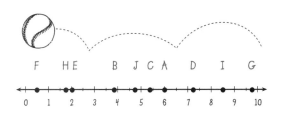

10.

Page 139

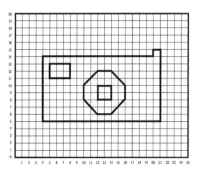

Page 140

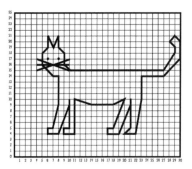

Page 141

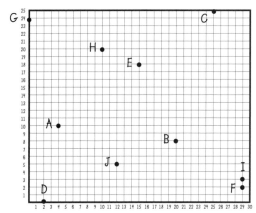

Page 142

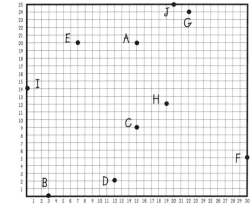

Page 143

1. (12, 6)
2. Laundry Mat at **W** and City bank at **Y**
3. (6, 12)
4.

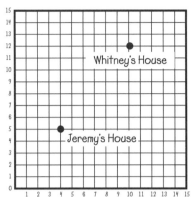

5. 13 blocks

Page 144

1. (7, 12)
2. Clothing Store at **C** and Cloth World at **D**
3. (12, 7)
4.

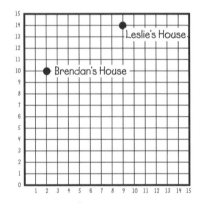

5. 11 blocks

Page 145

1. B
2. C
3. A
4. D
5. A
6. B
7. D
8. C

9.

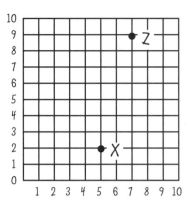

10. 9 blocks

Page 147: Stalagmice

Page 148: Six small slick seals

Page 149
Net will vary. One possibility is shown in each case.

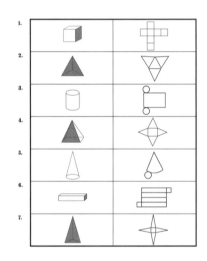

Page 150
Net will vary. One possibility is shown in each case.

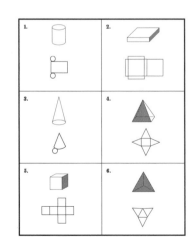

EMC 3018 • Basic Math Skills, Grade 5 • ©2003 by Evan-Moor Corp.

Page 151

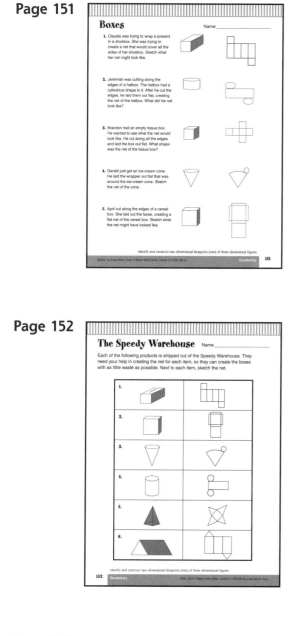

Page 152

Page 153
1. D
2. C
3. B
4. A
5. D
6. A
7. B
8. C
9. Answers will vary.
10. Answers will vary.

Page 154: Cheer him up

Page 155: Five fat French fleas

Page 156
1. turn
2. slide
3. turn
4. flip or turn
5. flip
6. flip or turn
7. slide
8. turn

Page 157
1. turn
2. slide
3. flip
4. flip
5. flip or turn
6. turn
7. flip
8. turn

Page 158

1.

2.

3.

Page 159

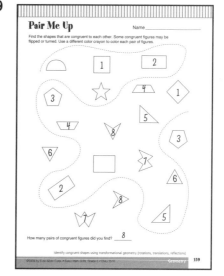

Page 160
1. C
2. A
3. D
4. B
5. B
6. D
7. A
8. C
9. Answers will vary.
10. Answers will vary.

Page 161: A drawbridge

Page 162: Casketball

Page 163
1. 2
2. 1
3. 3
4. 2
5. 1
6. 1
7. 4
8. 1

Page 164
1. 1
2. 8
3. 1
4. 1
5. 1
6. 0
7. 4
8. 1

Page 165
1. 1 line of symmetry
2. 2 lines of symmetry (one horizontal and one vertical)

Page 166
A-1
B-1
C-1
D-1
E-1
F-0
G-0
H-2
I-2
J-0
K-0
L-0
M-1
N-0
O-2
P-0
Q-0
R-0
S-0
T-1
U-1
V-1
W-1
X-2
Y-1
Z-0

Page 167
1. C
2. B
3. B
4. B
5. D
6. A (due to shading)
7. D
8. A

9. 1, vertically in the center of the O
10. Answers will vary; an example might be an equilateral triangle.

Page 169: An angle

Page 170: Catfish

Page 171

Linear	Capacity	Mass
millimeter	milliliter	milligram
centimeter	centiliter	centigram
decimeter	deciliter	decigram
meter	liter	gram
dekameter	dekaliter	dekagram
hectometer	hectoliter	hectogram
kilometer	kiloliter	kilogram

Page 172
1. M
2. M
3. C
4. C
5. C
6. M
7. M
8. M
9. C
10. C
11. M
12. M
13. C
14. C
15. M
16. C
17. C
18. M
19. C
20. M

Page 173
1. Answers will vary, but should address the root words *gram* for weight or mass and *meter* for length or distance.

2. Length–meterstick
   Mass–gram
   Capacity–2 liters

3. Metric: meters, centimeters, and kilometers
   Customary: inches, miles, and yards

Page 174
1. Answers will vary, but should address the root words *liter* for capacity and *meter* for length.

2. 1 centimeter, 1 decimeter, 1 meter, 1 hectometer, and 1 kilometer

3. Any measurement that is longer than 2 meters and shorter than 100 meters.

Page 175
1. D
2. B
3. C
4. A
5. C
6. D
7. B
8. B

9. Inch, because it is a customary unit of measurement and the rest are metric.

10. millimeter, centimeter, decimeter, meter, dekameter, hectometer, kilometer

Page 176: Pooped purple pelicans

Page 177: A firehouse

EMC 3018 • Basic Math Skills, Grade 5 • ©2003 by Evan-Moor Corp.

Page 178

1. 1 centimeter
2. 1 decimeter
3. 1 hectomeer
4. 1 dekameter
5. 1 kilometer
6. 1 hectometer
7. 1 decimeter
8. 1 hectometer
9. 1 meter
10. 1 hectometer

Page 179

1. 1 foot
2. 1 yard
3. 1 mile
4. 2 yards
5. 120 inches
6. 10 meters
7. 5 decimeters
8. 2 centimeters
9. 5 meters
10. 2 kilometers

Page 180
Answers will vary.

Page 181
Answers will vary.

Page 182

1. B
2. A
3. D
4. D
5. A
6. C
7. C
8. D

9. any line that measures 12 cm
10. 7 feet, because 2 yards is only 6 feet

Page 183: This disk sticks

Page 184: Because she ran away from the ball

Page 185

1. 2
2. 5,280
3. 9
4. 60
5. 5
6. 5,280
7. 72
8. 7,920
9. 4
10. 36
11. 144
12. 2

Page 186

1. 100
2. 1,000
3. 50
4. $\frac{1}{2}$
5. 400
6. 30
7. 3,000
8. 5
9. 3,000
10. 8
11. $\frac{1}{2}$
12. 5

Page 187

1. 4 centimeters = 40 millimeters
2. correct
3. 5 meters = 50 decimeters
4. 10 decimeters = 1 meter = 100 cm
5. correct
6. 3 hectometers = 30 dekameters
7. 2 kilometers = 2,000 meters
8. 4 centimeters = 40 millimeters

Page 188

1. 1 foot = 12 inches
2. correct
3. correct
4. 2 feet = 24 inches
5. correct
6. correct
7. correct
8. 3 miles = 15,840 feet

Page 189

1. C
2. D
3. B
4. D
5. C
6. D
7. A
8. A

9. Answers will vary, for example, 200 cm or 20 dm.
10. Answers will vary, for example, 6 feet or 72 inches.

Page 190: Chicken of the sea

Page 191: Is there a pleasant peasant present?

Page 192

1. 30
2. April, June, September, November
3. Thursday
4. Wednesday
5. 19th
6. 25th
7. 19th
8. 30th of the previous month
9. 22nd
10. Friday

Page 193

1. 7
2. 12
3. 31
4. 365
5. 366
6. February has 29 days.
7. Wednesday
8. Answers will vary.
9. Answers will vary.
10. Answers will vary.

Page 194
1. January, March, May, July, August, October, December
2. March (the month before has 28 days)
3. February 22
4. April 10
5. May 8

Page 195
1. February, only month with 29 days
2. January 26
3. Friday
4. 2004, because it's a leap year
5. His birthday only happens every four years.

Page 196
1. B
2. C
3. D
4. D
5. D
6. C
7. C
8. A
9. February has 29 days.
10. Sunday

Page 197: A knapsack strap

Page 198: A walkie talkie

Page 199
1. 60°
2. 42°
3. 64°
4. down 12°
5. up 19°
6. 91°
7. 59
8. 83°
9. −10°
10. −10°

Page 200
1. Thursday
2. Wednesday
3. Monday and Friday
4. up 4°
5. down 8°

Page 201
1. December 10
2. 7 degrees
3. Answers will vary; around 31°.
4. This information is not represented in the graph.
5. The 10th was 6° lower than the 9th.

Page 202
1. any temperature between 60° and 62°
2. any time between 8 A.M. and 9 A.M.
3. any temperature greater than or equal to 62°
4. 26°
5. any temperature between 46° and 54°

Page 203
1. C
2. A
3. B
4. D
5. C
6. C
7. C
8. B
9. Answers will vary.
10. 41°

Page 204: An itchy rich witch

Page 205: Walnuts

Page 206
1. 90°
2. 130°
3. 60°
4. 110°
5. 30°
6. 160°
7. 50°
8. 120°

Page 207
1. acute
2. right
3. acute
4. obtuse
5. acute
6. right
7. acute
8. obtuse

Page 208
Answers will vary.

Page 209
1. Answers will vary, for example, a half turn.
2. Answers will vary, for example, a full turn.
3. Answers will vary. Yes, it does matter which way the person turns.
4. Answers will vary. No, it does not matter which way the person turns.

Page 210
1. B
2. A
3. D
4. C
5. A
6. A
7. B
8. C
9. Answers will vary.
10. Answers will vary.

Page 211: Rigid wicker rocker

Page 212: A goldfish

Page 213
1. 18 units
2. 24 units
3. 30 units
4. 22 units
5. 16 units
6. 18 units
7. 24 units
8. 20 units
9. 28 units
10. 36 units

EMC 3018 • Basic Math Skills, Grade 5 • ©2003 by Evan-Moor Corp.

Page 214
1. 46 units
2. 32 units
3. 27 units

Page 215
Answers will vary.

Page 216

1. 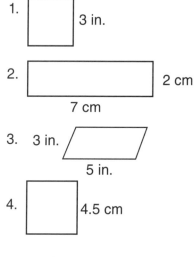 3 in.

2. 2 cm
7 cm

3. 3 in.
5 in.

4. 4.5 cm

5. 2.5 cm

Page 217
1. D
2. B
3. A
4. C
5. D
6. C
7. B
8. D
9. Answers will vary.
10. Answers will vary.

Page 218: Cheap sheep

Page 219: A drum

Page 220
1. 20 square units
2. 36 square units
3. 42 square units
4. 24 square units
5. 21 square units
6. 10 square units
7. 9 square units
8. 32 square units
9. 49 square units
10. 72 square units

Page 221
1. 64 square units
2. 49 square units
3. 153 square units

Page 222
1. 60 square yards
2. 540 tiles
3. 45 boxes, $1,800

Page 223
1. 135 square feet
2. 1 can
3. 328 square feet
4. 1 can

Page 224
1. C
2. D
3. C
4. D
5. A
6. C
7. D
8. D
9. Answers will vary.
10. 6
6

Page 225: An octoplus

Page 226: It was a hi chair

Page 227
1. 60 cubic inches
2. 30 cubic inches
3. 42 cubic inches
4. 80 cubic inches
5. 280 cubic inches

Page 228
1. 21 cubic centimeters
2. 24 cubic centimeters
3. 48 cubic centimeters
4. 168 cubic centimeters
5. 432 cubic centimeters

Page 229
1. She has different units of measurement.

2. Answers will vary, for example, she could change the 10 centimeters to 4 inches.

3. Answers will vary, for example, if she changed it to customary units, the answer is 144.

4. Answers will vary, for example, if she changed it to customary units, the answer is cubic inches.

Page 230
1. 2 × 4 × 5
2. 3 × 4 × 6
3. 2 × 5 × 7
4. 5 × 8 × 9

Page 231

1. B
2. D
3. C
4. B
5. D
6. B
7. A
8. D
9. 140 cubic inches
10. Answers will vary.

Page 233: Quick kiss

Page 234: Boo jeans

Page 235

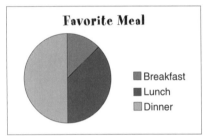

Page 236

Stem	Leaves
7	0 2
8	2 8 8 9
9	2 3 4 4 5 5 5 7
10	0

Page 237

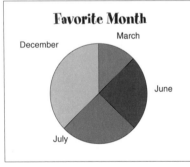

Page 238
Answers will vary.

Page 239

1. B
2. A
3. C
4. D
5. C
6. B
7. A
8. D
9. Answers will vary.
10. Answers will vary.

Page 240: Tapeworm

Page 241: A palm tree

Page 242
Mitch is 7, Kenny is 12, Sarah is 10, Michael is 15, Kathy is 5, Sally is 2

Page 243

1. 94°
2. 95°
3. Answers will vary but should be around 94°.
4. Answers will vary, but should address the fact that this graph doesn't give that information.
5. 2°

Page 244
Answers will vary.

Page 245

1. Answers will vary, for example, the y-axis starts at 40, not at 0.
2. Answers will vary, for example, using uneven spacing on the scale.
3. Answers will vary.

Page 246

1. D
2. B
3. D
4. C
5. B
6. C
7. C
8. D
9. Answers will vary, for example, find the middle value; 75 pages
10. 12 in the stem and 4 in the leaves

Page 247: Spookhetti

Page 248: Catch you later

EMC 3018 • Basic Math Skills, Grade 5 • ©2003 by Evan-Moor Corp.

Page 249

1. 13
2. 43
3. 48
4. 70
5. 4
6. 29
7. 35.5
8. 62
9. 9
10. 5
11. 15.5
12. 24
13. 9
14. 6 and 8
15. 25
16. 3

Page 250

1. 7, $14\frac{1}{2}$, 15, 15
2. 5, 6, 6, 6 and 7
3. 0, 21, 21, 21
4. 20, 40, 40, none
5. 6, $7\frac{1}{2}$, 9, 10

Page 251

1. any number greater than 37
2. 25 or 27
3. 10
4. 52

Page 252

1. ⌐ ⌐ 49
2. ⌐wers will vary, for example, 40 and 40, 41 and 41, 44 and 44, or 47 and 47.
3. 40
4. Any two numbers that when added together total 34, for example, 16 and 18.
5. Answers will vary, for example, 7 and 7.

Page 253

1. C
2. B
3. A
4. D
5. A
6. B
7. B
8. C
9. any number other than 8
10. 11

Page 254: Kooky kite kits

Page 255: Your shadow

Page 256

1. $\frac{1}{6}$
2. $\frac{1}{6}$
3. $\frac{2}{6} = \frac{1}{3}$
4. $\frac{3}{6} = \frac{1}{2}$
5. $\frac{3}{6} = \frac{1}{2}$
6. 0
7. $\frac{1}{2}$
8. $\frac{1}{2}$
9. $\frac{3}{8}$
10. $\frac{3}{8}$
11. 0
12. $\frac{6}{8} = \frac{3}{4}$

Page 257

1. $\frac{1}{6}$
2. $\frac{1}{6}$
3. $\frac{2}{6} = \frac{1}{3}$
4. $\frac{3}{6} = \frac{1}{2}$
5. $\frac{3}{6} = \frac{1}{2}$
6. 0
7. $\frac{4}{12} = \frac{1}{3}$
8. $\frac{8}{12} = \frac{2}{3}$
9. 0
10. $\frac{2}{8} = \frac{1}{4}$
11. $\frac{3}{8}$
12. 0

Page 258

1.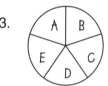
4.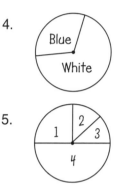
2.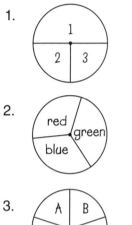
5.
3.

Page 259

1. 2, 2, 2, 5, 5, 7
2. 3, 3, 5, 7, 9, 11
3. 2, 6, 10, 11, 12, 13
4. 4, 4, 4, 4, 4, 4

Page 260

1. A
2. C
3. C
4. D
5. C
6. D
7. A
8. D

9. Answers will vary.
10. 0, because 7 does not appear on any side of the die

Page 261: Mothematics

Page 262: Come kick six sticks

Page 263

1. red pants and white shirt
   red pants and black shirt
   green pants and white shirt
   green pants and black shirt

2.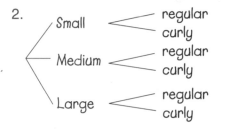

3. 6

Page 264

1. Answers will vary, for example:

Size	Flavor
small	orange
medium	orange
large	orange
small	cola
medium	cola
large	cola

2. Answers will vary, for example:

Cone	Flavor of Ice Cream
sugar	chocolate
waffle	chocolate
plain	chocolate
sugar	strawberry
waffle	strawberry
plain	strawberry
sugar	vanilla
waffle	vanilla
plain	vanilla

Page 265

1. Answers will vary, for example, add a different color.

2. Answers will vary, for example, add a different type of vehicle.

3. Answers will vary, for example, add 2 different types of vehicles.

Page 266

1. Julie left out the silver 4-door and has the silver 2-door listed twice.

2. Yes, the list is complete.

3. 2 more combinations need to be listed: waffle, vanilla, chocolate; waffle, vanilla, vanilla

Page 267

1. D
2. B
3. D
4. A
5. C
6. B
7. B
8. D

9.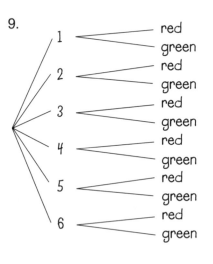

10.

Coin	Spinner
heads	1
heads	2
heads	3
heads	4
heads	5
tails	1
tails	2
tails	3
tails	4
tails	5

EMC 3018 • Basic Math Skills, Grade 5 • ©2003 by Evan-Moor Corp.